9N/

60/186

NAPOLEON'S ST. HELENA

NAPOLEON'S ST. HELENA

✦✦

Gilbert Martineau

*Translated from the French
by Frances Partridge*

JOHN MURRAY

First published in Great Britain 1968
by John Murray, Albemarle Street, London
and printed by William Clowes & Sons Ltd
London and Beccles
7195 1821 0

A MA MÈRE

CONTENTS

This Geographical Plan of
THE ISLAND & FORTS OF
SAINT HELENA
is Dedicated by permission to
Field Marshall His R.l Highness
The Duke OF Kent AND Strathearn
By Lieut. R. P. Read

ILLUSTRATIONS

MAP

FOREWORD

by H. Montgomery Hyde

It is a privilege for me as well as a pleasure to introduce this revised and enlarged English edition of M. Gilbert Martineau's work, originally published in France under the title, *La Vie Quotidienne à Sainte-Hélène au Temps de Napoléon*. The author is particularly well fitted for the task which he has discharged with expert knowledge. A profound student of Napoleon and his times, M. Martineau has made a special study of the Emperor's last years in captivity in St. Helena. In this no doubt he has received inspiration from the office of French Consul in the island, which he has held for the past few years. As such he is responsible for the maintenance of the property belonging to his Government in St. Helena. These include Longwood, the house in the interior of the island, where Napoleon spent most of his exile and where M. Martineau now lives as its official custodian; the little pavilion at The Briars, where Napoleon passed his first weeks, while Longwood was being got ready; and the empty tomb in the valley near Longwood, where his remains rested from his death in 1821 until they were removed, nineteen years later, to *Les Invalides*. From personal observation, in the course of a recent visit to St. Helena, I can readily testify to the loving care with which Gilbert Martineau has carried out this duty.

Napoleon arrived in St. Helena from England, after a voyage of ten weeks, in the autumn of 1815. He died at Longwood less than six years later, as much from boredom as from the cancer which Dr. Antommarchi's autopsy revealed. No individual in history has probably had his actions and words more minutely recorded than Napoleon during this last phase. Every day is accounted for, and, in the earlier months, almost every hour of his existence, in the shape of meticulous reports to the Governor, Sir Hudson Lowe, who had been expressly charged by the Cabinet in London with the captive's security. There was a real fear on the part of the British authorities that Napoleon might try to escape. Lowe's industry is embodied in ninety MS. volumes of Lowe Papers in the British Museum, supplemented by a further twenty-nine volumes of his official correspondence in the Public Record Office. To these must be added several hundred accounts written by a variety of persons who were in the island at the time and had some contact with the exile or his entourage, setting down their impressions and conversations. In the aggregate the amount of material relating to this period of Napoleon's life is immense. That M. Martineau should have distilled its essence so effectively for the purpose of his narrative is no mean achievement.

With such an existing wealth of original material, it might be assumed that nothing fresh of any significance could be forthcoming. But M. Martineau has made an interesting and important new discovery in the personal papers of Major Gideon Gorrequer, Aide-de-Camp and Acting Military Secretary to the Governor. With the exception of Lowe himself, Gorrequer occupied by far the most important position of all those concerned with Napoleon's captivity. A fluent French speaker, with a most retentive memory, Gorrequer proved to be an extremely diligent secretary, who was always at hand with his notebook, and his minutes form the basis of Lowe's lengthy reports to Whitehall. Thus it is largely due to his efforts that we possess such a detailed record of Napoleon's life in St. Helena.

Gorrequer went further. He also kept copious notes for his private use of everything he observed going on in the island, particularly at Plantation House, where he lived with the Governor and Lady Lowe. He had the reputation, confirmed by outward appearances, of being a whole-hearted supporter of his master's rigid and unimaginative treatment of Napoleon, although one acute observer of the local scene—Baron Stürmer, the Austrian Commissioner—described Gorrequer as 'a sly dog'. As the result of a family lawsuit brought after his death, Gorrequer's private papers were impounded, and for many years they remained under the seal of the Court. They have recently been released, and M. Martineau has obtained access to them, the first student, so far as I am aware, who has been able to do so. Among other things they show that the hard-working A. D. C. was by no means the Governor's partisan that he outwardly appeared, and that in reality he shared Lady Lowe's feeling that Napoleon was shabbily treated by the British Government at home and by her husband in Plantation House.

M. Martineau has added a new chapter to this first English edition, in which he examines the theory advanced by a group of Swedish scientists that Napoleon was killed by arsenic secretly administered by a member of his personal suite. It has been suggested that the villain was Count de Montholon, who stood to benefit by the sum of two million francs under the Emperor's will. I agree with M. Martineau that there is no substance in this assassination theory. It is true that tests recently carried out in two reactors at the atomic research establishment at Harwell on specimens of Napoleon's hair have revealed traces of arsenic. But this does not prove that Napoleon died from this poison. In his time arsenic was widely used in the treatment of undiagnosed stomach complaints, such as cancer. Also, he may have absorbed arsenic from the local water, soil, or fish, all of which were in some degree impregnated with small quantities of the poison. Recently there has been a suggestion that the green curtains which surrounded his bed at Longwood contained arsenic. However, it seems virtually certain that the pathological cause of Napoleon's death was cancer of the stomach.

Napoleon's happiest time in St. Helena was at the beginning of his exile when he lived at The Briars and enjoyed the company of the good-hearted Balcombe family, particularly young Betsy Balcombe who amused and delighted him with her outspoken remarks. At Longwood, where he was irked by Lowe's petty restrictions, one can see him peering at his guards through the holes he had made in the shutters, or else working in the garden or riding round the small compass of the estate which was permitted. One thinks too of his last moments, when he was racked with pain, and the peace which his mortal remains found in the isolated wildness of Geranium Valley. In 1840, when those remains were disinterred and his body exposed to view, he appeared almost miraculously preserved, as it were in the prime of his martial glory, while Marshal Bertrand and the others who had shared his exile and returned nineteen years later to remove his remains to France, looked weatherbeaten old men.

'He was the greatest enemy of England, and of myself also,' Sir Hudson Lowe exclaimed when he saw Napoleon lying dead in

Longwood, 'but I forgive him.' England might well have treated him more generously than she did after he had surrendered and thrown himself on her mercy, just as Sir Hudson Lowe might have carried out his instructions with more sympathy and latitude. The tale of these years has been vividly told by M. Martineau in the following pages, and I commend his account to what deserves to be a wide circle of English readers.

I

PRISONERS OF STATE

✛✛

The *Northumberland*—Arrival at St. Helena—Porteous
House—The plateau of Longwood—The Briars—The
Balcombe family—British regulations.

✛✛

On August 9, 1815, Napoleon and his companions in exile left
England on board the *Northumberland*, escorted by the brigs *Zephyr*,
Icarus, *Redpole* and *Ferret*, and the troop-ships *Bucephalus*, *Havannah* and *Ceylon*; they came within sight of St. Helena on October 14.

Memories of the stupendous events of the last fifteen years had
faded, the dreams of a great European empire were over, the gilded
drawing-rooms of the imperial palaces were deserted, the attentive
chamberlains in gaudy uniforms had fled; and the formidable
leader who had known everything, and controlled everything, to
whom everything was possible, was a powerless prisoner in the hands
of the Allied powers. The man whom the English agreed to call
'General Bonaparte' had a mere handful of followers at his command.

So this gloomy rock was to be his home. Leaning on Marchand's
arm, he studied it through the fieldglasses he had used at Austerlitz.
The French were appalled. 'It is not an attractive place,' Napoleon
muttered. 'I should have done better to remain in Egypt.' Seen from
the sea, this massive rock, this maritime fortress bristling with guns,
certainly presented a gloomy picture; it seemed to have risen from
the waves fully armed, like Pallas Athene. 'The devil must have s..t
the island as he flew from one world to the other,' one of the ladies
of Napoleon's suite is supposed to have remarked. The tall sombre
barrier hid the horizon and darkened the sea; the steep cliffs seemed
to melt into the grey sky, the walls were spiky with artillery, and the
wretched townlet of Jamestown could be seen huddled in a gigantic
cleft in the rocks, with its few pallid houses among clumps of

I

greenery, and the Union Jack floating free in the wind above the bleak walls of the fortress.

They had hoped for something better after the extreme discomforts of the *Northumberland*: the poetic landscape of Elba, perhaps, or the picturesque and smiling shores of the Mediterranean; men's dreams are not always reasonable, even those of vanquished and exhausted prisoners. Exhausted they certainly were, for the passage had been a painful endurance test. The *Northumberland* was an ancient ship, already marked down for demolition when the British Admiralty fitted her out in great haste; she was unsuitably rigged, ill equipped and miserably provisioned for so long a voyage, and her decks swarmed with soldiers, women and children. More than a thousand souls took part in that interminable procession, and the dreary journey was made even more tedious by the fact that, for some obscure reason, the English Admiral chose the longest route. During those twelve weeks, though the Emperor's propensity for walking restlessly to and fro with his hands clasped behind him was well known, he had to put up with a small cabin; the Admiral refused to give him the saloon, which was for general use, or the adjoining room. 'Tell the General', he said to the Grand Marshal when he came to ask permission, 'that it is contrary to regulations to lend the Admiral's cabin to anyone at all, least of all to a prisoner of war.'

The discomfort of his lodging was increased by the boredom of getting to know new faces: replacements for some members of the imperial household had had to be found at the last moment— General de Montholon and his wife, Count de Las Cases and his son. Of his familiar companions the only ones left him were the Grand Marshal, General Bertrand, and his wife, and General Gourgaud, his aide-de-camp.

The look-out-man's cry of 'Land!' was therefore heard with a sense of relief by those on board the Admiral's ship. To free men this is the signal for a return to family happiness in their native land and marks the end of the loneliness of the voyage, but for those on board the tall warship it stood for consignment to oblivion. Some of them, no doubt, hoped in their heart of hearts for some change of fortune, for one of those dramatic surprises so typical of the man in their midst; and during the six years of their coming captivity their evenings were to be soothed and their imaginations inflamed by the

St. Helena, from a drawing by Lambert and Scott, engraved by G. Vander Gucht

St. Helena by J. Clark and J. Hamble, *c.* 1806

wildest projects. But for the moment, arrival in sight of the island signified the prospect of material comfort; they were hoping for the wide open spaces of the Isle of Elba, the genial friendliness of Latin races, and some degree of independence.

Taking advantage of a favourable wind to sail round the southern shore of the island and enter Jamestown bay from the west, the *Northumberland* dropped anchor on the morning of October 15. A boat was lowered at once and Admiral Sir George Cockburn went ashore with Colonel Bingham, the new commanding officer of the garrison, to pay their official respects to Colonel Wilks, Governor for the East India Company. The Admiral also had to produce his instructions, which were to safeguard the government of the colony and arrange for 'General Bonaparte and his suite' to be installed there.

A postscript to the instructions had been added by the Secretary of State for the Colonies, Lord Bathurst, who was responsible for the administration of the island—and therefore for Napoleon's detention: 'His Royal Highness . . . relies on Sir George Cockburn's known zeal and energy of character that he will not allow himself to be betrayed into any improvident relaxation of his duty.' Nothing could have been better calculated to stiffen the determination of a professional sailor, and Cockburn was nothing if not that. An admiral at forty-three, this brilliant officer had served under Nelson and made his name by taking the town of Washington in 1813. Rigid, even a little haughty, he at first felt very little sympathy for Bonaparte and his suite, who often struck him as noisy, exacting and bad-mannered. But during the voyage he had had time to modify his attitude, and in the end he too capitulated to the spell of his terrible prisoner's personality: he tried to please him by speaking French and having it spoken at table, he allowed the Emperor to preside at meals, he stood up when he left the room and shared his walks on deck in the evenings. But if duty did not forbid such marks of kindness and courtesy, it did not admit of weakness.

Once on land, Cockburn, Bingham and Wilks studied the long document written by the directors of the East India Company:

'Napoleon Buonaparte having surrendered himself to the Government of this country, His Majesty's ministers, deeply sensible of the high importance of effectually securing the person of a man whose conduct has proved so fatal to the happiness of the world, and judging that the island of St.

Helena is eminently fitted to answer that purpose, have proposed to us that he shall be placed there under a system of government adopted to serve the end in view. . . . As the East India Company hold the principle of rendering their means and faculties, on all practical occasions, conducive to the national interests and objects, we have not thought ourselves at liberty to decline a compliance with the proposal thus made to us in so remarkable a case. . . . For the ministers of the King being responsible to the Nation and the other powers of Europe for the safe custody of Buonaparte they deem it necessary that such custody should be committed to the care of a general officer of the King's Service, particularly known to and selected by them, to be assisted with a body of King's troops and, as requisite to the object of his appointment, to be invested also with the government of the island whilst the service in which he is employed continues. . . . Being entirely satisfied with the conduct of Colonel Wilks and having had no intention that the system on which he has carried on the government should be interrupted, we regret that this unexpected occurrence is likely to deprive us of his service.'

When the Admiral returned on board at noon with Colonel Wilks, the latter was now in a subordinate position and could therefore talk freely with Napoleon, who found him frank and good-natured. They discussed the island and its climate, as well as India, for Wilks had served there and was writing its history.

Cockburn's first concern was to find his passengers a large house, conveniently situated from the point of view of security, and lending itself to alteration and enlargement at the least possible expense. He devoted October 16 to this quest, and went ashore early that morning to explore the island, while the Emperor and his companions, forced to remain on board, relieved their boredom by watching the reinforcements for the garrison disembarking, and the transhipment of stores and merchandise. At six o'clock the Admiral returned, fatigued by his long ride under the October sun, and announced that he thought he had discovered a suitable lodging; the residence of the Lieutenant-Governor, Colonel Skelton. It was a large house on the plateau of Longwood, and after certain alterations and extensions it could be made to house 'the General and his family', as they were already described on St. Helena; but when he went on to say that the work would take at least four months there were loud protests from the French, for they were well aware that Cockburn had orders to keep the prisoners on board his ship until the work was completed, for obvious reasons of security. Wanting to be magnanimous, and as Las Cases added 'with evident satisfaction', the Admiral explained that he had taken it upon himself to rent an inn 'by the week' to accommodate the French during the alterations: it was a pleasant enough house, situated in the town near the Castle—where he would be taking up residence himself—and it was clean and spacious. They could take possession next day. In order to escape the curiosity of the inhabitants already crowding the quay, Napoleon decided to disembark at seven o'clock after dinner, the hour when darkness falls in the tropics.

On the morning of the 17th, Bertrand went to inspect this temporary lodging; he returned in low spirits, saying that it was a very modest establishment, clean certainly, but dreadfully uncomfortable: there was no garden or courtyard, it was right on the street, and thus fully exposed to incessant noise, heat and the curiosity of the passers-by. What a contrast to the Castle next door, with its crenellated walls, moat, and beautiful reception rooms! But Cockburn, imbued with the British principle that a house must conform to the rank of its inmates, was determined to keep this for himself, as the seat of the government of the colony and of authority once Bonaparte was installed on the island; it did not seem to him, therefore, altogether a bad idea, politically speaking, that Porteous House—as the inn provided for Boney was called—should cut a poor figure beside the Castle. This was in keeping with the social order, and it would give Bonaparte his first lesson in humility!

The news that the Corsican ogre was to disembark on the evening of October 17 had already reached shore and been spread by mysterious bush-telegraph throughout the island; the information that he was to be exiled on St. Helena had arrived with the *Icarus*, which was separated from the *Northumberland* by bad weather off Madeira, but afterwards steered a better course, struck more favourable winds, and reached the island five days before the rest of the convoy. The inhabitants were thunderstruck; news from Europe generally arrived so late as to have no sort of bearing on local interests, and like other islanders they were unenthusiastic about anything but their own affairs. But this time tongues were set wagging with a vengeance, for they heard of the escape from Elba, the battle of Waterloo, and the Emperor's final abdication all at the same moment.

The wildest fears were rife, for Boney had an unsavoury reputation based on gossip brought by sailors putting in at the island, English caricatures, the adventures of French émigrés as retailed by the news-sheets, and stories told by the island nurses to frighten the children. 'The earliest idea I had of Napoleon was that of a huge ogre or giant,' young Betsy Balcombe admitted, 'associated in my mind with everything that was bad and horrible.'

It is easy to imagine the curiosity mixed with terror that seized hold of the population. The people of St. Helena normally disliked anything that interfered with the reassuring and monotonous routine of their lives, or forced them to behave in an unusual or improvised manner, and this little world of bewildered officials, planters and soldiers was filled with misgivings at the thought of a dethroned sovereign with his suite, troops of soldiers and a new governor suddenly being thrown among them, like a stone into a quiet pool.

'We were so eager to see the illustrious exile,' Betsy Balcombe continues, 'that we determined to go in the evening to the valley to witness his disembarkation. It was nearly dark when we arrived at the landing-place, and shortly after, a boat from the *Northumberland* approached, and we saw a figure step from it on to the shore, which we were told was the Emperor, but it was too dark to distinguish his features. He walked up the lines between the Admiral and General Bertrand, and enveloped as he was in his surtout, I could see little, but the occasional gleam of a diamond star, which he wore on his heart.'

She might have added that this bright star shining among her childish memories suddenly thrust the obscure island into the lime-light of fame: it was a strange sort of fame no doubt, but it would endure as long as the last inhabitant of our planet. As Heinrich Heine, the author of *Drummer Legrand*, has so superbly written: 'To the end of time, French youth will sing and tell of the dreadful hospitality of the *Bellerophon*, and when those songs of scorn and tears sound across the Channel a blush will rise on the cheeks of every honourable Briton. But a day will come when their songs will be heard and there will be no Britain any more; the proud race will be dashed to the ground, the graves of Westminster will lie in ruins, the royal dust which they enclosed will be forgotten. St. Helena will be the holy grave where the races of the East and West will make their pilgrimages in ships flying bright pennons, and take courage from the great memories of the deeds of the worldly saviour who suffered under Sir Hudson Lowe, as it is written under the gospels according to Las Cases, O'Meara and Antommarchi.'

But at this moment, it was the General Bonaparte who had been defeated at Waterloo, 'prisoner of State of His Britannic Majesty', whom the motley, silent crowd was watching, as a party of officers escorted him to the shabby inn. 'The pressure became so great that it was with difficulty way could be made for him, and the sentries were at last ordered to stand with fixed bayonets at the entrance from the lines to the town, to prevent the multitude from pouring in.' Whites and blacks stood silently watching the most important prisoner in history go by, as if he had been a 'wild beast': no one spoke or shouted, there were no demonstrations of sympathy or hostility. Nothing but silence. It was symbolic. For them, as for Walter Scott, Bonaparte had been deprived of the means of a second avatar or reincarnation on earth.

It is interesting to note that the construction of the quay at Jamestown has been altered since the 1815 disembarkation. All those tourists and historians who say they have trod the same steps as the Emperor are completely mistaken. There are three flights of steps leading to this quay, from east to west. The oldest is the central flight, now only used by fishermen—the two others are recent—and it was here that the Emperor came ashore in the *Northumberland*'s dinghy. It is also untrue that, as some writers suppose, the Emperor walked on the part of the quay we still use today; at that time the road penetrated the fortified wall and entered the town at a point further to the east than it does at present. It ran along the inside of the wall on a level with the battlements opening on to the sea, and led to a drawbridge over the moat which can still be seen near the tennis-court.

Porteous House was not much to look at, and only a sailor could have been so blind as to imagine for a single moment that a large and varied party of masters and valets, women and children, could be housed within its four walls. There were three windows on the ground floor and five on the first, and the only staircase was narrow and gave on to the street. Of course Admiral Cockburn had only landed the day before and could not be held responsible for this unfortunate and tactless choice, any more perhaps than Hudson Lowe was for selecting Longwood House. Who was to blame? Wilks? Unquestionably, for it was he who accompanied the Admiral on his tour of inspection and acted as his guide. Owing to some curious aberration of judgement, Wilks always appears in the history books as a white-haired dandy, tall, distinguished, affable and witty, and every historian supplements his predecessor's text with a few bouquets to the man who received the Emperor and his generals on their arrival and answered their questions wittily. He could in fact have ruled out Porteous House at once as not good enough, and Longwood House for its exposed position and dampness; Cockburn would have listened to his advice. But Wilks was too much of a soldier, in the worst sense of the word, to express decisive opinions; he was a skilful diplomatist and preferred to approve the Admiral's choice while at the same time taking the courteous initiative of going to greet 'General Bonaparte' on board ship. This was in no way a spontaneous and frank gesture of deference: it was his duty as Governor to greet important visitors, and the instructions from London described the prisoner as 'an officer of the highest rank'; Napoleon had a right therefore to expect the Governor's visit in virtue of the subtleties of colonial protocol. As to the choice of houses, how could such a good soldier as Wilks realise his mistake? In 1805 Porteous House had been honoured by the presence of a certain Arthur Wellesley, the future Duke of Wellington, on his way back from India, and surely a house which satisfied the victor of Waterloo ought to be quite good enough for his defeated enemy; as for Longwood House, it was the property of the Lieutenant-Governor of the colony, and apart from Plantation House it was the second best choice. It was useless for the French to storm and fret: they must realise that the conventions had been observed.

The French ladies in particular showed little signs of appreciating this special logic when they gathered in the sole sitting-room of the Porteous Inn. This boarding-house had been described as clean, but it was in fact crawling with bugs. After the prisoners had left, the owners made capital out of their visit, displaying the words 'Honneur et Patrie, 1815' written in General Gourgaud's hand, and renting 'the Emperor's room' at a high price, right up to a day at the end of the century when purifying fire put an end to these relics and their exploitation for money.

The Emperor's valet, Marchand, who disembarked before his master, prepared his room according to his long-standing and unalterable habits on campaign; the other officers installed themselves as best they could. Napoleon flung himself on his bed, but sleep eluded him: he got up and called Marchand who was dozing in a neighbouring closet, made him light a candle and indulged in his usual passion for carrying on a rambling conversation with his servant. He complained of the inconvenience of the house and spoke of Longwood House: 'I will go and see it tomorrow, and unless it's in a very bad state I will arrange to move in there.'

Early next morning, when the freshness of dawn had enabled Napoleon to sleep, the Admiral arrived to escort the French party to Longwood. He was kept waiting while the Emperor got ready, and expressed his irritation rudely. 'The Admiral is an ill-mannered man' was all Napoleon could say in reply: it was not easy for a man who had so long been the master to learn to be a prisoner, even a prisoner of State. Would anyone at the Tuileries ever have dared to stand up to him? Napoleon expressed this reflection one sad day some time later when the Grand Marshal had been emboldened by the audacity of the English to criticise his master: 'You would not have spoken to me like that at the Tuileries; then everything I did was right.' Absolute power spoils a man, and Napoleon, whose profoundly human qualities still astonish us, must have suffered more at St. Helena from having to adapt himself to ordinary life even than from remoteness, isolation and illness: his long battle with Hudson Lowe was centred entirely round his view that sovereignty was essentially permanent, and the anointing of a king had incontestable validity.

The road from Jamestown to Longwood is long, rough and difficult, but even under the oppressive October sun it had charms for the riders after the inactivity of the voyage. The procession, headed by Cockburn and Napoleon, with Bertrand, Ali and the Admiral's aide-de-camp behind, advanced slowly up the 'side path', as the inhabitants called the track painfully hollowed out of the rocky flank of the hill, which reached an altitude of nearly two thousand feet in two-and-a-half miles. The Frenchmen's eyes were attracted to a pleasant clump of trees slightly set back from the track: this was The

Briars, the property of William Balcombe of the East India Company. Some little girls were watching the procession from a hillock crowned by a Chinese pavilion. 'We were still doubtful whether Napoleon were of the party,' the youngest girl was to write later; 'we had already learnt to look for the grey surtout and small cocked hat, but no figure in that dress could be distinguished.' As the horses slowly advanced, their riders had plenty of time to examine the landscape, which made an unfamiliar and kaleidoscopic impression on Europeans accustomed to gentler contours, softer colours and veiled contrasts. On their right was the valley of Jamestown, like a gash made by a gigantic wedge, in which the few humble dwellings of the capital were huddled; beyond was a horseshoe-shaped waterfall, reduced to a mere thread in October and surrounded by thin shrubs wilting in the torrid heat. After the horses had panted up several bends in the road, they reached the top of the plateau, and were confronted by the imposing bulk of Alarm House, surrounded by stunted trees, and with a few soldiers busy around it. The alarm-gun was sunk in its metal slumber, unaware that it had just had the honour of announcing the arrival of the man who only a few weeks ago had been directing the storm of battle.

Suddenly, lit up as in a nightmare, the travellers saw opening to their left beneath a rocky spur the valley known as Sane, Seine or Geranium Valley; it was variously named and spelled up till 1821, when by common consent the Valley of the Tomb took its place in the geography of St. Helena. This ravine with its gloomy decor of lava, rubbed black rocks, and shrubs ceaselessly twisting and untwisting in the wind, gave shelter only to a few goats and pheasants. The upper part of it, reached through Hutt's Gate, had been christened the Devil's Punch Bowl, a wonderfully descriptive name for this unlovely basin through which warm, ragged clouds swept month after month and year after year, blighting the trees with their unwholesome breath, corroding the rocks, and exhausting anyone who walked there.

In the distance, squatting on the plateau of Longwood, a group of low buildings was silhouetted against the sky, with their backs to the wind in the feeble shelter of a few slender eucalyptus trees: this was Longwood House. We shall never know what thoughts passed through the Emperor's mind at this moment. Did he suspect that this was to be the final setting for his exile and his grave? Or did hope, that bird that goes on fluttering until a man's last breath, rouse dreams of yet another triumphal return?

The Lieutenant-Governor, Colonel Skelton, and his wife lived here in the summer; they knew the island too well not to realise that winters on the plateau were murderous, and only from October until February did they leave their house in Jamestown opposite Porteous House, and come to seek the cool freshness of the trade-winds at Longwood. During the other months this sinister landscape was deserted; lower down were a few houses nestling in the shelter of the south slopes of Fisher's Valley, but on the plateau itself no life was to be seen. With feminine desire to please, Mrs. Skelton provided an excellent luncheon, and showered attentions on the Emperor; she enjoyed showing off her knowledge of French and was distinctly thrilled to find herself entertaining the defeated sovereign.

Napoleon's quick judgement and observant eye must have grasped the drawbacks of the establishment instantly. What was this old converted farm-house like? A drawing-room had been added to the front of the house and also served as a hall; there were a dining-room, three bedrooms, and outbuildings arranged on the usual plan of the cottages in the colony. 'The Emperor was only moderately charmed by the house,' Marchand tells us; 'it possessed neither shade nor water, and was exposed to the prevailing south-east wind which was blowing violently at the time.' Its only advantage was that the large plateau would lend itself to rides and drives in the shelter of the eucalyptus grove. But what a lot of work would have to be done before these few rooms could be made ready for the 'General' and the thirty members of his suite!

At three o'clock the Emperor sent for his horse and said goodbye to the Skeltons: it was hot and the sun was shining brightly as the little party returned to Jamestown by the same winding road. As they descended, the abundant vegetation of the plateau, nourished by constant humidity, gave way to an arid landscape of cacti and wild geraniums, and the rounded shapes of the valleys to sharp ridges of volcanic rock parched by the heat of the sun; the Emperor must have dreaded the return to Porteous House, the distressing curiosity of the inhabitants and the stifling airless street no less than his Grand Marshal did. It may have been some such idea, or the desire to put a few miles between himself and the Admiral, or the romantic beauty of the grounds of The Briars, suddenly glimpsed among tall trees at the foot of a waterfall, that made the Emperor express a wish to go there. It belonged to Balcombe, purveyor and agent of the East India Company; he was in bed with an attack of gout at the time, but his family came out on to the lawn, trembling with emotion as the Admiral made the introductions. Betsy, the youngest girl, afterwards described the scene:

'On a nearer approach Napoleon, contrasting, as his shorter figure did, with the noble height and aristocratic bearing of Sir George Cockburn, lost something of the dignity which had so much struck me on first seeing him. He was deadly pale, and I thought his features, though cold and immovable, and somewhat stern, were exceedingly beautiful. He seated himself on one of our cottage chairs, and after scanning our little apartment with his eagle glance, he complimented Mamma on the pretty situation of the Briars. When once he began to speak, his fascinating smile and kind manner removed every vestige of the fear with which I had hitherto regarded him.'

It was four o'clock and the sun was slowly sinking behind the great wall of rock barring the horizon to the west, and spreading a softer and more peaceful light over the valley; there was a shady arbour, and fish gliding in a pond. The Emperor was charmed by his halting-place and conquered by its friendliness and peace: he asked about a pavilion adjoining the house. It was a summer-house built by William Balcombe for his children and their friends to have supper-parties in, and it consisted of a single room a few yards square, attractively decorated in the Regency style, with very large windows opening to the south, east and west. An attic, six feet square, above this room had to serve as a bedroom for Las Cases and his son, who were fetched by Bertrand to join the Emperor, while Marchand and Ali slept in front of their master's door, wrapped in cloaks and lying on rotten old mattresses from the *Northumberland*.

Napoleon spent nearly two months camping there, and one is tempted to call them the halcyon days of his exile. Kindly forgetfulness was already beginning to heal the effects of the terrible nervous strain of Waterloo, his abdication and flight across western France: the tranquillity of this simple but attractive abode, the respectful courtesy of the Balcombes, the pretty ways of the children, Betsy's unselfconscious chatter, and the silence of the park, disturbed only by the cries of the farm animals, all combined to bring him relaxation and rest.

But first the pavilion must be furnished. The Balcombes gave Marchand a few chairs, an armchair and a table to serve as writing-desk and dining-table. The camp bed was set up by one of the windows, the silver-fitted dressing-case glittered from the top of a chest of drawers, and the Balcombes were astonished by a wonderful washhand basin, made by Biennais, the Emperor's goldsmith in the days of his splendour. Miniatures of the King of Rome and the Empress hung on the walls, as they did on those of his tent during campaigns.

The catering problem was dealt with next; the first dinner had been a disagreeable experience, as the dishes had been brought from the town, arrived cold and were swallowed with distaste by lamplight. Next day the Emperor's polite and tactful valet, Marchand, managed to get hold of a cottage stove, and sent for Pierron, the official chef, and Lepage, his assistant, as well as silver and linen. Cipriani Franceschi, the major-domo, remained in the town with the Archambault brothers, Rousseau, Gentilini and Santini to look after the officers of the household. These servants had not yet succumbed to boredom, and they waited on their master with as much devoted zeal and affection now that he was a prisoner, as when he was the sovereign of the Tuileries.

To complete these arrangements, Colonel Bingham, the new commanding officer of the garrison, came to The Briars and offered the help of his soldiers in setting up a marquee on the lawn opposite the pavilion, to serve as dining-room and study. For work was to be Napoleon's chief occupation during his short stay with the Balcombes. He had begun dictating *The Italian Campaign* to Las Cases during the voyage, and this occupation invited or even demanded that daily intellectual effort which is the natural relaxation of men of action, and which Napoleon's prodigious memory, gift for historical narrative and critical sense especially fitted him for. Faithful to the promise he had made on taking leave of the Guard at Fontainebleau ('I will write about the great things we have done together') he had embarked on a study of his finest campaign as soon as he was on board the *Northumberland*.

Work thus helped to fill his days at The Briars to overflowing: he got dressed early, took a short stroll among the lac-trees and date-palms in the park, breakfasted about ten, took another stroll, and then embarked on his task. First Las Cases read what he had dictated on the previous evening from a fair copy, made by his son that morning; this was approved or corrected by Napoleon, who then began dictating a new lot of pages. At about five o'clock they broke off for a walk in what the exiles had christened the 'philosophers' avenue', and dinner followed soon afterwards at six o'clock. Then Napoleon would enthral his listeners by conjuring up scenes from his past, his triumphs and his meetings with great men, and firing off names and dates. These preliminary gymnastics stimulated his memory, and were the best possible preparation for his next session of dictation, but when he closed his eyes Napoleon probably forgot that he was in the middle of the ocean in enemy hands. In rapid, jerky sentences he sketched in the background of events and painted the portraits of the chief characters, with obvious concern to explain and dissect, for the edification of posterity, the machinery of his reign, and particularly of the great institutions he was so proud of, the Council of State, the University, the Legion of Honour and the Bank of France.

Las Cases soon began urging him to start dictating his account of the Egyptian campaign, the Consulate and the return from Elba; these would be taken down by the generals, while Marchand and Ali the valets were to turn themselves into copyists: in this way everyone would be kept busy.

When darkness fell—and this happens early in the tropics, between six and seven—Napoleon used to send Las Cases over to the Balcombes to find out if they were alone, in which case he would spend the evening with the family. 'They are excellent people,' he said. The head of the house used to lie with his gouty foot up on a sofa, and his wife and children kept him company; there would be a homely conversation about novels; the little girls asked ingenuous or absurd questions, and burst out laughing whenever Napoleon said anything. 'It's like a fancy-dress ball,' said Napoleon, charmed by this relaxed atmosphere. Sometimes they played whist, or young Betsy sang *Ye banks and braes,* and Napoleon gave a spirited rendering of *Vive Henri Quatre,* and afterwards announced in tones of finality that English music was the worst in the world; only the Italians knew how to compose an opera.

Outside was the stifling stillness of the hot tropical night; slaves came and went with trays of drinks; crickets vibrated in the silence; large insects fluttered round the lamps. They were submerged in the same exotic atmosphere that had delighted Napoleon when Bernardin de Saint-Pierre's *Paul and Virginia* took French society by storm. These were certainly the halcyon days of his exile. Although the Emperor was leading a bourgeois life, he was treated with suitable respect; within his domain he was a king surrounded by a little court, and his meals were announced by the traditional 'His Majesty is served', while his officers were kept busy galloping between The Briars and Jamestown to carry out his orders. British surveillance was discreet: when Napoleon caught sight of the captain, sergeant or the few soldiers who were billeted on the Balcombes, he at once complained and the soldiers were withdrawn, while the captain was ordered to wear mufti.

Within this little corner of the island he was to all intents and purposes free: free at least to go for walks, visit the master of the house, or stroll along the stony paths surrounding the estate. No risk was involved in these escapades, for, from his office in the Castle, the Admiral had woven a web in which the French were caught like flies and kept under complete control. On October 17, the actual day of disembarkation, there had been a meeting of the council, and Colonel Wilks, Colonel Skelton, William Doveton and Robert Leech solemnly legislated concerning the Emperor's fate: he was Gulliver in the hands of the Lilliputians. These four obscure members of the East India Company laid down rules that would transform the island of St. Helena into a prison and the rock into a fortress:

'Whereas His Royal Highness the Prince Regent acting in the name and behalf of His Majesty has been pleased to command that General N. Buonaparte and the French persons attending him should be detained on the Island of St. Helena—and the Honourable the Court of Directors have been pleased to issue to this government certain orders consequent on such determination.

This is therefore to warn all inhabitants and other persons on this Island from aiding and abetting hereafter in any way whatsoever the escape of the said General N. Buonaparte and that of any of the French persons who have arrived here with him and to interdict most pointedly the holding of any communication or correspondence with him or them excepting only such as may be regularly authorised by the Governor, or by Rear-Admiral Sir George Cockburn, in whose immediate charge the said General N. Buonaparte and his attendants are particularly placed.

Any person after the promulgation of this ordinance presuming to act in violation thereof will be immediately sent off the Island and be liable to be further punished as the circumstances of the case may appear to deserve.'

After these preliminaries came the details:

'Whereas during the detention at St. Helena of General N. Buonaparte and the French persons attending him, it appears essentially necessary to adopt some additional precautions on the Island, and particularly by night —this is therefore to give notice to the inhabitants and other persons of every description that after this date nobody whatsoever will be permitted to pass in any part of the Island (excepting within the immediate precincts of the Town) between the hours of 9 at night and daylight in the morning without having the parole for the night—the sentries and patrols having orders henceforth to secure and hold as prisoners until morning all persons they may find between the said periods not possessing the parole, and the officers of the different guards are to cause all persons so taken up to be sent prior to being released next morning to the Governor with a State-ment of the particular circumstances under which they were apprehended.
. . .

Whereas it has been deemed expedient that the whole coast of this Island and the vessels and boats frequenting it be placed, until further orders, under the immediate control of Rear-Admiral Sir G. Cockburn.

This is therefore to make known the same to all the inhabitants and others now on the Island or that may hereafter arrive here, and to direct that all persons possessing boats do immediately make a return thereof specifying the description of the boat, and the use generally made of her. . . .

His Royal Highness the Prince Regent having been pleased to command the detention of General N. Buonaparte on the Island of St. Helena and having further signified his pleasure that the said General N. Buonaparte should be respected and considered on all occasions as a General, the respective officers of this garrison therefore whenever the said General Napoleon Buonaparte may pass, or they may in any way meet him, are to turn out guards and otherwise show him the same marks of respect pre-cisely as a General in His Majesty's Service not in chief command would be entitled to.'

Las Cases' *Mémorial* and Betsy Balcombe's *Recollections* have familiarised us with several strange incidents of Napoleon's stay at The Briars. The Balcombes had an old Malay slave called Toby, who had reigned over the garden for the last forty years; he called Napoleon 'the good gentleman' and was always ready to bring him the finest fruit from his trees in exchange for a few gold coins. The Emperor offered to buy him and give him back his freedom, but the Governor refused to agree to his request, probably thinking that the news would act as inopportune propaganda among the other coloured inhabitants. So Toby remained the Balcombes' slave, but began to figure in popular history as illustrated by engravings or on printed stuffs. On another occasion Napoleon was staving off boredom by making an inventory of his treasures: snuff-boxes, gold boxes, cameos, miniatures and dressing-cases. When Las Cases admired one of these the Emperor gave it to him: 'I have had it a long time; I used it on the morning before Austerlitz. Emmanuel shall have it. By the time he is eighty it will be quite a curiosity. He will be able to say "The Emperor Napoleon gave it to my father at St. Helena".' We also have details of the daily life and games of the Balcombe children, as described by Betsy, which throw an unexpected light on Napoleon's psychology; now that he was free from the tyranny and the trappings of power, and had recovered from the physical and moral prostration that followed his last campaign, he seems to have been transformed into a teasing old uncle. Once he pretended to be an ogre to frighten a little girl friend of the family, ruffling up his hair and growling like a wild beast; he allowed Betsy to threaten him with a sword, hid her first ball-dress, played hide-and-seek, gave away cakes and sweets, and discussed the most serious subjects with the little girl in a bantering tone.

While Napoleon, hurled from the heights of supreme power, was whiling away the boredom of these first months by playing with children and dwelling on the past, the Admiral, in the silence of his study, was putting the final touches to the regulations. The instructions received from London were explicit, and Rear-Admiral Sir George Cockburn, Knight Commander of the Bath, veteran of the battle of Cape St. Vincent and the American war, certainly hoped to profit from his zeal and punctiliousness, by giving complete satisfaction to the Prime Minister and the Secretary of State for the

Colonies, with both of whom he had had extremely confidential conversations; he did not propose to leave a single detail to chance, and his sailor's eye would keep a sharp look-out for squalls from any quarter.

Colonel Wilks still held the title of Governor, but he was bound hand and foot by the instructions of the East India Company:

'As the officer destined to be the new governor of St. Helena is not yet arrived from the Continent and it is judged expedient to convey Buonaparte to that Island without delay, Rear-Admiral Sir George Cockburn, who commanded the squadron appointed to guard him there is invested by His Majesty's Government with the temporary care and custody of him, until the new governor shall arrive; and as Sir George Cockburn is charged with the whole responsibility of this service it is proper he should for the time direct the measures which he may deem necessary and you are hereby ordered to execute these measures upon his requisition and responsibility.'

All security measures were therefore planned by Cockburn and Wilks, and the other members of the council merely had to give them legal force by converting them into proclamations:

'The disposition of the military allotted to guard him must be left to the Governor, the Governor being instructed to attend to the wishes of the Admiral in the instances hereafter to be mentioned. The General must always be attended by an officer appointed by the Admiral or Governor as the case may be. If the General be permitted to move beyond the boundaries where the sentries are placed, the officer should be attended by one orderly at least. In the event of ships arriving, so long as they continue in sight the General must be confined within the boundary where the sentries shall be placed. He must during that interval be prohibited from all intercourse and communication with the inhabitants. They who accompany him to St. Helena must be subject at this period to the same regulations. They are to reside with him; and it is left to the discretion of the Admiral in the first instance, and to the new Governor afterwards, to establish such regulations with respect to them at other times as may appear expedient.
. . .
The General must be given to understand that, in the event of his attempting to escape, he will be afterwards subject to close custody; and they who go out with him also understand that, if they shall be detected in contriving means for his escape, they will be separated from him and placed in close custody. All letters addressed to him, or his attendants, must be first delivered to the Admiral or to the Governor, as the case may

St. Helena, a drawing by Durand Brager

Betsy Balcombe as a young woman, from a photograph
taken in 1857 by G. W. Mellis

The Briars from a photograph taken in 1857

be, who will read them before they are delivered to the persons to whom they are addressed. All letters written by the General or his attendants must be subject to the same regulation. No letter which has not been transmitted to St. Helena by the Secretary of State should be delivered to the General . . . if it be written by any person not resident in the Island. . . . The General must be given clearly to understand that the Governor and the Admiral are strictly instructed to forward to His Majesty's Government any wish or representation which he may think proper to make . . . but the paper on which such application or representation may be written must be left open for their joint inspection, in order that in transmitting it they may be enabled to accompany it with such observations as they may think expedient. Until the arrival of the new Governor, the Admiral must be considered as entirely responsible for the security of General Buonaparte's person; and His Majesty's Government entertains no doubt of the disposition of the actual Governor to concert with the Admiral for this purpose.'

The division of power between the Admiral and Governor Wilks seems curious and deserves a moment's consideration. It would appear that the decision to make neither of the two completely subordinate to the other was made precisely in order to keep the situation indefinite and equivocal—a favourite procedure in British diplomacy. If the Admiral's name had figured alone on this document, Wilks might well have sulked in his tent and waited for a retirement which would be more profitable than this burdensome post. In order that the Damoclean sword of reprisals (which were bound to be exemplary) should remain suspended day and night over both their heads, depriving them of happiness and sleep, the two officers had to share the responsibility; and with one nudging the other whenever his vigilance failed, His Majesty's Government could expect that its subordinates would set about their task with a will.

They were to be supported by Colonel Sir George Bingham, who commanded the garrison and had at his disposal fifty officers and seven hundred men of the East India Company, as well as the troops from the transports of Cockburn's convoy—namely eight companies of infantry and a detachment of artillery.

While a vigilant guard was to be established over the prisoner, the aspect of the little island was to be transformed by the arrival of these eleven hundred soldiers and the ships' crews. Red tunics and

3

sailors' blue jackets would make cheerful patches of colour in the landscape, but pickets, sentinels on the ridges and at cross-roads, would act as reminders that this was not just a military review, but that they were guarding the man referred to in a letter from Count Gneisenau to Hudson Lowe in 1817:

'Over and over again I have thought of that vast and solitary ocean and that interesting rock on which you are preserving the peace of Europe. Our safety depends on your watchfulness and your strength of character; once you relax your tight guard over the most cunning scoundrel in the world, once you allow your subordinates to grant him favours out of ill-judged pity, our tranquillity will be jeopardised and the honest people of Europe will be abandoned to their former fears.'

Gneisenau and all Europe could enjoy the return of peace: Admiral Cockburn and Colonel Wilks were paving the way meritoriously for the official Governor, who was still in London, and in the intervals between making a late marriage and being received into the distinguished Order of the Bath, was putting the finishing touches to the system which was to make him the most famous gaoler in history.

II

DAILY LIFE AT LONGWOOD HOUSE

✦✦✦

The move to Longwood—Description of Longwood
House—The Emperor's companions—The servants—
Organisation of the imperial household—Boundaries—
Work—The Emperor's day—The question of money—
Catering—Expenses—Contacts with the imperial
family—Food—The climate of Longwood—The
Emperor's health.

✦✦✦

'How far is Saint Helena from the field of Waterloo?
A near way—a clear way—the ship will take you soon,
A pleasant place for gentlemen with little left to do.'

RUDYARD KIPLING

By the last days of November 1815 the sojourn at The Briars had
come to an end, to the satisfaction of all concerned. Napoleon
suffered from the heat in his wooden pavilion, as well as from the
proximity of the servants and neighbours, and the fact that his
officers were so far away. The Montholons and Bertrands, crowded
into inadequate lodgings at Jamestown, were beginning to pick
quarrels over the domestic arrangements; the servants had danger-
ously little to do and gossiped with the landlord. And finally, the
Admiral was anxious to establish a permanent régime based on an
elaborate network of effective surveillance, and thus remove the
tireless and dangerous gossips he considered the imperial suite to be,
out of reach of the town and visiting ships.

Cockburn decided to give a ball on November 20; this was quite
a normal event, for it was a delightful change from the sluggish inactivity of the tropics to spend the cool summer evenings staying out
late on the candlelit terraces of the Castle, with the sea splashing
below in the moonlight. Neat, well-trained Chinese servants moved
silently about carrying silver trays laden with drinks; bandsmen in

scarlet tunics played soft music, women vied with one another to be charming, and men wore their best uniforms. The invitations were sent out by the Admiral's aide-de-camp: one was addressed to General Bonaparte, for Cockburn had naïvely asked Gourgaud a few days before: 'If I give a ball do you think the General will come?' The Emperor glanced at the invitation, shrugged and said shortly: 'Send the card to the addressee. Last time I heard of him was from the Pyramids and Mount Tabor.'

All the rest of the French came to the reception, however: the men in formal uniform, Countess Bertrand and Countess de Montholon dazzling in Paris creations sparkling with diamonds and emeralds, the relics of a past that was so very recent but none the less 'the past'. Fanny Bertrand's regal graciousness silenced the humble provincial society; Madame de Montholon's jewels eclipsed the trinkets of the other women. This sort of success is hard to forgive, and at dinner the French were given inferior places, while the Admiral offered his arm to the wife of Colonel Wilks. Gourgaud was furious; next day he complained to Napoleon, who rebuked the Grand Marshal. Before accepting the invitation he should have insisted on the French being properly treated. This was the first lesson for those who thought that at St. Helena, as at Tilsit or Vienna, titles, rank and function in the Emperor's service were valid currency.

Such treatment gave a glimpse of what was in store: nor was there long to wait, for the Admiral decided that work at Longwood House had advanced far enough for General Bonaparte to go and take up his residence there. Of course there was still much to be done before the French colony were decently lodged, but that could be seen to later. Since the Emperor had received reports about the state of the new house, and heard that painting was still in progress and hammering going on all day long, he decided to reject the Admiral's suggestion, and pointed out the inconveniences of a premature move. Cockburn was not the man to mince words: the General must submit to his decision, if not he would send a hundred men to camp at The Briars under his very nose.

Napoleon was outraged, but he fixed December 10 for the date of the move: it was a Sunday, and at about two o'clock the Admiral arrived, in a state of slight embarrassment. He was received politely and without a trace of animosity. Before getting into the saddle

Napoleon said goodbye to his hostess, presented Balcombe with a gold box bearing the imperial monogram, and invited him to pay a visit to Longwood with his family. Betsy burst into tears, and ran to the window to watch the procession move off and vanish from sight. At three o'clock, Marchand, who had gone on ahead of his master, heard the guards' drums beating a salute to the riders. The Admiral hurried forward, helped the Emperor to dismount, and did the honours of the house. The prologue to the tragedy was over; all the ensuing acts would be played out against the dull, monotonous and cramped decor of Longwood House. Inquisitive travellers, lines written by poets, the hostility of European courts and the devotion of the faithful were to make its name famous, and its harsh syllables would take their place in the story of the Empire, victory and exile merging together in one great warlike saga.

It was in fact a strange house, built on no definite plan, and without special beauty or ugliness: in fact it might have been expressly designed as a prison that dared not admit its purpose. The rooms set aside for the Emperor's use were all situated at the front of the house, in full view of both English and French; around a muddy courtyard were some sheds used as offices by the English servants who kept control over everything that came to the house for General Bonaparte; a little further back was the main building where the 'family' were to live—that is to say the Montholons, Las Cases, Gourgaud, and later on the priests Vignali and Buonavita, and Dr. Antommarchi, not to mention the invisible but ever present English orderly officer.

The house, or rather Napoleon's part of it, was entered by a flight of a few steps leading through a veranda straight into the long, light, spacious billiard-room, whose wooden ceiling and walls had rapidly been nailed in place by carpenters from the *Northumberland*. Next came the drawing-room, only moderately large but with a handsome black stone chimney-piece; it was here that the Emperor received the Admiral, standing with his hat under his arm so as to spare himself the displeasure of seeing the Englishman pull up a chair and sit down without his permission. It was in this room, between these two windows and under the King of Rome's portrait, that on May 5, 1821, his amazing life history came to an end in splendid isolation and biblical abandonment, ministered to only by unskilled

and indifferent medicasters, to be buried by foreign hands. The third
room was dark, lit only by the pallid light from the glass panel of
a door into the garden; this was to be the dining-room. It led into
the Emperor's two small private apartments and a tiny passage later
fitted up as a bathroom. The other wing of the house, with one large
room and several small ones, was to be for the use of the Montholons,
until it could be made into a library. Las Cases and his son were
housed in an attic above the kitchens, reached by a ladder. Faced
with this lack of space, the Grand Marshal decided to look for
lodgings a mile and a half away in a colonial house surrounded by
trees: there he could dream of the sumptuous table he had kept in
Paris in the name of the Emperor and King, at a cost to the Treasury
of two million francs a year.

✤   ✤   ✤

After the abdication, the stay at Malmaison, the hasty flight west-
wards to Rochefort and the exhausting voyage in the *Northumberland*, all those who from devotion or self-interest had undertaken the
ordeal of exile were at last united on the plateau of Longwood. A
better understanding of their daily life on this strange rock will be
gained by rapidly turning the pages of the gilt-edged album of their
lives, from the moment when the Emperor's star first rose one evening in the month of *Brumaire* in the lowering skies above St. Cloud.

General Bertrand had been the Emperor's aide-de-camp since
1807; the role suited this tall native of the Berry, who had left the
military academy with more ideas than experience. He possessed the
Grand Eagle of the Legion of Honour, had governed the Illyrian
provinces of the Empire and commanded a corps of the *Grande
Armée*, and when Duroc died he was chosen to carry out the brilliant
functions of Grand Marshal of the Palace. The dazzling uniform in
which he presided at official banquets, granted favours, and lived
extravagantly at the Tuileries, can today be seen hanging, faded, in a
glass case in his house at Châteauroux. He was still young, under
forty-five years old, but slight and somewhat round-shouldered and
beginning to go bald, timid and self-effacing. An engineer rather
than a soldier, he was more notable for his good-natured loyalty than
for his political sense.

His wife Fanny belonged to the influential but reckless Irish Catholic family of Dillon. Her father had fought with the Revolutionary army and perished during the Terror; her mother had quarrelled with Josephine de Beauharnais, her sister married La Tour du Pin, one of Napoleon's prefects, and went over to the royalists in 1815. but the Dillons could boast a distant relationship to the Empress Josephine, and this gave them a certain credit at court. Fanny was tall and elegant; her face was dominated by one of those prominent noses that reveal character and breeding. With the help of her intelligence, will-power or tears according to circumstances, she ruled over the husband the Emperor had chosen for her, to whom—so it was said—she would have preferred a prince or a duke. She held herself like a queen when she swam into a room, dressed in her best, and her memories of the years as vicereine in Illyria, with parties, receptions and carriages drawn by six horses, embittered her time at St. Helena.

Charles Tristan de Montholon was now thirty-two years old; thanks to the fact that he had been at an expensive school with Jerome and Louis Bonaparte and Eugene de Beauharnais, he had later been received by the new Empress. His military career had been more eventful than Bertrand's, but less successful. A Colonel on Berthier's staff at twenty-six, he left the service 'for reasons of health' and got himself made chamberlain to Josephine in 1809; from what we know about his character and his frenzied ambition, it is not surprising that he gave up camp life in the army for the anterooms of the palace where he rubbed shoulders with all the influential men of the moment. In fact he soon became French minister plenipotentiary at Würzburg, and the way seemed open to further advancement if a pretty widow had not made him commit the unpardonable sin of displeasing the Emperor. Already twice divorced, the vivacious Albine married him secretly, but disciplinary action followed immediately, and Montholon was recalled and dismissed from his post. The 'honourable functions entrusted him by His Majesty' were incompatible with this irregular marriage, which to make matters worse, bore fruit rather too soon. When the Allies invaded, Montholon was Colonel of a corps of volunteers from the Loire; he lost no time in bombarding the Bourbons with reminders of the long and faithful service of his stepfather's family, the Sémonvilles, and was at least given the rank of colonel. However, at the time of the return from Elba, he again presented himself before Napoleon, once more assumed the gold-trimmed uniform of chamberlain, and was made a general in June 1815. Perhaps he was not altogether disinterested in rallying to his old master's side, for those in control at the Restoration were tactless enough to institute an inquiry into the disappearance of certain funds from the Puy-de-Dôme, where Montholon had taken refuge when he left his department of the Loire before the Allied advance. As one of the Emperor's generals, he embarked upon the adventure of the Hundred Days, nor was any further volte-face possible: he therefore begged to be included in the 'Household' of St. Helena and his wish was granted. His company was agreeable to Napoleon, who sometimes showed a liking for the old nobility, and had made the Marquis of Montholon-Sémonville a count of the Empire. Elegant and well groomed, fairly tall, with dark curly hair, his manners were attractive and he expressed his opinions with a certain arrogance—this had its effect on the English, who nicknamed him Veritas.

Albine Hélène de Montholon is one of the most interesting figures of the Longwood party, even if only because of all the rumours that were current about her intimacy with the Emperor. She was born Vassal or Le Vassal, one of a family that had been ennobled by Louis XVI. Married first to a certain Bignon and afterwards to the Baron Roger, a Swiss business man, she had only been divorced a few weeks when she met Montholon. An accommodating or ignorant mayor performed the marriage ceremony in extremely irregular circumstances, and what was done could not be undone. Portraits of the Countess show an agreeable, distinguished and lively-looking woman, obviously an accomplished coquette; she brought freshness and good humour to the mixed company at Longwood, as well as submissiveness to the whims of the master of the house; she sang quite well, could play the piano, and knew the Italian arias that Napoleon liked to hum out of tune. The room allotted to the Montholons was only separated from the Emperor's by the pantry; the park was used by all, and when he strolled in the shrubbery or went to the stables Napoleon would stop and exchange a few words with the Countess or play with the children. This was probably why he preferred the company of the Montholons to that of the Bertrands, who had chosen to isolate themselves.

The third officer, General Gourgaud, proudly displayed the braided blue uniform of aide-de-camp to the Emperor; ever since he had been chosen to take the famous letter from the island of Aix to the Prince Regent ('I come like Themistocles to seat myself on the hearth of the British people') he had dreamed of playing the principal role beside the defeated sovereign. There may seem some irony in the fact that Gourgaud was connected with the Dugazon family, who bequeathed their name to a special branch of theatrical activity. His grandfather, who went on the stage under the name of Gourgaud, was a lively Marseillais who later became insane; three of his sons were actors, and the last—the general's father—became the King's violinist. It was from this talkative and noisy world that General Gourgaud, Baron of the Empire and Commander of the Legion of Honour, escaped to become a student of the Ecole Polytechnique and an officer of the artillery, in which the Emperor had begun his own brilliant career. In 1811 he was made aide-de-camp, after having fought at Austerlitz and Saragossa. Eaten up with ambition and the desire to cut a figure, he hatched innumerable schemes to get into touch with this sovereign who was a judge of men, and could not, so he thought, fail to take notice of a handsome and spectacularly brave officer with a slightly theatrical air. He achieved his aim by being officially recommended for the post he longed for, with the flattering comment: 'Has education and talent, has fought well, is an accurate observer who can describe what he has seen; a good draughtsman; speaks Spanish and German'. He followed the Army and the Emperor to Russia, was wounded at Smolensk and was the first to enter the Kremlin and find a bomb left there by the Russians: for this he was made a Baron of the Empire. During the agonising retreat from Russia he swam across the Beresina, saved his master's life (so he said) when surrounded by Cossacks and became first aide-de-camp, a post specially created for him. He received his colonel's epaulets and commander's collar in March 1814, and after being discharged at Fontainebleau with the rest, he joined the Bourbons who made him a Chevalier of Saint-Louis, with the result that he was not received when he presented himself at the Tuileries after the return from Elba. Always inclined to behave theatrically, Gourgaud protested, stormed, raged and wept—he was given to weeping—and finally threatened to kill himself under the Emperor's windows. Napoleon gave in and reinstated him in his post. He took part in the Belgian campaign and was promoted brigadier-general on June 21, 1815, a few hours after the abdication. As with Montholon, his fate was now linked with that of the defeated Emperor, not merely because a second volte-face was inconceivable and unacceptable, but because he saw in his new situation a means of getting even closer to this extraordinary man, whose name was heard all over the world, even in the hour of defeat, and whom he admired and envied for always playing the leading role. His tyrannical devotion was often tiresome to Napoleon, who exclaimed one day at St. Helena: 'I'm not his wife; after all I can't go to bed with him!' After five years on the staff, Gourgaud was hurt when he found himself kept at arm's length and supplanted in his sovereign's intimacy by newcomers, Montholon and Las Cases in particular; impulsive and full-blooded, he found the celibacy of his exile hard to bear and having no family pleasures to distract him, wanted to be all in all to the Emperor, and the Emperor to him. He irritated Napoleon so much by his constant display of his feelings, his services and his talents, that when the moment came he was too exasperated to make any move to keep his oldest and perhaps most faithful companion at his side.

Count de Las Cases, the fourth of the leading actors, was a man of an entirely different stamp: he was the stage confidant, the Burrhus of Racine's tragedy, always ready to listen, to enjoy and stimulate conversation while content to remain in the background himself. Confronted by such great talkers and sometimes boasters as his colleagues, Marie-Joseph-Emmanuel-Auguste-Dieudonné de las Cases, son of the Marquis de Las Cases, lord of la Caussade, Puylaurens, Lamothe and Dourne, made a rather depressing impression with his smooth manners, his small stature, his round shoulders, short sight, and air of a provincial nobleman subdued by the presence of dashing cavalry and artillery officers. A naval lieutenant at the time of the Revolution, he was not attracted by the new ideas, and attached himself to the legitimate royal family; when the royalist army disbanded, he found himself walking the pavements of London, like many other exiles, and earned his living by giving lessons while arranging for the publication of his *Historical, Genealogical and Chronological Atlas*. Returning to France in 1802, he threw in his lot with Napoleon and asked for the Legion of Honour, which was refused him (perhaps he forgot that he had received the Cross of St. Louis from the Duc d'Angoulême in London) and had to fall back on an appointment as chamberlain, after being created Baron of the Empire in 1809. The entry on his application gives a pleasant impression of him: 'The Baron de Las Cases, ex-officer in the navy, author of the *Historical Atlas* published under the name of Le Sage, enjoying an income of 30,000 francs in his own right and that of Mlle de Kergariou whom he married. A very well-educated and well-bred man, he has long wished for the honour of being attached to His Majesty's Household, has been presented to him, and enjoys the highest possible reputation.'

Chamberlain and Maître des Requêtes in 1810, he was entrusted with several missions, and a member of the National Guard; before the disaster of 1814 he was promoted to naval captain and councillor of State. After the return from Elba his appointment as chamberlain was confirmed and he accompanied the Emperor from the Elysée to the island of Aix, wearing a splendid naval uniform and soliciting the right to the cross for gallantry he coveted so keenly. This desire was gratified and he insisted on being one of Napoleon's suite in exile.

'Do you realise where this may lead you?' asked the Emperor.

'I have not thought about that at all, Sire, but my most fervent desire will be satisfied if you grant my request.'

Such fidelity is rare, and Napoleon was not displeased by this decision. Hastily collecting some money, Las Cases said good-bye to his wife, and removing his son from the *lycée* joined the party for Rochefort. Born in 1766, he was the oldest of the Frenchmen on St. Helena, and ever since 1815 historians have been trying to decide what motives inspired him, a man in his fifties, to follow the dethroned Napoleon and abandon family, fortune, country and career, when—having taken so little part in the Hundred Days—he could have paid court to the new king, like so many others. Will this question ever be answered? Las Cases never revealed the underlying reasons for his quick decision, unless it was in the preface to the first edition of his famous *Mémorial*, published in 1822. Even so, he expressed himself extremely vaguely: 'Extraordinary circumstances kept me for a long time in close contact with the most extraordinary man who has appeared for centuries. Admiration made me follow him when I did not know him; as soon as I got to know him love bound me to him for ever.' Literature, the words of an effective writer, but without a trace of genuine feeling, and giving no reasonable explanation.

For lack of proof, we must therefore judge the man on the evidence and pause a few moments in front of his portrait. We know he was small, and Lord Rosebery showed subtle psychology in saying that Las Cases pushed 'chamberlainism' to the length of being a shorter man than his master. Rather thin, he had a long, narrow, distinguished face; his pointed nose gave him a ferrety look, but the forehead under his greying locks was broad and well-shaped. The constant care he devoted daily to writing his *Mémorial*, and the interest he showed in each new edition of this historical best-seller, prove that he was sufficiently a writer and a man of business to get the most he could out of an exile which in fact only lasted thirteen months.

When he was subsequently arrested for carrying on a clandestine correspondence, and detained at St. Helena before being deported to the Cape and Europe, his chief concern was to save his precious manuscript at whatever cost; he wrote letter after letter to the Governor: 'In consequence of a trap, according to all appearances laid by my servant, I was on the 25th instant removed from Longwood and all my papers were seized'. The 900 pages of the first draft of the *Mémorial*, copied by young Emmanuel de Las Cases, obviously constituted the most valuable item in the little chamberlain's wordly goods, and he mentioned them before even criticising the manner of his arrest and isolation.

It was undoubtedly as a man of letters that Las Cases followed Napoleon to St. Helena: a more detailed study would prove this point; yet his motives were in no way discreditable, for although the *Mémorial* did bring its author notoriety and affluence in the end, it also set in motion a current of feeling in regard to the Emperor's misfortunes and exile that has not yet died down. It was read in town and country, in foreign courts and cottages all over Europe, and Las Cases's unusual talent conveyed the actual atmosphere of Longwood and the sound of the Emperor's voice.

Napoleon's ex-chamberlain—'The Jesuit' as the rest of the French called him among themselves because of his punctilious

manners, or 'Rapture' because of his effusive admiration—was one
of his favourite companions, for he was an intelligent, devoted and
hardworking man, with a useful knowledge of English and naval
matters, and quick to grasp an idea or an implication. His style did
not displease Napoleon: he was the author of several rolling phrases
which have passed as the Emperor's in the history-books. A case in
point is the excellent letter written at sea from the *Bellerophon* and
addressed to Admiral Lord Keith: 'I appeal to history; it will say
that an enemy who for twenty years waged war against the English
people came voluntarily to them in his misfortune to seek refuge
under their laws'. He listened with all his ears to the impassioned
talk of his new master and was rewarded by finding his attentiveness
appreciated. And then there was the journal. Napoleon had been
told by Ali, who helped make a fair copy of it, that Las Cases and his
son spent their evenings in their tiny lodgings, copying out each
day's entry by candlelight. Of course everyone was keeping a private
diary, but the more the merrier, and Napoleon skilfully distributed
his historical studies, seeming on the whole to have reserved the
politics of his reign for his conversations with Las Cases, and his
memories and essays on Julius Caesar, Charles XII, Hannibal and
his own campaigns for the soldiers of the party. Sharply criticised by
historians who have made use of the writings of Gourgaud and
Montholon alone, Las Cases nevertheless remains an important
witness of the Emperor's last years, when a chronicler's pen could be
of greater service to him than an aide-de-camp's sword.

✤   ✤   ✤

The servants of Longwood, the 'Service' as they are still called,
deserve to be considered in detail: their pell-mell existence without
privacy brought them into close contact with their master. Although
they only had walking-on parts, and entered the stage from behind
the wings of the private apartments, they might be called on to act
as confidants, spies, questioners or copyists at St. Helena, and some
even kept detailed journals full of talent.

Louis Marchand was head valet. Born in Paris in 1791, he had
been employed in the palace in 1811 when his mother was nurse to
the King of Rome. He had experienced the splendours of court life

and of Napoleon's visit to Holland with Marie-Louise; then came the abdication. When Constant, the Emperor's chief valet, became the first deserter he was appointed to that coveted post. On Elba, his discretion and zeal gained him the Emperor's esteem; during the Hundred Days and the severe trials that followed, he never relaxed his assiduity, and he served his master during exile as attentively as at the Tuileries. He was responsible for the presence in Napoleon's baggage of everything that added beauty and material comfort to the exile's life; if it had not been for Marchand he might well have been reduced to wearing shirts given him by the English. . . .

When he arrived on the island, the young valet was only twenty-four years old; his portrait shows sensitive, refined features, laughing eyes and long curly hair. Amongst Napoleon's suite, he was the most typical of the humbler class of Frenchman—clever, devoted and self-sacrificing—and he was also a representative of the younger generation with which the imperial government had always been concerned.

A man is never a hero to his valet, so it is said, but few masters could be as simple and accessible as the Emperor was at St. Helena. The last echo of his days of power and glory had faded away and the final ordeal was at hand; a dying man lay on his bed, a man whose sheets must be changed, who must be turned, washed and shaved, not to mention more sordid details. What patience Marchand needed when the doctors ordered clysters, cauteries, emetics, salts of mercury, salt-water baths, foot-baths, frictions and fomentations! Napoleon was aware of his devotion and paid tribute to it in his will:

'His services were those of a friend'. And the little valet was to have the unique distinction for a man who has worn livery of being executor of the ex-Emperor's will, in company with Generals Bertrand and Montholon.

Louis-Etienne Saint-Denis, known as Ali, was born at Versailles, the son of a servant of the Ancien Régime, and received a good education in a notary's office before entering the Emperor's service as groom. He had taken part in the campaigns in Spain and Germany and, like Marchand, accompanied their Imperial Majesties on the state visit to Holland. When in 1811 Napoleon expressed a desire for a new mameluke—the one he had brought from Egypt had to be dismissed for bad character—Saint-Denis was chosen, dressed in oriental costume and rebaptised Ali. On campaigns, he used to be seen carrying field-glasses, dressing-case and brandy; at St. Helena his good education, and reserved and discreet character, endeared him to his master, and he was promoted to librarian. When he had finished his work in the Emperor's apartments, and cataloguing his books, he sometimes had to do copying for one or other of the party, for a great deal of writing was going on at Longwood, whether making fair copies of what the Emperor had dictated, or of documents drawn up by the generals, or notes to be smuggled abroad, which had to be carefully written in tiny letters on small pieces of material. All the books in the library at Longwood were inscribed by Ali: THE EMPEROR NAPOLEON.

Cipriani Franceschi, known as Cipriani, remains the most enigmatic of the servants. A Corsican and allied—in the Roman sense—to the Bonaparte family (his son was in the service of Cardinal Fesch in Rome), he was fanatically devoted to the Emperor. His eventful career had involved him with Saliceti during the siege of Capri, just at the time that an officer called Hudson Lowe was in charge of espionage in the British army there. Leaving the Mediterranean, he joined the Emperor on Elba in 1814, and undertook a secret mission to Vienna at the time of the Congress. He was certainly not outstanding either as a spy or a detective, but he was an astute man, a heavy drinker, able to talk and above all make others talk. At St. Helena he organised an information bureau that gave the English a lot of trouble; he was clever at making fools of the soldiers guarding him, and he threw himself into feverish activities which may perhaps have had some bearing on his cruel death in 1818. He died in a few days of appalling 'pains in the intestines' suggestive of poison, although peritonitis has been considered a possibility. To throw light on his end it would have been necessary to trace his grave; his tomb cost the Emperor a small fortune but it has vanished today—although there are plenty of tombstones of the same date in the cemetery at Plantation House.

The rest of the staff was made up of under-servants who played a less conspicuous part: Noverraz, a Swiss employed in the Emperor's apartments, Pierron, the official chef; the two Archambault brothers; in the stables; Rousseau, in charge of the silver; Gentilini, a footman

from Elba who fluttered the hearts of the Englishwomen on the
island; and finally Santini, keeper of the portfolio, a little man who
did everything from cutting hair to mending shoes.

✢   ✢   ✢

All these people could not be accommodated in a small house
without complications arising. As we have seen, Napoleon occupied
the most comfortable rooms, an anteroom, a drawing-room, two
private apartments, a dining-room, a library and a bathroom; the
Montholons had three large rooms, Gourgaud one, and an office in
another part of the building. Las Cases and his son had to climb up
into two attics above the kitchens, until they were moved to the south
wing—on the ground floor, it is true, but in the most insalubrious
part of the house, exposed to wind and rain. The servants had to
make the best of the low-ceilinged, gloomy attics where they stifled
in summer and shivered in winter. Marchand was to sleep over his
master at the west end of the house, and Noverraz over the library;
as for the rest, the English bluejackets hastily improvised some sort of
cells like ship's cabins for them, into which the reluctant daylight fell
through tiny skylights.

The servants' offices surrounded the inner courtyard: silver room,
pantry, linen-closet and kitchen, the latter only a few yards square
and fitted with a wretched smoking stove.

The Bertrands had turned up their noses at Longwood and chosen
to live a mile and a quarter away; Hutt's Gate was an unremarkable
house, but it had the distinct advantage of providing isolation and
independence. Napoleon had been piqued by their decision, however,
and when Bertrand came to ask for his approval of his choice, he said
shortly: 'Do as you please; anyway Montholon will stay here with me.'

Finally installed in this new imperial residence—his last—Napoleon at once began organising everyone's duties as if on the battlefield, or camping in Poland or Spain; he was determined to affirm
his royal status, but the British opposed him openly in this, address-
ing him as General Bonaparte, or Sir, or at best Your Excellency.
They might even write, as Admiral Cockburn did to Bertrand in
reply to a French note of protest: 'You oblige me officially to explain
to you that I have no cognisance of any Emperor being actually upon

this island, or of any person possessing such dignity having (as stated by you) come hither'. As might be expected, Napoleon held an entirely contrary view; certainly he had abdicated the French throne, and he was no longer Napoleon, Emperor of the French, but he was and would remain the Emperor Napoleon, a title conferred on him by his people and confirmed when he was consecrated and anointed by the Pope himself. A prisoner in the hands of the Allied powers, treated like the general of a *coup d'état*, he wished to maintain before this little group of conceited and boastful English, as well as in front of the whole world, some semblance of protocol. He has been criticised for this insane attachment to his past grandeurs, but this shows complete lack of understanding of the feelings of all isolated and inactive communities, and particularly of the white population of St. Helena. The English colony on the island will be considered in a later chapter: it was on their account, and because of their interest in what was going on at Longwood House, where the man now lived whose word had been law throughout Europe, that Napoleon put himself to so much trouble. If he established court etiquette, if his valets wore livery and his generals appeared before his august person in uniform, the English might still go on calling him 'General', but they would soon feel envious of those among their number who received an invitation to an audience; and Napoleon did not fail to realise, and to declare, that an enemy disarmed is a conquered enemy, and that it was essential, at whatever cost, to make sure of such contacts. An immediate advantage of this elaborate ceremonial was the discouragement of possible familiarity on the part of the English, or even of the French, who were soon to relapse into a form of camp comradeship.

Bertrand, as a high officer of the Crown, was still to be addressed as 'Monseigneur' by the servants; the other officers of the Household were to give him the title of Grand Marshal which he still held. As he was not living at Longwood itself, Montholon was more or less permanently delegated to act in his name and control domestic affairs: to the English, Montholon was therefore Lord Chamberlain. Gourgaud was to be in charge of the stables, where about ten sluggish horses and a four-wheeled carriage were entrusted to the brothers Archambault. These expert coachmen drove full tilt along the narrow winding lane from Longwood to Hutt's Gate when Napoleon went

4

to visit the Bertrands; his usual outings were to the wood of gum-trees behind the house. Las Cases was put in charge of the stores and Crown property (all provided by the British government, needless to say, as Marchand had permanent charge of the Emperor's personal belongings), but he was far from enthusiastic about this sinecure, which kept him away from his beloved journal, and allowed it to be taken from him by Montholon, who dreamed of collecting more and more functions.

As major-domo, Cipriani was to be in control of food supplies under Montholon's supervision; while Balcombe, master of The Briars, was to administer and organise the provisioning of the establishment for the British, a thankless task in an island which was short of almost everything. A few English sailors, dressed in the green and gold imperial livery, helped Napoleon's servants; they were lent by the Admiral to work in the stables, silver room, kitchen and pantry. Saint-Denis and Noverraz were told off to take turns on guard duty, and spent alternate nights in the little anteroom next the Emperor's bathroom; as soon as the bell rang they had to go to him for orders. Santini waited in the dining-room by day and also had the duty of opening the door for the Emperor or the generals to go into the private study or drawing-room. The handsome Elban, Gentilini, was given charge only of laying the table.

✤   ✤   ✤

On December 11, 1815, early in the morning, the Emperor and Gourgaud made an inspection of the surroundings of Longwood, a sort of landowner's tour of the four-mile-long wall limiting the domain in which he could wander without being escorted by a British officer—this independence and liberty was purely relative, for on every crest and along all the roads were posted the red-coated sentinels of the 53rd regiment. The 'permitted' area in fact only provided a few outings, and repetition soon made these intolerable; the boundary passed along the road from Longwood to Hutt's Gate and from Hutt's Gate to Miss Mason's cottage on the south slope of Fisher's Valley. Of course Napoleon could have galloped along any of the island roads, but only when guarded by a British officer; he therefore declined this privilege and spent six years at Longwood in ignorance of the other, more attractive side of the island where he had not been allowed to live, except for two brief escapades to Mount Pleasant on the south coast, in 1816 and 1820.

Pickets of soldiers and non-commissioned officers guarded all the roads leading to Longwood and even the gateway into the grounds; as soon as it grew dark each evening they entered the garden and took up a position under the windows of the house. After this, no communication was possible without the password and the escort of the orderly officer.

The rusty pulleys of the aerial telegraph installed by a previous governor were cleaned; and an office was set up at Longwood making it possible to communicate immediately to the authorities the information that:

'All is well with respect to General Bonaparte and family.
General Bonaparte is unwell.
General Bonaparte is out, properly attended, beyond the cordon of sentries.
General Bonaparte is out, but within the cordon of sentries.
General Bonaparte has been out longer than usual, and is supposed to have passed the sentries not properly attended.
General Bonaparte is missing.'

This last signal, a blue flag, was of course never used.

Such close supervision left Napoleon no alternative but to shut himself up indoors, and he took to doing this with obsessional tenacity. The rhythm of his life therefore varied little for six years, except at moments of real crisis, when he was ill, or after the departures of Las Cases and Madame de Montholon.

Work had been the daily diet and sole religion of Lieutenant Bonaparte, as of the First Consul and the Emperor; his contemporaries, ministers, and generals have all spoken of his powerful intellect, his ability to dictate simultaneously and his habit of walking to and fro during interminable councils, holding forth and discussing, fresh and lucid, while the rest of the company were dropping with sleep. Throughout his life he had driven his mind at full pressure, just as he had conducted his most successful campaigns: he dictated fast, was a rapid reader, and exhausted an investigation in a few minutes. This strange passion saved him from a speedier and more miserable end at St. Helena. If he had been merely Chateaubriand's 'proud genius of action', boredom and obesity would have made his intolerable exile even worse by depriving him of power and physical outlets; but like Diocletian growing his salads at Salona, or Cincinnatus pushing his plough, Napoleon used his intellectual gifts to make the transition from the exercise of power to rustic life, and set aside an unvarying number of hours for study and research. The projects, calculations and reforms outlined by him at Longwood were purely mental gymnastics.

'We are off to the wars,' said one of the copyists mockingly. 'His Majesty is reorganising the army.'

When it was not a question of modernising the infantry or improving the equipment of the cavalry, he would become absorbed in the question of irrigating the Nile valley, or in algebraic calculations, educational reform, new rules for games and a thousand other subjects, from algebra to physics and from history to literary criticism.

✢   ✢   ✢

Once installed in his new home, he adopted a system of dividing the days almost equally between work, recreation and conversation. He woke at six or seven, rang for the valet on duty and ordered the sash-windows and shutters to be opened.

'Let in God's good air', he used often to say, as he slipped into a pair of white wool trousers and a quilted dressing-gown. With his feet in red leather slippers, he sat at a small table drinking a cup of black coffee, while his valet made preparations for his toilet.

It was a very austere room, and must often have reminded the exile of bivouacs in every corner of Europe. His iron bedstead, an old friend of his campaigning days, was pushed into a corner beside the small mahogany breakfast-table, and between the windows was a simple writing-desk with a green baize top. At right angles to the fireplace stood a sofa surrounded by a Chinese screen; on the other side, the large dressing-case—made by Biennais, a goldsmith from the Faubourg St. Honoré—stood open, casting reflections of vanished splendour on the humble walls. On these walls and over the fireplace hung miniatures of Marie-Louise and the King of Rome, and there were other mementoes, such as Frederick the Great's watch, between the candlesticks and an incense-burner.

Having swallowed his coffee, Napoleon began his toilet; he had always been, and still remained, very particular—even meticulous—in matters of hygiene. Since the Consulate, he had taken the precaution of shaving himself, in front of a mirror held by his valet at a convenient height. One after the other, his cheeks were turned to the light and left smooth under the attentive gaze of his servant, who also had to answer questions. Had any corner escaped his blade? Had he left any stray hairs? He went on to perform his simple ablutions in a silver basin, for he seldom took baths in the morning. His teeth were carefully brushed, his face sponged, his torso rubbed with eau de cologne by the valet.

'Rub harder', the Emperor used often to say banteringly, 'as if you were rubbing down a donkey.' He felt the better for these frictions, and joked with anyone who was present at his levée, such as Bertrand, or the doctor.

'Bertrand, do you rub your body like this?'

'No, Sire.'

'You should, it's a protection against many diseases.'

This was the moment when the valet used to announce the doctor's arrival. After the defection of his usual doctor, Maingault, on the *Bellerophon*, Napoleon accepted the services of the Irish ship's surgeon, a young man of thirty-three called O'Meara. The English gave their consent for him to become the 'General's' doctor, and his name remained on the Royal Navy list as filling a post in which both glory and danger were involved. Hudson Lowe wanted to use him as a spy; so did the French. He was finally sent away from St. Helena in 1818 and dismissed from the Navy, but he consoled himself for this material disaster by publishing his *Voice from St. Helena* in two volumes. This proud and aggressive testimony, directed against Hudson Lowe rather than in favour of Napoleon, brought him warm expressions of sympathy as well as a good deal of money, and Lord Byron, always ready to fight for a desperate cause, wrote the defiant lines:

> 'And the stiff surgeon who maintained his cause
> Hath lost his place and gained the world's applause.'

Napoleon used to question the Irishman also: What were the Governor and the Admiral up to? What was the gossip, what were people saying? At this period, the needs of Dr. O'Meara's illustrious patient were simple: his health was still good in spite of a number of colds. Santini, the Corsican usher, sometimes came and carried out his new function of barber in his master's room, and Napoleon would joke with him in patois:

'*Eh brigante! mi voi tagliare une orecchia :* Hey, you rascal! do you want to cut my ear off?' But the man performed his task conscientiously—his heart was in his work if talent was lacking; the few caricatures of the time show us Le Petit Tondu with a shock of hair that can hardly have been to his taste.

His toilet finished, Napoleon got dressed: he would then go out or stay indoors according to the weather. If he stayed shut up in his room dictating, he would put on a dressing-gown, tie a coloured cotton handkerchief round his head, and appear as in Steuben's picture, with his shirt collar undone, his left hand in the pocket of his white trousers and a sheet of paper in his right, while General Gourgaud, dressed in uniform, tried to keep up with his rapid delivery. The dictation sessions took place either in the little study or in the billiard-room, on whose table the Emperor could spread his maps and plans, to be studied in comfort; his two fine globes were close at hand and can still be seen in the corner of this room. If the weather was good he would dress for riding, in a hunting coat with silver engraved buttons, white breeches and waistcoat and top boots. Marchand had slipped the ribbon of the Legion of Honour under the coat and he now pinned the star on his breast. If he were only going for a walk he wore shoes with gold buckles and embroidered white silk stockings instead of boots. Later on, especially when working in his garden, he adopted the planter's dress which so delighted British caricaturists: white nankeen shirt and trousers, wide-brimmed straw hat with a black ribbon, and leather slippers; a billiard cue did duty both as a cane and yard measure.

Before leaving his room, he followed an old habit of filling his coat pockets: a handkerchief, a small lorgnette, a box of liquorice sweets, and of course the inevitable snuff-box; no jewellery, except a gold watch on a chain made from the Empress's hair. He was to offer this to Bertrand one day, with a melancholy remark about the happy hours the watch had once recorded.

His rides could hold no surprises for him and he soon tired of them; they were limited to the gloomy Deadwood plateau where the British army was encamped beside the black silhouettes of the Barn, Goat's Mount—grey, bleak and hostile—and Alarm House, in which lived Sir Thomas Reade, *âme damnée* of Hudson Lowe, and where government spies kept watch. He would return by Miss Mason's cottage on the south side of Fisher's Valley; here there lived an eccentric, slightly mad, old Englishwoman, who was made fun of by the other colonists because she saddled and rode a bullock and showed exaggerated respect to Boney. To get back sooner to Longwood, he sometimes cut across this valley, down which a small stream flowed through damp marshy land; here stood the cottage of a farmer called Robinson, whose daughter Mary Ann had never before seen such dashing horsemen, and curtsied and offered them flowers. Napoleon laughed and said teasingly to the taciturn Gourgaud:

'She pays more attention to you than to me because you are a bachelor. These poor girls think of nothing but getting married.'

It takes very little to set gossip going, and soon the whole of Europe was talking about this girl, and knew that the Emperor had christened her the Nymph and the valley where she lived the Valley of the Nymph, while pictures were published of the girl with a bunch of flowers in her hand, smiling ingenuously at the imperial visitor and his officers.

On his return from the morning's ride or walk 'His Majesty's luncheon' would be served, according to strict etiquette: if the meal was to be eaten in his private room the head cook brought the dishes as far as the bathroom, where the servant on duty took charge of them and handed them to Marchand who had the honour of offering them to the Emperor. By now it would be ten o'clock; Napoleon had undressed on returning from his exercise, throwing his clothes as usual on chairs and the floor, and would be wearing his dressing-gown. He usually invited Las Cases to join him, or sometimes one or two of the officers; when all four members of his suite were asked it was a sign that their master was in a specially good mood. Weather permitting, the table was laid in the garden, under the arbour or in the shade of an evergreen oak.

The menu was simple: first came soup, served very hot (Napoleon was particularly fond of it, and never tired of praising the beneficial effects of chicken broth or consommé à la reine). A meat course followed, preferably chicken or mutton, both on the list of his favourite dishes; vegetables usually consisted of beans or lentils. It was a soldier's meal, washed down with a glass of well-watered Bordeaux, and lasting a bare ten minutes; coffee was served as hot as the soup and hardly prolonged the meal. Then the party left the table, and Napoleon went off at a slightly rolling stride to the billiard-room, where he worked; he either dictated or took a siesta according to the weather and inclination. Dictation and research work had been shared between Las Cases and the three officers, so that each of the four men should have an audience with the Emperor in turn, and his apportioned task to pass the time. The sound of pacing footsteps echoed with curious resonance in this long room, where the billiard-table still stands today, not so much because of its proportions but from its lack of foundations—there was nothing between the floorboards and the beams supporting them. With his hands clasped behind him, Napoleon paced up and down, for this was how ideas came most easily to him, and the silence was broken only by the squeaking of the pen and the sound of his heels on the wood. Occasionally he would revolve the beautiful terrestrial globe on which the various stages of his great adventure were marked— the adventure he was now trying to analyse, explain and justify. It was a tedious task for the generals, choking in their high collars and hampered by their braided uniforms, yet they must always respond at once to the famous cry: 'Write!' Outside, the summer heat had put an end to all activity, and the tropical sun beat down on the thin roof. Or the rain might be streaming from it in cascades, whipped by the south-east wind, or a thick fog sweep into the garden enveloping everything and everyone. But there was always the same penetrating silence, winter or summer; when the workmen had finished their task and gone away, nothing was heard but the cooing of turtle-doves, the neighing of horses or the cry of a child. That was all, and it was very little after the sound of armies marching all over Europe and treading the streets of all its capitals, after the bustle of camp life, the salutes and marching songs (*Pour l'Empereur, La Carabinière*, or *La Canardière*), and the swarms of aides-de-camp competing to receive the orders of the Emperor and his marshals. How far away it must all have seemed, and yet so very close!

'How far is Saint Helena from an Emperor of France?
I cannot see—I cannot tell—the crowns they dazzle so.
The Kings sit down to dinner and the Queens stand up to dance.
After open weather you may look for snow.'*

Sometimes Napoleon would sigh, stop in his tracks, and apply the old Austerlitz field-glasses to a hole in the shutters—not, this time, so as to see Murat's cavalry charging and the white tunics in retreat, but to watch one of Hudson Lowe's men trotting past, or the British troops manoeuvring on the plateau of Deadwood.

Dictation over, it was time for the Emperor's bath—no unimportant matter. For the last hour the valets and the Chinese servants had been busy round the ancient circular contraption of pipes heated by a crackling fire. The hot water ran in a thin stream into an enormous copper bath; as Napoleon insisted on having his bath boiling hot, Marchand used to urge on the Chinese servants with cries of 'More water! More heat!' Napoleon took these prolonged daily baths as a sort of medical treatment; up to his neck in water, his body relaxed, his nerves soothed, he would talk to Las Cases, Marchand or one of the generals, or skim the pages of a book lying on a rest, or even eat his luncheon. Then Marchand helped him dress in white shirt, black tie, white stockings and buckled shoes, white waistcoat, coat, and hat with a cockade, and he went to the drawing-room to receive visitors. The generals gathered there, talking and waiting for him to come. During the first years, in 1816 and 1817, a great many foreigners were received: besides the officers and important inhabitants of the island there would be arrivals by sea, high officials of the Crown on their way to India or returning from the East, who set great store by having an audience. 'English travellers on their way to or from the marvels of the Ganges used to visit this other marvel on their way: India, accustomed as she was to conquerors, now had one chained at her very door.'†

The Grand Marshal handed them an invitation card and the Governor added a pass, similar to one I have at present lying before me. An ugly piece of paper, such as admits visitors to see ordinary prisoners, had been printed by a local firm: 'The officer commanding the Guard at Longwood will permit the bearer hereof, Mr.——, to

*Rudyard Kipling.
†Chateaubriand, *Mémoires d'outre-tombe.*

pass to the residence of General Bonaparte, on the ——. Given at Head Quarters, St. Helena, this ——, 18—. Memo: This ticket will be delivered to the officer of the guard, who will transmit it to the Governor the following Morning.'

What motives can have inspired these unknown persons to seek the strange honour of meeting an exiled sovereign—'a prisoner who was no prisoner'? Curiosity is the besetting sin of the English, and these travellers were anxious not to return to Europe without a sight of the man of the century, no longer in splendid isolation on his throne in the Tuileries, but in his overgrown cottage dwelling; they speculated as to the expenses of upkeep on the way. The man who had made England tremble was at present supplied by her with eau-de-cologne and snuff: it was well worth the journey to see such a thing. And since the applicants for an audience all kept 'private' journals which they published on their return, it was a fine thing to be able to sandwich between chapters on 'The Kaffirs of the Cape' and 'Anchor at Spithead', one entitled 'Interview with Bonaparte; observations upon his appearance, manners and situation'! So this was the man who had disturbed the whole world, and worse still threatened the ancient and noble country of England: they gazed at him with the ferocious curiosity and morbid attentiveness of explorers. The result was to be seen in pages of lively and well-described detail, useful to historians no doubt, but with very few exceptions quite devoid of pity for a man who was expiring of boredom and inactivity.

These audiences continued for two years, and Napoleon was glad of them in the intellectual desert surrounding him; the visitors were usually cultivated people, and full of fresh impressions of the Orient —the same impressions that had once excited a young general who had treated Europe like a molehill and dreamed of crossing the Alps and seeking glory in Asia. Conversation set his memory and his astonishingly alert intelligence to work: he asked questions, volunteered opinions. There were others who were received more or less as friends: the Wilks, who had been in India before they came to St. Helena and had an exceptional knowledge of that vast country, the Skeltons, who took the first messages home to Europe, General and Lady Bingham, and Admiral and Lady Malcolm, who succeeded Cockburn and his wife.

To impress his questioners, Napoleon instituted an elaborate ceremonial for audiences. A servant in livery, either Santini or Noverraz, would be waiting in the garden to escort the visitor to the billiard-room; there he would be received by an officer, or perhaps the whole Household, in full uniform, welcomed in the name of the Emperor, and informed that His Majesty would receive him. The Grand Marshal then appeared framed in the door into the drawing-room, and signed to him to enter. In spite of their confidence and familiarity with the ways of society, the strangers were embarrassed by the personality and present situation of the man waiting to see them, and it was Napoleon who at once set the tone of the encounter. Lady Malcolm declared that she was afraid of meeting the hero who had made Europe a battlefield for twenty years, but Napoleon quickly put her at her ease by questioning her, for he was well aware that women like talking about themselves. Had she been seasick on the voyage? Was it her first? Had she been bored? Did she do embroidery?

He would stand in front of the fireplace, with his hat under his arm: ever since Admiral Cockburn had sat down without a word in his presence he preferred to give audience standing, until he was dropping with fatigue, rather than see the English take a chair without asking leave. With his favourites, like the Balcombes and Malcolms, he would have long conversations that left them astounded: his erudition, knowledge of facts, men and history amazed them, for the London press had always presented Bonaparte as a stupid and pretentious vulgarian. Lady Malcolm was Scottish, and he gave her a lecture on Ossian that would not have disgraced a literary critic. If he laid himself out specially to please her, it was because she was gazing at him with all her eyes; this over-painted woman, dressed like a macaw, was a warm-hearted aristocrat and a connoisseur of manners, and she detected a born sovereign in the portly exile. When she got home she jotted down notes of her conversations which were the basis for yet another journal:

'His hair of a brown-black, thin on the forehead, cropped but not thin in the neck, and rather a dirty look; light blue or grey eyes; a capacious forehead; high nose; short upper lip; good white even teeth but small (he rarely showed them); round chin; the lower part of his face was very full; pale complexion; particularly short neck. Otherwise his figure appeared well proportioned, but had become too fat; a thick, short hand with taper fingers and beautiful nails, and a well-shaped leg and foot.'

When the audience was over Napoleon would bow and retire, leaving one of his officers to escort the visitor to the door.

At about four o'clock, General Gourgaud, who was in charge of the stables, ordered the carriage to be harnessed for the daily drive. Madame Bertrand or Madame de Montholon usually sat beside Napoleon, while Bertrand and Las Cases squeezed into the front seat and Gourgaud galloped beside them. The six horses were driven by the brothers Archambault, who had plenty of experience and were not daunted by the island roads. They galloped at breakneck speed across the plateau of Longwood, round the wood or as far as Dead-wood, and if the Bertrands were not of the party they paid them a visit on the way to Alarm House. In spite of its exposed position, Madame Bertrand had succeeded in arranging her house charmingly; it was embowered in camellias and tall trees. Though nothing like their apartment at the Tuileries, where two million francs a year had been spent on the gayest dinner-table in Paris, as she sadly told an English friend one day, it was a pleasant enough colonial house. The Emperor dismounted in front of the veranda, went inside and sat down to play with the children. One day he took a walk to the bottom of the valley beneath the house: a tiny stream ran through it and fine trees gave refreshing shade, while their foliage was shot through with silver reflections from the sea. The spring water was kept cool by a screen of three weeping willows, and every day thenceforward one of the Chinese servants was sent to fetch two large carafes full of the water from 'my spring' as Napoleon called it. One day he told Bertrand: 'If my body is left in the hands of my enemies when I die, you must bury me there'.

Sometimes he took a walk instead of a drive in the barouche, and in spite of the smallness of the park it often seemed to go on for ever. Up and down they walked while Napoleon talked and talked in-defatigably, till the women in their cumbrous dresses were quite exhausted. 'If we got too tired,' Madame de Montholon tells us, 'we tried to slip away down a side path, but however adroitly this was done it never escaped the notice of the Emperor, although he might be absorbed in conversation. Even when he was several paces ahead he always saw that one had vanished and never failed to say "There's Madame de Montholon (or someone else) running away".' Subjects of conversation were numberless and depended on his mood, the weather and events in Europe; they provided material for the journals of Gourgaud, Bertrand and Madame de Montholon, and Las Cases's *Mémorial*, not to mention the notes made by Marchand and Ali, while the Emperor—who was well aware they were all scribbling away—was not at all averse to repeating himself to make sure of being properly understood.

When the garrison cannon announced that the sun had set, the temperature grew cooler and a light sea breeze sprang up; they returned to the house with relief, and everyone was free to go and wash and change their clothes while Napoleon retired into his study to read a book or news-sheet.

They all met again in the drawing-room, the women rivalling one another in their low-cut evening dresses, the officers in braided uniforms, and were soon joined by the Emperor for more conversation or some games of chess. Surprisingly enough, he played fast and therefore badly, and cheated shamelessly. 'Sometimes', relates Madame de Montholon, 'he would insist that a piece touched was a piece played, but only for his opponent. It was quite another matter in his own case; he always had a good reason why it did not count, and if anyone commented on it he merely laughed.'

The dinner-hour was changed more than once during the six years of exile: from seven o'clock to eight o'clock and then to nine o'clock, but protocol was always observed. At the appointed time the dining-room door was opened, and Cipriani, dressed in a green coat embroidered in silver, black silk breeches and buckle shoes, bowed deeply and announced: 'Your Majesty's dinner is served'. The Emperor went into the dining-room, followed by the ladies and officers: his place was in the middle of the table with his back to the fireplace, with Madame de Montholon on his right and Las Cases on his left, Gourgaud, Montholon and young Las Cases opposite. When the Bertrands were present, the Grand Marshal's wife took precedence over Madame de Montholon, provoking some acid comment. In the early days some of the English were invited and were astonished by the style up at the 'House'. 'It was a most superb dinner,' wrote Colonel Bingham to his wife, 'which lasted forty minutes, at the end of which we retired into the drawing-room to play cards. . . . The dinner was stupid enough. The people who live with Bonaparte scarcely spoke above a whisper, and he was so much engaged in eating that he hardly said a word to anyone. He had so filled the room with wax candles that it was as hot as an oven.'

There was an abundance of silver on the table and in the room; candlesticks on the furniture and table-cloth; dishes, covers and centre-pieces all gleamed with a thousand soft reflections. Marchand had brought a considerable amount of plate, and even after 120 pounds of it had been sold, there still remained 234 plates, 34 dishes, 96 dish covers and numerous accessories. Saint-Denis and Noverraz waited on the Emperor, and stood behind his chair wearing green coats with gold embroidery; the other guests were looked after by Gentilini, some British sailors dressed up in the imperial uniform, and Bernard, the Bertrands' valet who came as an extra. The fare was more abundant than at lunch: soup, a remove, two entrées, a roast and two vegetables, followed by sweetmeats. Pierron was a marvellous confectioner and sent up some inventions of his own by way of dessert, to be eaten with silver forks on the beautiful Sèvres service with its green and gold borders patterned with swords and laurels around scenes from the battlefields of Egypt and Europe.

Cipriani supervised the serving of dinner assiduously and with authority, treating the British extras sternly, and attentive to his master; and when the drawn curtains shut away the view of the bare garden there was a certain splendour about this modest room, with its silver, the women's evening dresses, the officers' epaulets, the stars glittering on their breasts, and the impassive face of the man who had rocked the world, though it was a little like a vision in a soap-bubble, that might vanish at the first breath. To be reminded of the sad realities of exile it was enough to hear the rain streaming down the tarpaulin on the roofs, or the challenging cries of the sentries. After dessert, they went into the drawing-room, where coffee was steaming and another Sèvres service was laid out. 'The coffee cups were the most beautiful I ever saw,' wrote Bingham; 'on each cup was an Egyptian view, and on the saucer a portrait of some Bey or other distinguished character. In France they would have cost twenty-five guineas a cup and saucer.' A lower price would have been surprising for the designs were by Denon, the decorations in gold and Sèvres blue, the portraits in grisaille. The evening seemed long: usually they played cards—reversis or piquet—or listened to Madame de Montholon singing and accompanying herself on the piano. The evenings most dreaded by the French were those when the Emperor sent for a book and read aloud: Corneille or Voltaire, the Bible, Ossian or Homer, *Manon Lescaut* or *Paul et Virginie;* those most enjoyed were devoted to his recollections. The Emperor's memory was stocked with endless material for discussion, and he could talk all night long about Santo Domingo, Robespierre, prefects, sovereigns, generals, soldiers, marquises and courtesans. Then suddenly he would change his tone. 'The Emperor asked for *Zaïre*', Gourgaud tells us, 'and read until midnight. We were all dropping with sleep and boredom.' For Napoleon was an extremely bad reader and had no sense of prosody. It was in vain that he said laughingly: 'We are going to the theatre to hear Talma or Fleury'; he then proceeded to massacre both poetry and prose in an emphatic monotone.

'Madame, you're asleep,' he barked at Madame Bertrand, who was at the end of her tether.

'No, Sire.'

'What time is it? Bah! What does it matter? Let's go to bed.'

Somewhere between eleven and midnight he allowed them to withdraw, and retired into his room, where Marchand was waiting to help him undress and get into bed; often he kept Las Cases, Montholon or Gourgaud to read to him. When he was asleep at last, Marchand blew out the candles, lit the nightlight and went off to his attic, leaving the valet on duty. The night bell rang often: the Emperor suffered from insomnia; now that his body was no longer exhausted by work, he could not rest; he would get up, summon his valet, talk, read or walk up and down in his two rooms and remain awake until the small hours.

✤   ✤   ✤

This elaborate procedure was laid down and organised by Napoleon himself, with the evident and laudable intention of giving the British the impression that he was a sovereign living incognito rather than a prisoner of State, and of letting his faithful adherents in Europe know that though their Emperor was detained against his will he was still waited on by a court of officials, and that he worked, wrote and meditated, while possibly waiting for events to become favourable to fresh plans. But what was going on behind this screen of etiquette? How were they all living behind the drawn blinds of the billiard-room and the imperial apartments? And first of all, the key question: where was the necessary money coming from to pay for all this pageantry?

When the French party had gone on board the *Northumberland* in August 1815, British instructions indicated that it would be a favourable moment to search the General's belongings: 'The Admiral will allow baggage, wines and provisions which the General may have brought with him to be taken on board. . . . His table-service shall be understood as included, unless it be so considerable as to seem rather an article to be converted into ready money than for real use. His money, his diamonds, and his saleable effects (consequently bills of exchange also), of whatever kind they may be, must be delivered up.' On instructions from the Grand Marshal, Marchand the valet, who was told off to help in this humiliating operation, left behind in the strong-boxes only 4,000 napoleons, or about 80,000 francs, and these were seized by the English 'to be used for General Bonaparte's needs on St. Helena', and a receipt given.

'They were astonished that so little luggage remained for them to in-vestigate; probably measuring the Emperor's worldly wealth by the heights of his glory, they expected to find piles of valuables instead of a few odds and ends hardly worth looking at. They did not know that, as the Emperor was heart and soul for France, he had never thought of anything but his country's grandeur and prosperity, and was so disinterested that he would have been left without a centime after Waterloo if some of his friends, like the Dukes of Vicenza and Bassano and the Count de Lavalette, had not been concerned to collect and deposit for him with M. Laffitte a few million francs which were to provide the legacies in his will six years later.'*

The 4,000 napoleons were now in enemy hands; but there still remained another 12,500 or 250,000 francs, which had been divided among the eight belts worn round their waists by members of his suite until they disembarked at St. Helena. Marchand collected the money and Napoleon called it his 'reserve' or his 'nest-egg'; with the

*Marchand's Memoirs.

help of monthly economies it had been increased to 300,000 francs by 1821, and enabled the legacies of the first codicil to be paid. The Emperor had also left several deposits in France: 800,000 with Prince Eugene de Beauharnais, and with Perrégaux and Laffitte the bankers 3,400,000 francs (400,000 in 1814, and three million taken from the Tuileries with Fouché's consent on June 28, 1815). Beside this, Joseph Bonaparte seems to have received some capital, exactly how much is not known but possibly as much as a million. Last but by no means least, Napoleon could count on the immense fortune of the ex-king of Spain, in land, diamonds, pictures and cash. Joseph had transferred this estate of Mortefontaine to the name of his sister-in-law Clary, to prevent its being confiscated; the château of Prangins was outside the French frontier, and diamonds valued at five millions had been buried in its park. Madame Mère had sold her house in Paris and taken refuge in Rome with her brother Cardinal Fesch, who had succeeded in saving his magnificent collection of Italian paintings. Jerome Bonaparte was in Württemberg with his father-in-law; and even if his position was precarious he was reckoned to be worth two millions. Lastly Lucien, protected by the Pope, enjoyed the opulence suitable to a Roman prince, and was filling his fine mansion to overflowing with old masters. All this wealth, the fruits of the astonishing success of the head of the family, should be according to Corsican custom at the disposal of any relative in need or distress. But family feeling, alas, has its limits! The party at Longwood, or a few of them at least, had some property: Las Cases had managed to collect 4,000 napoleons in great haste from his banker in Paris, and offered them to the Emperor—who accepted them; Bertrand had deposited the considerable sum of £15,000 with a London financier. As for Gourgaud and Montholon, neither of them had anything.

The English, on their part, had arranged for the cost of detention to be borne by the British Treasury, in conformity with the agreement signed by the Allies on August 2, 1815; but, shortly after his arrival on the island, Hudson Lowe received formal instructions from Lord Bathurst to keep expenses within £8,000 a year, anything above this amount to be paid by General Bonaparte himself. This strange measure, involving the absurdity of making a prisoner pay for his own detention, is not surprising from a nation which required a

5

condemned man to pay the cost of the hangman's rope! It was there-fore without much trepidation that Hudson Lowe decided to have an interview with the people at Longwood, having first discovered that in the absence of any control the British Treasury had hitherto paid out about £20,000 sterling a year—more than double the allowance envisaged. The rate of expenditure current in August 1816 meant a budget of £11,700 for Napoleon's house and board, £3,445 a year for wines, £2,020 for outside board, £939 for workmen, £1,250 for the stables and £675 for the English servants.

This expense seems, even now, so large that some attempt must be made to account for it. Provisions for the Emperor's table, costing nearly £1,000 a month, were abundant—the purveyor furnishing every day 90 pounds of beef, 6 chickens, 74 lb. of bread, 5 lb. of butter, 2 of lard, 9 of sugar, 1¼ of coffee, 1 of tea, 9 of wax candles, 30 eggs, 1 lb. of cheese, 5 lb. of flour, 7 lb. of salt meat, 2¾ hundred-weight of firewood, 3 bottles of beer, vegetables, fruit, oil and vinegar. Every fortnight the purveyor also sent up: 8 ducks, 2 turkeys, 2 geese, 2 sugar-loaves, half a sack of rice, 2 hams weighing not more than 14 lb., 45 bushels of coal, 7 lb. of butter, salt, mustard, pepper, capers, lamp oil and peas, also fish to the value of £4 and milk to £5. The cellar was supplied every morning with 7 bottles of Champagne or Graves, one bottle of Madeira and one of Constantia, 6 of ordinary red wine, and besides this, each servant was entitled to a bottle of Cape or Canary wine every day.

Of course to these lists must be added the foodstuffs bought by the French themselves: every day, a dozen eggs and 8 lb. of butter, 2 lb. of candles, 3 fowls, 5 lb. of sugar, 1 lb. of cheese, 2¼ lb. of salt pork, 1 lb. of lard, a bottle of oil, 1 lb. of rice, 5 lb. of coarse sugar, a bottle of vinegar, and rolls; every week, 2 turkeys, one ham, a pig for roasting, gherkins and olives.

When Hudson Lowe arrived at Hutt's Gate, the Grand Marshal was already at luncheon, but he left the table to receive him:

'I came to see you the other day to discuss a matter we have already spoken about; the expenses at Longwood appear to be £18,000, according to the statement I have here. The government fixed a lower sum.'

'What sum did the government fix?'

'Eight thousand pounds.'

'As soon as the Emperor's friends in France, Italy and Europe are informed of what he needs, I am quite sure they will hasten to provide it, but I must draw your attention to the fact that he has had no news from his men of business: as you know, he has received no letters from them, nor can he write to them, because he is only allowed to write open letters, and this is equivalent for him to a prohibition.'

'I did not come here to talk about that matter. It was settled with General Montholon and . . .'

'If you have arranged the matter with Montholon you had better finish it with him! For my part, I desire to have as little communication with you as possible.'

'I can assure you, sir, that wish is quite reciprocal on my part,' retorted Hudson Lowe, and left in a rage. Without a moment's pause, he galloped off to Longwood and demanded to see 'the General'; he was told that the Emperor was in his bath. The Governor then buttonholed Montholon and showed him the British minister's instructions. Lowe insinuated that Prince Eugene, Napoleon's stepson, was worth more than forty millions, that he owed everything to the Emperor and should be written to and asked to provide funds. Montholon promised to do so.

Next day was Sunday, and despite the fact that it was a day of rest for all Anglicans, Hudson Lowe, who was determined to come to grips with the financial question, again set off for Longwood, accompanied by the Admiral, his deputy adjutant general Sir Thomas Reade, and the secretary Major Gorrequer. It had rained all night and all morning, and Napoleon had taken advantage of a bright interval to go out, to visit first Las Cases and then Madame de Montholon, with whom he was now walking in the garden; he was in a cheerful mood, and was teasing the young woman about her behaviour, urging her to examine her own conscience and confess, since his capacity of anointed of the Lord authorised him to hear her confession. Madame de Montholon was protesting amid general laughter, when a servant came to announce the Governor's arrival. At first the General sent a message that he was out, but as the English were insistent he left Las Cases and Madame de Montholon, and went up to the group of visitors and walked a few steps with them. From the house, the servants saw a procession forming: Napoleon walked in front with the Governor and the Admiral, and Las Cases, Madame de Montholon and Major Gorrequer followed a few paces behind. Napoleon took no notice of Hudson Lowe, but chatted to the Admiral for a while, referring to several unimportant matters. The Governor grew impatient and fidgety, and finally took the bull by the horns and interrupted this dialogue, from which he was so pointedly excluded:

'I am sorry to importune you on any disagreeable subject, but the very improper conduct of Count Bertrand renders it indispensable. Having received instructions to limit the expenses at Longwood, I mentioned the subject to Count Bertrand and Montholon; the latter fully met my wishes, but I was desirous to converse with yourself that I might be enabled to make such arrangements as would be most agreeable to you. I came here for that purpose, but was told that you were in the bath, and that you requested I would communicate with Count Bertrand. In compliance with this request I went to see the Count, who received me in a very extraordinary manner; nevertheless I told him my business and put the necessary papers in his hands. He took them and said he would show them to the Emperor. I proposed to explain, when he abruptly replied: "The less communication you and I have either verbally or in writing the better." I replied the wish was reciprocal, and left him. I think the conduct of Count Bertrand to me as Governor of this island highly improper, and particularly so as I called on him at the request of the person he acknowledges his sovereign.'

Lowe paused. There was a long silence. Napoleon seemed to be searching for a plan of attack. Suddenly he turned to the Admiral and burst out:

'Count Bertrand is a man well known and esteemed in Europe; he has been distinguished, and has commanded arms. The Governor treats him like a corporal. Madame Bertrand is a lady well born, who has been accustomed to the first place in society; he does not treat her with the regard that is her due; he stops her letters and prevents her seeing those that wish to visit her, except under restrictions.'

Then turning to face Hudson Lowe:

'Since your arrival we have experienced nothing but vexations. Your instructions are the same as Sir George Cockburn's—he himself told me so—but you execute them with fifty times more rigour.

Of course I had reason to be displeased with some of his proceedings, but our conversations were not fruitless. There is no talking to you, you are quite intractable; you suspect everything and everybody. You are a general, yet you behave like a warden. You never commanded any men but Corsican deserters. You vex us hourly, by your little ways. You do not know how to conduct yourself towards men of honour, your soul is too low. Why do you not treat us as prisoners of war? You treat us like Botany Bay convicts.'

He suddenly stopped and was silent, waiting. The Governor knew that he was being watched by the witnesses of the scene and he controlled himself:

'I have every desire to make your situation as agreeable as it is in my powers. . . . General Bertrand has written to me that I render your situation dreadful; he accuses me, as you do now, of abuse of power and injustice. I am the subject of a free government; I hold every species of tyranny and despotism in execration, and I will repel every attack upon my character, as a calumny against a man who cannot be attacked with truth.'

'Some men are respected, others are not,' Napoleon retorted, obviously alluding to the mission entrusted to Lowe by the British government.

'I understand the tactics well: slander is the last resort when other weapons fail.'

Breaking the silence that followed, the Admiral tried to intervene and prove that ever since his arrival the Governor had been anxious to show his goodwill and pay attentions to the Emperor: this misunderstanding was entirely a matter of different temperaments, and errors resulting from the interference of third parties. Napoleon turned to him quickly and said:

'Do you know that he had the meanness to keep a book back from me because I was described on the cover as Emperor, and that he has boasted of having done so?'

'I boasted of it?' exclaimed Hudson Lowe.

'Yes, the late Governor of Bourbon, Colonel Keating, told me so.'

'Permit me to explain this affair of the book,' said the Admiral. 'Sir Hudson showed it me and told me the author had desired him to give it or not as he thought proper. It was a work of little consequence and Sir Hudson is forbidden to give you the title of Emperor.'

'But he has sent me letters addressed to "the Emperor",' Napoleon insisted.

'Yes indeed, but they came through the Secretary of State's office and from your own relations, not Englishmen.'

Napoleon had been controlling himself with great difficulty and he now burst out into scathing reproaches:

'But he has also had the meanness to speak of the contents of our letters, that came to him open. My old mother, although I forbade her to write to me, wrote to say she would come to St. Helena and die with me. This was told round the island.'

'Not by me,' cut in Hudson Lowe.

'Yes, by you, Balcombe told me so.'

Then suddenly he lost his temper completely:

'I am an Emperor in my own circle and will be so as long as I live: you may make my body prisoner but my soul is free. Europe will be the judge of my treatment and the shame of it will fall on the English nation; even the poor English sentinels weep for my unworthy treatment. You ask me for money to pay for my living? I have none, but I have friends, a great many friends, who would send me whatever sum I required if I could write to them. Put me on rations, if you please. I can dine with the officers of the 53rd regiment, and if not with them, with the soldiers. . . .'

Hudson Lowe said calmly that he had not asked for the post of Governor of St. Helena and would confine himself to carrying out his government's instructions.

'If you were ordered to assassinate me, would you do so?'

'No, I would not. My countrymen do not assassinate.'

'I see that you are afraid I will escape—you take useless precautions. Why do you not tie me hand and foot? Then you could have some peace. You are not a general, you're only a clerk. To-morrow you will receive a letter from me which I hope may be known in all Europe.'

Turning to the Admiral again, he complained that Hudson Lowe had thought it his duty to forbid his communicating in writing with the inhabitants of the island, although Cockburn himself had allowed it; Malcolm tried to calm the troubled waters like the good sailor he was, and argued that bad use had been made of the permission, for a few days before, Madame Bertrand had tried to carry on a clandestine correspondence with the French commissioner.

'The Governor tells you so, but it is false!' interrupted Napoleon, turning on Hudson Lowe. 'It was disgraceful of Lord Bathurst to send a man like you to guard me. You are no Englishman.'

'That makes me laugh,' said the Governor bluntly, perhaps wanting to cut short a dispute which threatened to grow more violent.

'What! Laugh, sir?'

'Yes, sir; I say what I think. I say it not only makes me laugh but it excites my pity, to see how misinformed you are with respect to my character, and for the rudeness of your manners. I wish you good morning.'

And the Englishman withdrew, scarlet in the face and obviously furious, followed by his officers. It had been such a stormy scene that Napoleon himself regretted it: 'I must not see that officer again; he makes me lose my temper and forget myself. I said things to him that would have been inexcusable at the Tuileries. If they are excusable here it is because I am in his hands and in his power.'

In fact he kept his word so well that the Governor had no further chance to quarrel with him: he did not see his prisoner again until May 6, 1821, when he had suffered an eternal change. Napoleon was dead.

After this skirmish, Hudson Lowe received the letter in question; it had been composed by the Emperor himself, read to his officers, altered more than once and signed by Montholon. Known to history as the *Remonstrance*, it goes at length into the position of the Emperor Napoleon as established by the convention drawn up by the Allied sovereigns on August 2, 1815. Copied on pieces of silk by Ali and Marchand, it was smuggled into Europe where it created a sensation. The postscript was devoted to money matters:

'I had already signed this letter, sir, when I received yours of the 17th; accompanied by the estimated account of £20,000 sterling, which you consider indispensable for the expenses of the establishment at Longwood after having made all the deductions you thought proper. It is not for us to enter into any discussion of this estimate. The table of the Emperor is barely supplied with what is strictly necessary; all the provisions are bad in quality, and everything here four times as dear as in Paris. You demand from the Emperor £4,000 sterling, your government allowing only £8,000 for all expenses. I have already had the honour to tell you that the Emperor has no funds, that for a year past he had neither received nor written any letters; that he is entirely ignorant of everything that is happening or may happen in Europe. Taken by force to this rock, two thousand leagues away, unable to receive or write letters, he finds himself at present entirely at the mercy of British officials. The Emperor has always desired and still desires to be personally responsible for all his expenses and he will do this as soon as you make it possible by re-moving the ban on the forwarding of his correspondence, by merchants visiting the island, and as soon as it is free from any inquisition on your part or that of any of your agents. As soon as the Emperor's needs are known those who are interested in him will send him the necess-ary funds.'

At the end of this dispute Lowe decided on his own account to raise the sum allowed for expenses at Longwood to £12,000: it was exactly the amount of his own annual salary.

However, as all circumstances must be taken into account and this unfortunate official be given his due, it is only fair to emphasise that considering the cost of living on the island on the one hand, and the number of persons living at Longwood on the other, this allowance would have been enough but for the enormous wastefulness that went on in the catering department of the House. Examples abound. In September 1816, the Governor made a new and conciliatory approach to Montholon on the question of wine. 'A watch should be kept on the consumption of wine,' he said, 'and no bottle should ever be uncorked unless it is needed.' Measured language, and on the whole admirable on the part of a 'gaoler'; but mere waste of words, alas, in view of the determination of the liveried staff to console them-selves for the terrible hardships of exile by material advantages and cheerful evenings. Current rumours alleged that provisions were sold at the back door of Longwood House and bought by English soldiers and the islanders; there was laughter, drinking and even dancing late at night in the servants' lodgings, with these same soldiers and the women of the town, to whom the password was no secret. In an island where everything was in short supply and wine was a luxury, everyone was amazed that 630 bottles should be delivered every fortnight to the 'prisoners'. It caused the Governor further exasperation that when he arranged for the empty bottles to be collected—they were scarce on the rock—the French servants smashed them and left piles of the pieces conspicuously in view. The humbler members of the party, who had shown a certain nobility and great selflessness at moments of crisis, could not be trusted to behave with suitable dignity when it came to trifling kitchen matters. Only Gourgaud, who in spite of his extravagance had a proud spirit, used continually to repeat: 'In our position we would do well to accept as little as possible.' As for the valets, accustomed as they were to the fabulous waste in official establishments, to the bottomless gulf of the catering department in the Tuileries and the extravagance at General headquarters, they refused to be guided by the pride indispensable to their new situation. Marchand remained cool and kept a detailed and careful account of the Emperor's private expenses the others only thought of profiting as best they could from an adventure whose outcome was inscrutable to them.

However, this sordid business of maintenance enabled Napoleon to strike a direct, skilful and effective blow at Hudson Lowe's policy on a certain day in October 1816. The Governor had told Montholon that the sum of 4,000 napoleons seized on board the *Northumberland* was now exhausted, having been used for the personal purchases of the French, and that it must now be renewed.

'Get Noverraz to break up all my silver with an axe and send it to him, and tell him to leave us in peace,' Napoleon ordered.

This operation caused as much of a sensation as he had expected. Next morning a list was made of all the silver, and after setting aside what was necessary for daily use, three lots had their chased eagles stripped from them and were broken with hammers.

'You see,' said Napoleon somewhat dramatically to Dr. O'Meara, 'this man destroys everything and forces me to sell plate to buy the necessities of life, which he either refuses me, or gives me in quite insufficient quantity.'

Balcombe was instructed by Lowe to credit the 'General's' account with the sum derived from the sale, but above all to give him nothing in kind. Three sales took place, on October 15, November 15, and December 30, 1816, at which 952, 1,227 and 2,048 ounces were sold respectively, making a total of about 500 lb. in all; they fetched £1,065—scarcely enough to cover the extra requirements of Longwood for three months. But from a psychological point of view Napoleon had scored a point, for there had been many witnesses of the weighing of the silver at Jamestown, among others some officers just leaving for England, who spread the news there.

'How is the Emperor?' one of them asked the astute Cipriani.

'Fairly well. How you would expect someone who has to sell his plate to live.'

Hudson Lowe was furious.

'Why do you need so much money?'

'To buy food, Excellency,' muttered Cipriani.

'What! Have you not enough? Then why do you buy so much butter, or so many fowls?'

When the British minister heard of this transaction from Lowe, he decided to increase the yearly budget for Longwood to £12,000, thus confirming the Governor's proposal; he also authorised the prisoner to write a sealed letter to those who held deposits on his account, in order to get supplementary credits. Lowe was probably afraid that the French would take advantage of this new privilege, for he took good care not to inform them of his chief's concession.

Cipriani's heavy witticism about the shortage of food had of course been made with a view to publicity, for the sums the Emperor was trying to collect in Europe by drawing on Prince Eugene and other members of the family were actually destined to pay the members of his suite. Since their arrival at Longwood their annual salaries had been fixed as follows: Bertrand, 24,000 francs; Montholon, 24,000 (which was reduced to 18,000 after Madame de Montholon's departure); Gourgaud, 6,000; Piontkowski, 3,000; Marchand, 8,000; Pierron, 4,800; Noverraz, 4,000; Saint-Denis, 4,000; the Abbé Buonavita, 6,000; the Abbé Vignali, 3,000; Dr. Antommarchi, 9,000; Coursot, 2,400; Chandelier, 2,400; Archambault, 1,800; Josephine Noverraz, 600. Including 1,000 francs paid monthly to Marchand for the Emperor's 'toilet', this made up nearly 100,000 francs a year, or about £4,000, to be found.

The money from the sale of the silver did not remain long in Balcombe's safe: the first lot served to pay off those members of the suite deported by Lowe in order to reduce the expenses of the Household—Piontkowski, and three servants. The rest was devoted to current payments, and disappeared rapidly. Napoleon next took advantage of a loan offered by Las Cases, who was also banished from the island in December 1816; and he seems to have covered the cost of personal expenses in 1817 with the help of three bills of exchange, each for £300, signed and accepted by Las Cases. As soon as the chamberlain got back to Europe, his most urgent task was to write to members of the imperial family and reveal the penurious condition of the head of the family. Madame Mère was the first to answer, and her letters, now yellow with age, have a majestic nobility:

'Everything I have is at my son's disposal, even if it should mean dismissing my household except for one servant. If the rest of the family have not sent you funds it is because they assumed that I would do my utmost for you before asking their help. My heart's desire would be to act for them all. The sorrow and affliction in which I have been sunk ever since his captivity began may be eased if I can do something to help him. I desire you to let me know as nearly as possible how much is needed a year to supply all the Emperor's needs, not only the amount needed to meet the bills of exchange drawn on St. Helena, but for all the requirements of his staff.'

Then, as a practical woman, she was impelled by her invariable desire to hurry to the help of any of her children in trouble, to write to her son Joseph:

'It is not for me to fix the amount my children should provide to pay for their brother's wants. My children are honourable and full of feeling, and all of them have more money and generosity than he has needs. I have just sent M. de Las Cases 30,000 francs to start the fund; you should each write directly to him. For my part I am ready to give the Emperor my last sou.'

As a result of this appeal, Las Cases collected 5,000 dollars from Joseph, 15,000 francs from Jerome and 20,000 francs from Prince Eugene. Cardinal Fesch, who was horribly mean, had the effrontery to tell the Emperor's old chamberlain: 'Do not hesitate to apply to my sister for anything that might mitigate the horror of the Emperor's predicament; she will give you as much as she can.' Madame Mère bitterly resented this cynicism; when people accused her of impoverishing herself for the exile, she replied 'What does it matter? When I have nothing left, I shall take a stick and go and beg alms for Napoleon's mother.' By October 1818, all contacts had been established, and she wrote to Joseph in the United States: 'I have already provided 60,000 francs a year. If necessary, I will provide 50,000 to 60,000 francs a year, and I am only waiting to hear if this sum is needed before reducing my own expenses.'

Las Cases had now been reimbursed by an advance from Prince Eugene and it seemed as if the Corsican clan, their loyalty strengthened by adversity, were prepared to put 100,000 francs a year at the disposal of the ex-sovereign. Unfortunately a promise does not always lead to its fulfilment, and Joseph living comfortably in America, Jerome at Trieste, and Lucien surrounded by his collections, all had other things to think about besides helping their brother; this at least seems to emerge from a letter from Madame Mère to Joseph, written in March 1820. After reassuring the ex-king of Spain as to the fate of the valuable pictures he wanted her to send him, she again broached the subject of the expenses at Longwood:

'As for the Emperor, his fixed expenditure on necessities amounts to £500 a month. He has given orders for this sum to be debited from the funds whose origin you know of, which he entrusted to a Parisian firm of bankers during the time he was at Elba. The £500 monthly has hitherto been paid from this fund, although the banker was untrustworthy enough to let some letters of exchange be protested for a sum of 70,000 francs. As I have heard nothing about this for the last three months, and as I have also made myself responsible for the payment of this sum, I suppose that all is now in order again and the situation has been put straight. My expenses for sending him wine, coffee, clothes, books, a medicine-chest, ornaments for his chapel, etc., and paying for the journeys of two priests—one of them a doctor—a surgeon, a cook and a major-domo, have amounted to about 130,000 francs, including the 65,000 francs I sent direct to Las Cases. Lucien can do nothing, with his very large family to support. Jerome has lost a great deal and I have had to send him money—even more than I have sent the Emperor. Pauline—I do not think she can be induced to do anything for other people. Louis lives well, but I do not know how much he has. It seems therefore that you and I will have to make sacrifices unless Providence comes to our aid.'

In fact the Emperor drew mainly on his own reserves during the last years of his exile, while his brothers and sisters, on whom he had showered kingdoms, principalities and governorships, titles, diamonds, mansions and furnished castles, were not in the least interested in paying his debts 'of honour'. The proof is to be found in a letter he wrote on April 23, 1821, a few days before his death, to the banker Laffitte in Paris:

'When I left Paris in 1815, I sent you the sum of nearly six million for which you gave me a double receipt; I cancelled one of these receipts and instructed Count de Montholon to present the other, so that after my death you might hand him the aforementioned sum together with interest at 5% dating from July 1, 1815, after deducting any payments you have made on my instructions.'

✤   ✤   ✤

The question of daily supplies of food is closely linked to that of finance and its effect on the health and morale of the exiles makes it an important element in the history of those six years.

A list of provisions supplied by the British contractor has already been given; it remains only to describe the quality of the goods. Even without the evidence of numerous nineteenth-century witnesses, it is possible to estimate it without great risk of error from present-day conditions in St. Helena. Local resources are still today extremely poor, but modern methods of preservation and the abundance of frozen foods makes existence possible, whereas a hundred and fifty years ago there were absurdly few bullocks and sheep on the island and meat was such a rare luxury that, immediately he got there, Hudson Lowe asked the East India Company to send forty bullocks and five hundred sheep every two months to feed the population, now increased by the arrival of the garrison to 7,000. 'Slaughtering a bullock', a witness tells us, 'was a State matter needing the permission of the Governor and council.' The rage of the population may be imagined when they heard that the Emperor sometimes asked for two sets of brains for his luncheon. The animals were imported from the Cape or the coast of Angola, and did not thrive on the wretched sun-scorched grass of the island pastures, which contained no nourishment whatever. Sheep hardly weighed thirty-three lb. and were often so transparently thin that the Longwood cooks used to put a candle inside the carcass and use it as a lantern. Flabby and tasteless, the meat melted when it was cooked. The pigs, fattened on the insipid farinaceous roots of the yam, were covered with a thick coat of fat which vanished in the cooking-pots like butter in the sun, leaving nothing to be carved except a few stringy tasteless hunks. Both common sense and harsh necessity therefore drove the inhabitants to use a great deal of salt meat, and the commissariat always held a reserve of two years' rations. Poultry, chiefly chickens, were allowed free range for the sake of economy, and after running about in the constant heat in search of scarce and poor nourishment they became nothing but nerves and bones; forced to multiply by inbreeding, they hatched out chicks which grew into ridiculously small birds hardly bigger than partridges. Fish of various sorts abounded, but did not provide such succulent dishes as most European species. The small ones were rather tasteless, like our freshwater fish; the flesh of the bigger ones was hard and compact, giving the Europeans indigestion and all sorts of allergies. Vegetable-growing would have been the despair of a European gardener. The soil was heavy and muddy in winter, hard and dry as a rock in summer, and only the most common vegetables would grow on it; cabbages, beetroots and turnips reached a gigantic size and were the staple food of the natives, but vegetables such as white men enjoy—beans, peas, artichokes, carrots and celery—drooped and dwindled in this unsuitable climate, and when they came to the table they were stringy and tough as leather.

✤   ✤   ✤

The climate is another very important factor in the daily life of a country. What of the climate of St. Helena? It is a thorny question. Some writers who have never tried it have declared it was excellent, while others who have suffered from it describe it as execrable; but in both cases they wished to prove a thesis. The climate of Longwood concerns us more than that of St. Helena as a whole, since between the time the Emperor went to live on the plateau in December 1815, and his death in May 1821, he never left it except for short outings, and even those were in the close vicinity. And Longwood with its winds, damp, fogs, and sharp changes of temperature, was very different from the overheated, dry, in fact tropical atmosphere of Jamestown, the tiny capital buried among its clay and laterite walls.

The first witness for the prosecution, specially fitted by his profession, is Doctor O'Meara:

'When it was understood that Longwood had been fixed upon for the abode of Napoleon, it at first excited some surprise in the minds of the islanders, as the situation was so bleak and exposed that it had never been inhabited by any family for more than a few months in the year ... Exposed to a south-east wind constantly charged with humidity, its elevated situation causes it to be enveloped in fog or drenched with rain for the greatest part of the year.'

Then follow some medical considerations, which, however out of date they may be, are still of interest:

'To sudden diurnal vicissitudes of temperature, especially when accompanied with rain or humidity, may be ascribed the greatest part of the diseases which affect the human constitution. Rapid transitions from heat to cold render the extreme vessels on the surface of the body torpid, impelling at the same time a quantity of blood upon some of the internal organs. Sudden atmospherical changes ... (produce) in some climates, such as that of England, affections of the lungs, in tropical ones, where the biliary system is so liable to derangement, affections of the liver. The great sympathy existing between the skin, liver and intestines, has never been more strongly exemplified than by the number of violent and fatal affections of the two latter organs, which have occurred, and are daily occurring, in St. Helena, where the atmospherical vicissitudes are so frequent and so rapid, and where such humidity prevails.'

These few sentences contain the essence of the truth.

On the plateau of Longwood the average rainfall is nearly twenty-four inches; this is about the same as the figure for the drier parts of Great Britain, but it is not the chief drawback of the climate. Seasonal differences hardly exist; in theory there is winter and summer, and the rainy period falls between the months of March and September, but the summer—which lasts from September to February—is by no means free from rain and extremely unhealthy. At this altitude and in this climate, the quantity of rain is not so serious as the time of year when it arrives. When summer showers fall on the overheated earth it sends up warm vapours to float round Longwood House; these are not fresh, like the morning mists that herald a warm dry day in Europe, but clammy and oppressive, making Europeans and natives alike complain of feeling low-spirited, sluggish and sleepy. There are also violent changes in temperature to be reckoned with, causing bronchial affections; these are still trouble-some today in spite of more comfortable houses and modern medi-cine. In the height of summer, when the thermometer stood at 25 degrees centigrade on the lawns of Longwood, as soon as the sun had set behind the grey walls of High Knoll fort the mercury would fall suddenly to 15 degrees, an alpine coolness following the tropical heat of the day without any transition. When they first arrived, the French were deceived by the heat, and wandered along the garden paths at dusk wearing silk breeches and white stockings or muslin dresses, with the result that they suffered from endless colds, sore throats, and bronchitis, or catarrh as it was called at the time.

The wind blows violently for months on end, rapidly exhausting the physical organism and exciting the nervous system strangely: its strength and persistence are revealed by the shapes of the trees, the whirling dust and the movement of the clouds. In winter it comes from the south-east and is glacial, in spring moist and damp, and when it veers to the north in February it is scorching hot and full of water like a vapour bath.

The difference between the temperatures of earth and air naturally gives rise to the formation of clouds—a well-known phenomenon in the islands of the Atlantic, and days when the sky is clear are few and far between. Usually the sun is hidden behind huge, almost motion-less clouds, diffusing strong light, or else sailing rapidly by, leaving intervals of blazing sunlight. A perfectly clear morning is often followed by heavy showers at noon; or a night of hurricanes, rain and uprooted trees may be succeeded by a morning as tranquil as a Japanese print. The most unbearable time of year is during the months of August and September: low clouds cover the island at a height of about 500 metres and completely envelop the plateau: the sky is dull, visibility reduced to a few yards, rain streams down on the vegetation, chimneys smoke, and cattle and donkeys take refuge behind low walls, soaked to the skin.

This alternation of heat and cold, dryness and humidity, stillness and high wind, is very harmful to both plants and human beings. Hardly has a shrub been encouraged by the torrential rain and warm air to put out a few buds, than it is stripped bare by a sudden drought or savage wind. If one walks a little way along the plateau to enjoy the noonday warmth, heavy drops of rain are sure to herald

Napoleon Bonaparte sketched at St. Helena
by a British officer

Longwood House drawn by James Wathen

Longwood old house

the advent of large woolly clouds. What a trial for men from temperate countries, where psychological pleasure in the changing seasons is reinforced by the slow and refreshing alterations between heat and cold! Napoleon, as a son of Corsica and its gentle climate, probably suffered more than his companions. English doctors declare that humidity is only unhealthy when there are sharp changes of temperature, and that a drop from 25 to 15 degrees is not 'excessive'; they point out that in 1815 there was a sanatorium for tuberculosis at High Peak on St. Helena, at the same altitude as Longwood but on the west of the island—and thus in a more sheltered and definitely healthier region. On all the evidence, and in spite of their theories, Napoleon certainly suffered considerably from the high degree of humidity in the air—it sometimes reached 88%—and Ali tells us in his memoirs: 'When he came in from his outing rather late and had got wet, he always caught a cold in the head; we were almost certainly in for a sleepless night if he got up after his first doze; then he began sneezing and after the first sneezes he would begin to cough more and more, until he seemed unable to stop. He coughed so loudly that it could be heard all over the house. The crisis would last for one or two hours of incessant sneezing, blowing his nose, coughing and spitting. Only the very slightest humidity was needed to give him a cold.'

The arrangement of the rooms and the construction of the house were not designed in the best possible way to dissipate this pervasive humidity: there was no cellar, no damp-course. Intended as a summer residence, its walls had been built on foundations of laterite—a porous volcanic stone. The clayey soil of Longwood plateau might perhaps therefore keep the house cool in fine weather; but in winter! ... In winter, clothes, leather, and even floor-boards had a thin white coating of mildew. It would be natural to suppose that fires would have been enough to dry out the air, but the relative amount of humidity increased with the temperature, so that when the Emperor, feeling chilly and having every reason to dread the sepulchral atmosphere of his apartments, ordered baskets of wood to be heaped on the fire, all was alas in vain—the wood was green! The damp remained, and the chimneys drew so badly that life indoors became even more uncomfortable than before. Hudson Lowe was well aware of all these inconveniences, and when the question of moving

6

the Emperor came up and Plantation House was suggested, he told the Russian Commissioner in confidence: 'I do not want to hand over Plantation House to the French. They would do too much damage there, and besides Lady Lowe would not be so well at Longwood, and I will never sacrifice my wife's health to Bonaparte's comfort.'

III

DAILY LIFE AT PLANTATION HOUSE

✦✦

Plantation House—Sir Hudson Lowe, his career and
character—Lady Lowe—The men surrounding the
Governor—The orderly officers—The garrison—The
Royal Navy—Lowe and the East India Company.

✦✦

A winding, leafy lane three miles long, in the form of a W, led from
Longwood to Plantation House which took its place in history
beside Longwood House when Napoleon arrived on the island. A
semicircular white railing, a keeper's lodge and a sloping path edged
with blue agapanthus, led to the terrace in front of the residence of
the governors of St. Helena. It was no more impressive than a rich
English gentleman's country house, and was only given an official
appearance by the Union Jack on the pediment: one storey, a flat
roof and a porch in the Georgian style made up a commonplace
architectural whole, but there was a splendid view of the sea and the
interior decoration was not without charm. In an island where shade
was scarce, vegetation sporadic, the wind overpowering and the
scenery unattractive, the traveller was surprised and enchanted to
find in this park of about 200 acres an abundance of different rare
plants, while the smooth, well-kept lawns and cool shrubberies gave
it a European air.

Built in 1791, it was of modest proportions, and as soon as he
arrived Hudson Lowe realised that it must be enlarged if it was to
accommodate the large staff working under his aegis. He added in
turn a library—made simply by roofing over the central courtyard—
a billiard-room, a nursery, an office and a servants' wing. He thus had
twenty-seven rooms at his disposal, all of them high, spacious and
airy, a little gloomy and austere certainly, but in which the activities
of government could be carried on both in office and drawing-room,
and in which everyone would want to be received and above all to

be seen. The 'servants of the Crown', to use the old-fashioned description given to British colonial officials, came to this drawing-room to ask the opinion of the all-powerful Governor; to the childish pleasure of spending several hours there, in futile conversation, glass in hand, there was added the sensation of being at the heart of political intrigues which it might be useful to know. Hudson Lowe soon discovered the advantages of lavish official receptions, and paid little attention to any aloofness or criticism he might encounter. Both civilians and soldiers were languishing in isolation, and he knew very well that a card bearing the magic inscription in gold letters 'His Excellency the Governor and Lady Lowe request the pleasure of Mr. ——'s company' would soon bring waverers, individualists and even enemies back to his camp.

On the ground floor, practically on a level with the park, were the official apartments: a hall, dominated by the royal portraits, a drawing-room, a dining-room to hold thirty, the Governor's study, the library and offices; while on the floor above were the private apartments, bedrooms, Lady Lowe's boudoir and suites for important visitors or staff officers. The only entrance was through the official apartments on the ground floor, and this made for a tiresome lack of privacy. It was somewhat like life in barracks, with communal meals, presided over by Lady Lowe and under the usually unamiable eye of the master of the house (who never put himself out to be polite to his subordinates) and seasoned with sarcasms from the clerks and backstairs gossip.

April 14, 1816, was a Sunday—in fact Easter Sunday; the weather was atrocious, for it rained all day without stopping. About noon the Alarm House gun announced the arrival of British ships, one of which was the *Phaeton*, commanded by Captain Stanfell, with Sir Hudson Lowe on board, accompanied by Lady Lowe, her daughter Miss Charlotte Johnson, Lieutenant-Colonel Sir Thomas Reade, the Governor's deputy, Major Gorrequer his military secretary, Dr. Baxter who was to run the hospitals, Major Emmett, Lieutenants Wortham and Wallace of the Engineers, Lieutenant Jackson, and a German staff clerk called W. Janish. As it would not have been suitable to carry out the ceremonial connected with the arrival and assumption of his functions of the Governor on Easter day, they did not disembark until next day.

Before following him to Plantation House, let us take a look at Sir Hudson Lowe, Lieutenant-General, Knight Commander of the Most Honourable Order of the Bath, Russian Cross of St. George, Prussian military Order of Merit, Governor and commander-in-chief of the island of St. Helena. Who was this man of obscure origins, who entered history by that narrow door reserved for actors of unsympathetic parts as soon as he set foot on the rock?

He was born in Ireland on July 28, 1769, under the same zodiacal sign and in the same year as Napoleon, who was eighteen days younger. Destined for the army, at eighteen he joined the garrison at Gibraltar, where his father was army surgeon, with the rank of ensign. Without money or useful connections, having only the few guineas of his pay, he had to rely on hard work, a good memory and ambition—like a certain Lieutenant Bonaparte. He learned French, Italian and Spanish easily, and as he was too obscure and impecunious to take part in the London season with its dandies, clubs and gossip, he spent his leave from the army visiting France and Italy. Afterwards he returned to Gibraltar, and his first wartime garrison was at Ajaccio with the 50th regiment. While there, he heard talk of Bonaparte, then in France, and saw Madame Letizia and her daughters, who in view of the special situation of their relation to Napoleon, were asked (so he said) to let their house be requisitioned by a British officer. When Corsica was evacuated he was sent to Elba, and then to Minorca, where he organised a troop of Corsican emigrants and deserters under the name of the Corsican Rangers.

We find him next at their head in Egypt; disembarking at Aboukir, he took part in the battle of Alexandria. After the evacuation of Egypt he went to Malta, where he lost his job and his troops when the Peace of Amiens was signed. He was put on half-pay and obtained an office post and then a special intelligence mission to Portugal in 1803 from his old chief, General Sir John Moore. When hostilities with France were resumed he set off for the Mediterranean, raised a further force of Corsican Rangers and became a lieutenant-colonel at the age of thirty-four. This was an honourable promotion and certainly justified by his ability in 'intelligence'—an activity which makes and unmakes the fortune of soldiers in all branches of the British army. Lowe and his recruits took part in various operations undertaken by the British in this part of Europe, and

particularly against the kingdom of Naples. Besieged on the island of
Capri, he was ousted and forced to surrender to the French, among
whom was a certain Cipriani Franceschi, who has already been mentioned as a member of Napoleon's suite and who was to die a sudden,
violent and mysterious death in 1818. After various missions to the
Ionian Islands, we find him in 1812 a colonel on leave in England,
and soon afterwards on his way to Russia and Sweden, where the
British army was recruiting a legion made up of prisoners and
deserters from the German Confederation. On May 20 and 21 he
was at Bautzen.

'In the morning,' he tells us, 'a body of the enemy's troops was observed
to be formed on a crest. Immediately in their front a small group was
collected, which by aid of spy-glasses was soon discovered to be composed
of persons of consequence in the enemy's army, amongst whom was most
clearly distinguishable Napoleon Bonaparte himself. . . . He was dressed
in a plain uniform coat and star, with a plain hat, different from that of his
Marshals and Generals which were feathered, his air and manner so
perfectly resembling the portraits given of him that there was no possibility of mistake.'

This was the first meeting, at a distance, between the future exile
and his gaoler, 'the man who only knew how to command and the
man who only knew how to obey'.*

A little later we come across Hudson Lowe attached to Blücher's
staff—in exactly what capacity is not clear, but the secret of his
mission is probably hidden in the intelligence files of the British
army—and he was privileged to be present as a spectator at the
'battle of nations' at Leipzig. In November 1813 he was galloping
along the roads of Germany on a mission which took him again into
Blücher's entourage. He rejoined the Prussian marshal at Vaucou-
leurs in January 1814, and remained with him until the fall of Paris.
He was present at all the battles of the French campaign: Brienne,
La Rothière, Champaubert, Craonne, Laon, and among the thirteen
in which he took part, Napoleon was commanding in person in
eleven. His memoirs are always precise and chiefly concerned with
his own advancement, and he remarks with a touch of that ingenuous-
ness that seasons all his narratives: 'During these campaigns I had
my full share of military responsibility besides being exposed to all

*Balmain.

the ordinary dangers of war: having been constantly near the person of Marshal Blücher, present on one occasion where he was wounded, on another where his Cossack orderly was shot by his side'.

His finest hour arrived when the French capital fell, for, as the only British officer attached to the Prussians, he was given the task and the honour of bearing the anxiously awaited news to London. He reached the Foreign Office during the night of April 9, almost at the same moment that news of another event—the abdication at Fontainebleau—was filling the daily papers. Hudson Lowe was rewarded by being made a Knight of the Bath, and became Sir Hudson Lowe, K.C.B.; his excellent relations with the Allied armies gained him a mention on the honours lists by which several nations celebrated the fall of the 'usurper'. Thus he received the Prussian military Order of Merit and the Russian order of St. George; 'these honours were accompanied by very amiable letters', he wrote. He always took trouble to keep on good terms with Great Britain's allies, believing this helped his career. He also carried on an active correspondence with various important persons. He was very proud of his European contacts, and when there seemed danger from the Russian commissioner at St. Helena he told his secretary Major Gorrequer: 'I have more influence than his protector at the Russian court'. The letters received by Lowe and still existing among his papers bear witness to his anxiety not to be forgotten. They always begin in the same way: 'It is with great satisfaction, my very dear and honoured general, that I have received your letter on September 15, which tells me that you have still preserved the remembrance of a man who is infinitely attached to you. . . . Your appointment . . . must place you in continued relation with Wellington; you would oblige me by conveying to that hero the sentiments of respectful homage I feel for him . . . Gneisenau.'

Or, 'Your letter, my dear General, I have duly received, and I feel very much obliged to you for the sentiments you have therein expressed towards me. . . . I wish you joy from my heart on the important post which the Prince Regent, in his confidence, has bestowed on you, and I rejoice that the choice has fallen upon a man so perfectly equal to fulfil the duties of it, in its whole extent. Blücher.'

Obviously Blücher understood human nature.

These two letters were written to congratulate Colonel Sir Hudson Lowe on his nomination, on June 14, 1814, as quartermaster-general to the British armies in the Netherlands, under the command of the Prince of Orange, with the rank of major-general. This promotion made him responsible, at a crucial moment in history, for the material organisation of the troops: commissariat, billeting and armaments. It was indeed a crucial moment, for it was rumoured that Napoleon had landed on the French coast; Sir Hudson Lowe was quartered near Brussels at the time, only a few miles from a village with an almost English name: Waterloo. In the month of April 1815 Wellington came to take command of the armies in Belgium and it seems that the relations between the Iron Duke and Lowe were somewhat cool. Wellington, like many great men, relied on his instinct rather than on documents and details, and he was irritated more than once by his subordinate's tentativeness. One day he was heard saying that Lowe was 'a damned old fool'. Whether as a result of a War Office decision, Wellington's wishes, or a request from Lowe himself, the 'old fool' was transferred from his post with the British commander-in-chief to command the English troops at Genoa.

The plan was that the army quartered at Genoa should join the Austrians and Sardinians and a squadron of the British fleet cruising off the coast of France, to attack in the south. Before leaving the region where the fate of the Empire and all Europe was so soon to be decided, Lowe was candid enough to ask for commendation, but Wellington only grumbled that 'he was accustomed to doing most of the work himself, and in any case he could make do with the first-comer'. On his way to Genoa, Lowe stopped at Heidelberg where the allied sovereigns then were: he was received by the Tsar Alexander and Blücher, and immediately sent a report of these flattering audiences to London. He finally took over his new command on June 19, the day after the fate of the Empire had been decided. Europe breathed again, England put out flags, the Emperor was galloping at all speed from the battlefield of Waterloo in the direction of Paris—a Paris that only longed for peace.

It was not therefore difficult for Lowe to land his troops on July 11 at Marseilles, and he met with hardly any resistance. Marshal Brune and the generals had surrendered to Louis XVIII on June 24: sporadic fighting in the region of Toulon was the only justification for the presence of the British troops and their commander. On August 1 he received from London his nomination to the post at St. Helena, with orders to return to the capital without delay. He hardly had time to accept from the municipality of Marseilles a very handsome silver vase 'in recognition of his personal conduct'.

Such was the career of the man who was to represent British authority on St. Helena in its most rigid and tactless form, and the goodwill of the Allied sovereigns in its most hypocritical aspect—all with the direct approval of Lord Bathurst, Secretary of State for the Colonies, who invested him with considerable and unrestricted powers. One thing is quite certain. This obscure man, who was to show that he himself could be broken when the time came, was the incarnation of two powerful emotions: the hatred of the English 'shopkeeper' class, as Napoleon called them, who had been ruined by the imperial wars, and the bitterness of European sovereigns and princes against their ambitious 'cousin' for occupying their capitals, carving up their domains, carrying off their armies into captivity and even marrying their daughter. 'Britannia, you own the sea. But the sea has not water enough to wash away the shame left you in death by the great departed. It was not your Sir Hudson, but you who were the Sicilian *sbirro* hired by perjured kings to avenge in secret on the man of the people what the people once inflicted on one of them.'*

It would of course be very unjust to condemn Hudson Lowe on the evidence of his denunciation by the Emperor and his companions, or even on the word of French historians alone; but there are also English witnesses, and no great research is needed to draw up a list of crushing indictments. Lord Rosebery, Foreign Secretary under Queen Victoria, had access to the archives of his department and was personally acquainted with survivors from the Napoleonic drama. With the slightly exaggerated arrogance of an English aristocrat he affirms that 'Lowe was, we conceive, a narrow, ignorant, irritable man without a vestige of tact or sympathy. . . . He was not what is in the best sense of the word called a gentleman.' Wellington, whose subordinate he was, did not forget General Sir Hudson Lowe, and in the serenity of ripe old age confided to his eager questioner, Lord Stanhope: 'He was a man wanting in education and judgement. . . .

*Heine, *Drummer Le Grand*.

I knew him very well. He was a stupid man. He was not an ill-natured man. But he knew nothing at all of the world, and like all men who know nothing of the world, he was suspicious and jealous'. The historian Sir Archibald Alison's more moderate opinion was that 'his manner was rigid and unaccommodating'; while the eminent jurist and Lord Chief Justice Lord Campbell pronounced a sentence to which there was no appeal: 'There may be tragedies on the death of Napoleon, in which Sir Hudson Lowe will be the *sbirro*'. There was an unprejudiced chorus, too, from the foreign commissioners, Stürmer the Austrian, Balmain the Russian, and the absurd Frenchman the Marquis de Montchenu. 'I do not know what fatality induces Sir Hudson Lowe to quarrel with everyone in the end. Crushed by the weight of his responsibilities, he torments himself and worries endlessly, and always wants to be a nuisance to other people.' 'The Governor is not a tyrant, but he is a busybody and impossibly unreasonable. . . . He cannot get on with anyone and sees treason and traitors everywhere.' 'What a man! I am certain that one could search everywhere and never come across his like.'

Lowe's physical appearance was as strange as his mentality. Most witnesses saw him at the age of forty-seven as of medium height but with a natural leanness which made his figure look elegantly slim even when padded out with the braid and epaulets of a lieutenant-general's uniform. His curly hair was reddish, thick and unruly; his face was freckled and rather ruddy, but grew very pale in moments of intense excitement; his pale eyebrows were so thick that they almost hid his restless, half-closed eyes. His long, narrow nose drooped above the tight lips and pointed chin. 'It is the face of a hyena caught in a trap,' Napoleon said mockingly.

To make up for his unattractive physique, Sir Hudson took great trouble over his uniforms, his appearance and manners; his walk was brisk, he dictated in a loud, firm, assured voice. Was this really a sign of a strong will and lively intelligence? This was the impression Lowe wished to give in any case, and the only person who could settle the question for us is his secretary, Major Gorrequer. Yet the major speaks of indecision, perpetual irritableness, changes of mood and insincerity. A letter would be written, torn up, re-written, crossed out, and written again ten times over. A proclamation only six lines long would take ten days to draw up, but it was incredible to see him, said Gorrequer mockingly, 'Shuttling about, knocking his aiguillettes against the chain and walking up and down full of affectation when dictating'.* When at last the Governor had an interlocutor or correspondent who felt out of his depths or anxious at his mercy, 'Sir Hudson's grin and demon look. His appearance like nauseous medicine to me'.* A particularly lively passage of the secretary's papers gives us some idea of the Governor's methods of work and tact:

'Working hard all days fabricating a short note to Old Frog (the Marquis de Montchenu). The frequent bursts of "scoundrel", "rascal", "black-guard", etc., let off at him whilst composing it and the frequent observations of "this is a most important note (to ask him who the persons were who had spoken of the wish to have the young Napoleon on the throne of Frogland), one of the most so I ever wrote, it requires a great deal of consideration". This was when he was puzzled what to say or how to turn his phrases in French. . . . Several of mine he was obliged to adopt after all. Not knowing in fact what to say but determined to pick a hole in Frog's coat and to harass him. Saying he had completely committed himself and he'd be damned if he let him out of that trap. He would make him feel, he would work him and not let him alone till he got him fairly involved. Then all at once giving up writing, saying he did not think it worth writing about. But the second day at it again with revived vigour and full of the high importance of doing something of it. At last sent it off with imprecations on Frog.'*

Such as the Governor was, both physically and morally, the French at Longwood and the English on the island had to put up with him. On the whole the French were perhaps in a better position to declare, either is no uncertain tones through the voice of Napoleon, or through protests published in Europe, what they thought of this man, this 'hired assassin', this 'Sicilian *sbirro*', this 'monster with the face of a man'. As for the English, they depended on him for everything—their jobs, promotion, freedom of movement, and freedom itself. They had to submit without a murmur to his domineering control, and only a few brave spirits, encouraged by Napoleon and dazzled by promises of material gain, dared stand up to him; of course they were losers in the game, but they won as much sympathy and popularity in Europe as they lost in St. Helena.

Yet Hudson Lowe was not merely that terrifying combination of

*Major Gorrequer's Papers (unpublished).

duplicity, meanness and narrow stupidity that historians and witnesses have combined to reveal to the public. His genuine good qualities had helped him to ascend all the ranks of the hierarchy with reasonable speed, at a particularly difficult period. Unfortunately the situation and personality of the man he had to deal with at St Helena, the trend of opinion, and the tendency of history to see events through the eyes of the victim—if he is also a hero—emphasised his numerous faults and changed some of his qualities into intolerable obsessions.

Conscientious he certainly was, and this would have been a virtue in a subordinate; his mania for looking at everything through a magnifying glass and making a note of it has bequeathed us the invaluable collection of documents known as the Lowe Papers, now in the British Museum, which contain the essential history of the years 1815–21. With his usual naïve self-satisfaction he tells us:

'There are perhaps few, if any, public administrations of any kind, of which the records are so full and complete as those of my Government at St. Helena. There is not only a detailed correspondence addressed to the proper Department of His Majesty's Government, reporting the occurrences of almost every day during the five years that Napoleon Bonaparte remained under my custody, but the greater part of the conversations held with Bonaparte himself, or with his followers, was immediately noted down with an ability and exactness which reflect the highest credit on my Military Secretary, Major Gorrequer.'

But how many faults have been committed in the name of conscientiousness? Where an astute politician would have realised that his mission allowed scope for generosity, Lowe succumbed to his mania for detail and stooped to miserable pettinesses, until he was quite unable to see the wood for the trees. Instead of behaving like a general concerned only with larger questions of conduct, he demeaned himself daily to carry out the unsuitable roles of tax-collector and detective.

He was honest also, this lieutenant-general who had recently been poor but now enjoyed a salary of £12,000 a year at a time when a captain earned £300 and a doctor £400, so that wealth, plenty and material comforts might well have turned his head, as had happened to some of his predecessors on St. Helena. His secretary shows him to us, disputing one by one every item of the expenditure which was burdening his country's budget, and spending weeks on end contesting a demand by an officer for a few pounds pay, because he thought it unjustified. Of the £70,000 he received in the course of his mission—a small fortune—little remained at the end of his life, and he died poor, ruined and heartily disliked, leaving nothing to his children except countless files of papers which found their way to the British Museum in exchange for a small pension by Queen Victoria's government to Lady Lowe's youngest daughter.

Who could possibly have shown greater zeal and obedience? Without these qualities would he ever have succeeded in climbing the rungs of the rigid British military hierarchy? The French, particularly Napoleon himself, could never understand his absolute submission to the regulations drawn up in London by Lord Bathurst. The argumentative spirit of the inhabitants of Longwood could not accept such automatism, and expected more diplomacy and breadth of vision from a general than they would have from a subaltern. But for Hudson Lowe, just as for a country policeman, a regulation was a regulation, and the remote situation of the island made no difference at all. Measures signed by respected chiefs in London were exactly enforced, without personal initiative.

Could anyone have made more blunders? Certainly not, but no one could have had worse luck, for Lowe could not guess that the abilities whose extent and variety were so highly praised in his dossier would be of no service to him in his very unusual task. He needed the diplomacy of Talleyrand or the generous outlook of a man of higher social standing.

✤   ✤   ✤

Lady Lowe does not seem to have had much influence over her husband; she frequently exasperated him by ill-timed or two-edged remarks, and Gorrequer often comments on the way the first lady rebuffed the Governor, or her terrible rages, when she 'rolled her eyes like a tigress'. At the age of forty-six, after amorous adventures in the Mediterranean resulting in illegitimate offspring (one day Lady Lowe thoughtlessly showed an Englishwoman the portrait of a natural child of her husband's and the news was soon all over the island), Hudson Lowe had married just before embarking for St.

Helena a Mrs. Johnson, *née* de Lancy, widow of a colonel and daughter of a colonial governor. She was nearly forty, dressed well, wore rather too much rouge, and if Gorrequer is to be believed was not averse to strong liquor. During their stay on St. Helena she presented her husband with a daughter and two sons, only one of whom survived. Being the first lady of the island went a little to her head: if there were countesses at Longwood, all the more important to be her Ladyship at Plantation House. With more financial means than her French rivals, Lady Lowe tried to eclipse them by her finery, receptions and the futilities of etiquette. She never went out without an aide-de-camp cantering beside the door of her carriage. 'Oh pride, oh vainglory,' wrote Gorrequer mockingly, 'would either of them, a few years before, have been warranted in anticipating all this high rank and honours and to have gentlemen to follow them as *staffieri* or *palafrenieri*?' She sulked, gave herself airs, and complained to her husband whenever she thought people were not paying her sufficient attention, she jeered at younger and better-dressed women than herself, and took to no one except Madame Bertrand, who must be a real lady since she had relations among the London aristocracy. Lady Lowe ruled the little world of Plantation House despotically, officers, couriers, servants and slaves alike, and meddled in everything. Gorrequer often accuses her of becoming involved in the love affairs of her servants and the relations between the officers and laundresses. What else was there for her to do? And what occupation was there for her two daughters by Colonel Johnson, whom Lowe had taken under his wing when he took their mother to his bed? There were none of the clubs or receptions beloved of Englishwomen; only the rather provincial dullness of parties organised in the regimental mess by a group of amateur actors. Only the gilded solitude of Plantation House, with its spurious air of grandeur, driving the lady of the house and her daughters to withdraw little by little from a world they no longer found to their taste, and content themselves with the obsequiousness of their timid menials. Of course Lady Lowe's chief concern was to marry her daughters, and Napoleon's death came too soon for her plans, as only the eldest had found a husband in the person of Balmain, the Tsar's commissioner, thus becoming to the delight of Sir Hudson and Lady Lowe a real Russian countess.

It was towards this on the whole well-matched couple that all eyes on the island were turned: the Governor represented the Crown, and thus the combined notions of rank, wealth and good manners, in the eyes of middle-class Englishmen. So they sneezed when Lady Lowe felt cold and vied with one another for the honour of drinking wine with her and the Governor—but chiefly with her, for she had written a toast for the edification of her children, which amused the guests enormously:

> 'God save the King
> God save the Queen
> Damn our Neighbour.'*

✣ ✣ ✣

The special status of St. Helena meant that Lowe's functions on the island were of two sorts: the most important was of course to guard General Bonaparte, but he also had to administer the colony on behalf of the East India Company. Sir Hudson therefore had two separate groups of subordinates to assist him: the garrison and head-quarters for military duties, and a council and the employees of the Company for civil administration. The former were centred at Plantation House, while he installed the administrative offices with their copyists, store-keepers and agents in the Castle at Jamestown.

The soldiers who made up his staff had all travelled out with him on the *Phaeton* and he had chosen them with care. Chief among them was Lieutenant-Colonel Sir Thomas Reade, thirty-one years old, who had been his chief of staff at Genoa and was afterwards employed in the intelligence department. For this he had been made a Knight bachelor—not a very considerable reward, but one which gave him the title of Sir, so keenly coveted in England. Short and plump, with a round baby face and a cheerful manner, Sir Thomas made quite a good impression, even on Napoleon, but this was misleading: his letters in the Lowe archives, the reports of the foreign commissioners and the gossip current in the island all with one voice reveal him as the most savage and the least scrupulous enemy the French possessed. Strictness, more strictness and even more

---

*Major Gorrequer's Papers (unpublished). The Neighbour was a nickname for Napoleon.

strictness might have been his motto, and if he had been Governor he would have brought that confounded Boney to his senses by taking away his pens, pencils, paper and even his books. When the Russian commissioner wrote to his court, he did not hesitate to say: 'Reade is the Governor's intimate friend, advisor and sole confidant, and on that account he has nothing to do with anyone at Longwood. He knows a little Italian, but has no education, is not an agreeable or intelligent man, nor a person one would care to meet. He is a John Bull in the raw. Napoleon will not condescend to see him or talk to him. The English are afraid of him.' In fact his influence on Lady Lowe was so great that Gorrequer admits bitterly: 'Do you know, Reade, what Lady Lowe says? That you are the Governor and Sir Hudson Lowe is your Deputy. That for herself she is a cypher.'

In 1819, his blind and persistent zeal gained Reade an unusual promotion for a colonel in the British army: Lowe nominated him superintendent of the St. Helena police, with a salary of £625 a year. The news that he had been chosen naturally spread consternation among the few rebel spirits and scandalmongers who tried to relieve their boredom by gossiping. 'The bulldogs of police prowling about the streets,' complained Gorrequer. 'And both these fellows of known bad character.' Sir Thomas and his ignoble *shirros* were to be found even among the Governor's circle, poking about and listening at doors, or searching the servants' rooms from time to time; this repugnant activity earned him the nickname of Nincompoop. To keep a closer watch over the contacts between Longwood and the rest of the island, Reade moved into Alarm House at the entrance to the winding road that led over the ridge to the French establishment: there, like a gaoler at his spy-hole, he could see and hear without being seen, and transform his house into an active centre where gossip and rumours were collected, paid for and exploited with gusto. The means employed were often dishonourable, such as the trap laid for the Emperor's valet Gentilini. He had an English mistress called Mrs. Snell, and Gorrequer tells us that in January 1820 'Sir Hudson Lowe saying to me today how Reade got everything from Snell's wife that Gentilini told her, the husband repeating to Reade all his wife got out of Gentilini. "I don't know how he continues to get his information but he gets hold of everything".'*

*Major Gorrequer's Papers (unpublished).

Lieutenant-General Sir Hudson
Lowe

Admiral Sir George Cockburn

Rear-Admiral Sir Pulteney
Malcolm

William Balcombe

La Comtesse de Montholon   Le Général Comte de Montholon

La Comtesse Bertrand   Le Général Comte Bertrand

Lowe's second assistant in order of rank was Lieutenant-Colonel Edward Wynyard, aged thirty-six, whose official position was military secretary, a sinecure involving being constantly with his chief. Wynyard was another old acquaintance: he had taken part in the operations at Santa Maura, Ischia and Procida, where he had been wounded, and was subsequently chosen for the staff at St. Helena. His indolence and stand-offishness gradually lost him his privileges in favour of Gorrequer, a bachelor living under Hudson Lowe's roof, and he was content to live in married bliss with his young wife at Rock Cottage, surrounded by the magnificent scenery of Sandy Bay. A more headstrong character than Gorrequer, his liking for independence did not endear him to the Governor. The occasion for his rejection was the expulsion of Doctor O'Meara in 1818; his manner of conducting this affair displeased his chief, who disapproved of the fact that after receiving his dismissal the doctor was allowed to communicate with his patient. Hudson Lowe stormed to his officers. Wynyard should never have been entrusted with such a mission. Reade would have been cleverer. Why did he let O'Meara communicate with Bonaparte? Why did that tall grenadier let himself be fooled by the doctor? Wynyard lost his job and returned to England in 1820, where he pursued an honourable career.

The vacant post fell to Major Gorrequer who thus combined the functions of military secretary and aide-de-camp. Sir Hudson trusted him completely:

'His ability and exactness reflect the highest credit on my Military Secretary, Major Gorrequer. This gentleman was not only a perfect master of the French language, but possessed a memory equally remarkable for its accuracy and tenacity, and was therefore eminently qualified to report the conversations at which he was himself present, and to detect any error to which a misapprehension of the meaning of foreigners might lead other persons who repeated what passed at interviews with Bonaparte and his followers.'

Gorrequer was thirty-five years old; he had served in Sicily and the Ionian islands, where he had come to the notice of Lowe and been chosen for St. Helena. As a bachelor, he either occupied an inferior room at the end of the corridor on the first floor of Plantation House or a summer-house in the garden. But he was on the war-path night and day: he knew everything because he heard everything, and

7

he heard everything because he did not hesitate to put his ear to the door, if need be. The only letters Lowe refrained from showing him were those from the Foreign Secretary, marked 'confidential'. Everything else was an open book to him: he listened, translated, copied, recopied, took part in conversations, luncheons, breakfasts, and Lady Lowe's card-parties, and when he had retired to his room at night and was relieving his mind by pouring out his ill-humour on to the pages of his journal, he was still at the mercy of a summons from Sir Hudson or the whims of his lady. His portrait shows him as young, baby-faced, with an intelligent nose, mocking eyes and a knowing expression. All those who wrote about St. Helena saw him as the Governor's tool, the power behind the throne, alarmingly shrewd and a proficient linguist. Even Balmain, the perspicacious and guileful Russian commissioner, was taken in by him, and while admitting that the aide-de-camp was a 'sly dog' he believed that his cunning was dedicated to the Governor's service. 'Major Gorrequer is an excellent young man,' he wrote, 'very agreeable and obliging, but he owes everything to the Governor.' With the proofs before me —for I have had the advantage of studying his private journal—I now know that the 'sly dog' deceived his companions. Whether from resentment at Hudson Lowe's tyranny, or indignation at seeing a man he was secretly sorry for persecuted day after day, Gorrequer is revealed to us as being in constant opposition to the Governor and condemning his policy unequivocally. A page of his correspondence deserves quoting for its revelation of the feelings of all the 'honest Englishmen' of whom the poet writes:

'Lady Lowe pitying the situation of Bonaparte and saying he really was to be pitied, contrasting his former situation with his present and Sir Hudson saying he deserves more contempt than pity—which gave rise to a lengthening reasoning between them and both looking at me alternatively, as they spoke and if it were engaging me in the conversation. I observed that something must be allowed for the personal feelings of a man who had (as he said trusting to the generosity of the British nation and expecting refuge in England) delivered himself into the hands of the British and instead of an abode in England found himself fixed at St. Helena.'*

The other individuals closely connected with the Governor played minor, or utility parts, as they are called in the theatre, and did not

*Major Gorrequer's Papers (unpublished).

enjoy such a comprehensive view of events as Reade or Gorrequer. Dr. Baxter, thirty-nine years old, was a product of the Edinburgh medical faculty and had served in the Mediterranean and with the Corsican Rangers; he had been with Hudson Lowe at the siege of Capri and his old chief had expressly picked him out for St. Helena, giving him the vague title of inspector of hospitals. A tall, heavily built, distinguished-looking man, he often joined Sir Hudson and Lady Lowe at meals, was always at their card-parties and echoed his chief's opinions without a single discordant note. Lowe had thought of getting Napoleon to accept the Scot as his personal doctor and so having a sure means of getting exact information about the prisoner's state of health and the life of his suite; but Longwood mistrusted this plan and it failed to materialise, for, as the Emperor said, 'it would be madness to accept a doctor offered by one's enemy'. He spoke more truly than he knew, since Lady Lowe told Gorrequer one evening that Dr. Baxter had been urged to explain Napoleon's illness as a mild disorder: his orders were to minimise all the symptoms.

Baxter stayed at St. Helena for a period of three years and returned to England in May 1819. Shortly before embarking he had several noisy interviews with Hudson Lowe, and declared afterwards:

'that he gave it to him well. He first found him very high but he soon cooled when he told him he had observed he withdrew his friendship from him, that he had devoted himself entirely to him and that he had lost the protection of his chief who would now no longer support him, that he had avoided writing anything about this place, that his name had been slandered in consequence of the share he had made him take in the Bulletins, that he had rendered, even by Sir Hudson's own representations, important services, that he thought his services respecting the General Hospital entitled him to something more than mere acknowledgement, that it would be much better, not only for himself but for Sir Hudson, that he should go home with a recommendation to His Majesty's ministers than to go as it were under his displeasure. . . . He also said that on Sir Hudson's telling the ministers would put many questions to him for information he answered he meant to go and live retired at Cheltenham and go near nobody, that besides he knew nothing of what had passed here and how could he expect he should give any information.'*

It seems that Baxter got his recommendation, and it is interesting to note that when he got back to Scotland he returned to his medical

*Major Gorrequer's Papers (unpublished).

studies and completed a thesis on remittent fevers, *De Febre Remittente*, from which it may be gathered that he had increased his knowledge of the subject in the Mediterranean, where a mild version of the disease existed, and in St. Helena, where it flourished in a severer form.

Thomas Lyster—an old man to the rest of the company—was over fifty, and Lowe had equipped him with the pompous title of inspector of the coast and militia; he too had belonged to the Corsican Rangers and been an officer in the garrison at Ajaccio during the British occupation. To add to his authority and influence, Lowe had accredited him with the local rank of lieutenant-colonel, to the annoyance of the other officers. But worse was to follow. One day the post of orderly officer at Longwood fell vacant, and Lowe had the idea of nominating Lyster: a storm broke out among the French, and it was in vain that he praised the virtues of his protégé as a man of gentle and harmless character, speaking French and Italian, and anxious to do all he could for the well-being of the detained persons and their dependants. He received a categorical refusal from Bertrand.

'We have noted with surprise that Lieutenant-Colonel Lyster is the same who was in command at Ajaccio, a city in which the Emperor's parental home is located. . . . He does not belong to the English army, or any other body, has been your satellite for several years and depends entirely on you; he will sign anything you tell him to, understand any of your orders, and say anything you please, for he has no other will, no other conscience beside yours—that is to say that of a declared enemy. Such a man undoubtedly suits you better than some captain of a regular regiment with a reputation and conscience of his own.'

Balmain, the Russian commissioner, knew all about this affair, which culminated in the Grand Marshal receiving a challenge from the inspector of coasts and militia, and he commented in a despatch to his court: 'What foolishness to send an ex-major from Ajaccio. It shows an inexcusable lack of tact.' Lowe had to give in and appoint a Captain Nicholls, who carried out his duties honourably.

Major Emmet (twenty-seven years old) and Lieutenants Wortham (twenty-two) and Jackson (twenty-one) were officers of the Engineers, entrusted with the task of enlarging Longwood House, building a house for the Grand Marshal, drawing up plans for Napoleon's new residence—Longwood New House—and also maintaining the batteries, forts, lodgings and other buildings belonging to the administration. Emmet, who was to have the melancholy honour of digging the Emperor's grave, spent his six years in authority at daggers drawn with Lowe, who does not seem to have realised that he had a certain moral independence. Nor did Wortham fare better; he was removed from Longwood in April 1821 as a sign of disfavour rather than because his work was finished.

Lieutenant Basil Jackson was of a different stamp from the rest. His youth, his handsome face and figure and his perfect knowledge of French, unexpectedly made him the Governor's tool. One evening Bertrand and his wife met the Russian commissioner and got into conversation. 'Balmain learned that Mr. Jackson was seeing a lot of Madame de Montholon. She was said to have thrown herself at his head. It was thought that she was all the more in love because of finding herself loved in spite of having made all the running. This was causing a lot of trouble among the others at Longwood; she never bothered about what she said and might let out anything . . . Jackson was keeping daily notes of everything and had conversations with the Governor lasting two hours.' It is easy to imagine Hudson Lowe's opinion of the young fool and the part he got him to play beside this ageing woman. Bertrand reported this conversation to the Emperor, who brought the subject up with Madame de Montholon that very evening. She merely complained that Jackson was 'a nice young man, but very simple-minded and unintelligent'. It was certainly a question of intelligence! Without beating about the bush Napoleon ordered her to stop seeing the seducer, but a few days later Bertrand admitted with annoyance: 'It seems that Jackson has found several opportunities of meeting Montholon. Nobody knows what will come of this.' Napoleon was furious, and returned to the attack on March 18: 'Montholon and his wife must give their word of honour not to see Jackson again, or else they must leave.' Montholon lost his head and wanted to leave on the spot; Bertrand calmed him, at the expense of the faithless wife's reputation: 'He (Montholon) gave Jackson away; the Emperor has done both him and his wife a service in getting rid of Jackson. His attitude has been to achieve his aim by going to meet it.' This was a bitter blow for the Governor and his intelligence system, and when Lowe heard that Napoleon had decided to force the Montholons to break with the enterprising lieutenant he was furious: 'They say the Governor is extremely angry with the Grand Marshal and Mr. Jackson for quarrelling, and that he wants to get rid of the Grand Marshal.'

What was the relationship between General de Montholon and the irrepressible Mr. Jackson? We shall never know. The only people who could have enlightened us were the beautiful Albine de Montholon, fast becoming a fleshless skeleton in a convent at Montpellier, her husband—who married an Englishwoman as soon as he became a widower—and the little lieutenant himself. All of them were extremely discreet, but there must have been something more in the affair, when all is said and done, than the commonplace situation between a young man and an ageing woman, for the legal husband showed not the slightest signs of jealousy, even when, as he ironically commented, 'we were practically living under the same roof'. A curious, or scabrous detail, according to taste, is that the handsome Basil left St. Helena exactly a week after Madame de Montholon's departure on July 9, 1819, and that, like her, he arrived shortly afterwards at Brussels where his new post awaited him.

It is impossible to doubt that the young officer was Hudson Lowe's tool, or rather plaything—a successful young man may well be blinded by his own ingenuous self-satisfaction. Many years later, destiny having decreed that Jackson should be the last survivor of the drama of St. Helena (he died in 1889 at the age of ninety-four) he wrote than when Sir Hudson Lowe was quartermaster-general in the Low Countries he had been one of his aides, and when he was posted in 1815 he saw him every day and had some conversations of a confidential nature with him. But the young rascal, as Gorrequer called him, had more than one string to his bow, and while admitting that he tried to please the pliable Albine de Montholon, and succeeded, it is certain that he combined love with other business without apparent embarrassment. It was probably for this reason that he was afterwards employed at Brussels to keep an eye on a woman who might well intrigue on the Emperor's behalf, and speak her mind when silence was what Europe desired.

✷   ✷   ✷

Hudson Lowe was represented night and day at Longwood by the orderly officer, who lodged under the same roof as the French and spent most of his time, when he was not saddling his horse to escort one of the 'detained persons' to Jamestown, watching, listening and making reports. There is little worth noting about the first of these captains, T. W. Poppleton; he was the only one to make himself agreeable to the French and even be thought well of by them. He had the unusual honour of being invited to dinner by Napoleon and when after two years his regiment returned to England and he had to resign his post, the Emperor sent him a snuff-box with the imperial monogram, to thank him for his 'honourable behaviour'. It must be admitted that the Englishman worked hard for this valuable present, and lavished attentions on General Gourgaud, who made a point of saying that Poppleton had carried out his duties with all possible tact. The Englishman set great store by this gift, and forty years later he had the curiosity to scrape away the lining at the bottom of the box—when he discovered a thin piece of paper bearing a message for Las Cases written in Napoleon's own hand.

Poppleton was succeeded by Captain Blakeney of the 66th regiment. He only stayed a year and aroused the violent dislike of the French, not so much because of his reputation as a heavy drinker as for his mania for inspecting the contents of their laundry-baskets, including the women's underclothes, in search of possible clandestine correspondence. After Blakeney, Lowe tried without success as we have already seen to impose Lieutenant-Colonel Lyster. This clumsy attempt only resulted in creating a breach between the Governor and the Grand Marshal, and gave Bertrand the chance to behave with honourable firmness.

Plantation House next chose Captain George Nicholls of the 66th regiment, a pleasant, rather ingenuous young man, who kept a meticulous journal of his duties—a document that throws much light on the difficulties and absurdities of his position. The account of his nineteen months at Longwood is a depressing list of the ludicrous games of hide-and-seek he had to play in order to get a sight of 'General Bonaparte', mixed with such occasional pearls as: 'This day the masons began on the new house at Longwood intended for the future residence of Napoleon. There was no ceremony used in laying the first stone.' There were many comical recriminations and complaints against the French for complicating an existence he had hoped would be easier. 'I was nearly twelve hours on my legs this day, endeavouring to see Napoleon Bonaparte before I succeeded; and I have experienced many such days.' 'I saw Napoleon this morning at his toilet.' 'I have been round the house several times since half past six, but he would not let me see him.' 'Count de Montholon said that Napoleon sometimes walked in the billiard-room after dinner and that it was likely I might see him then, and that if I could not see him through the window I might see him through the keyhole. I told the Count I certainly would not adopt such a plan.'

When Nicholls grew exasperated by this puerile pursuit and asked to be relieved, in February 1820, Captain Engelbert Lutyens of the 20th regiment arrived at Longwood. He stayed until April 1821, when he had to resign because he had accepted from the Emperor a book, a life of Marlborough, for the library of his regiment. Captain William Crokat was sent in haste to guard an already dying man. More fortunate than his predecessors, he was rewarded by a major's epaulets and a present of £500 for taking the news of the death of Great Britain's enemy to the Prince Regent.

We know the names of these subalterns from the memoirs of the Emperor's companions, but they all ended their lives in total obscurity. The good-natured Poppleton was the only one of them who always remembered his unusual mission, and it is worth quoting the words he had engraved on his tombstone: 'Honoured by the esteem of Napoleon, who was under his personal charge for two years in St. Helena.' The others had not realised that history would eventually make amends to 'General Bonaparte', and that when they were guarding Sir Hudson Lowe's 'prisoner of State' they were living in the shadow of the hero of their century. Nicholls and Lutyens, however, had the sense to leave behind writings explaining certain unusual items in the orders they were carrying out. They not only had to confirm the actual presence of Bonaparte, as might have been expected since this was Lord Bathurst's sole stipulation, by trying to get a sight of him twice a day, but also to satisfy the Governor's strange and inexhaustible curiosity. These captains had been trained in the school of the Napoleonic wars and thoroughly understood discipline. Lowe never failed to remind them that the orderly officer held the most important post on the island after his own, and that if he knew how to write and was intelligent he would find every possible chance of advancement at Longwood. So the poor devils went through a thousand torments, hurried to and fro, rummaged, mobilised gardeners and Chinese servants, corporals and sergeants into a spy network for collecting bits of information; they did not even hesitate to collect material for their reports by spying on the Emperor in his bath—'the General was *in naturalibus*' Nicholls told the Governor one day—or on his close-stool being given an enema.

In spite of so much repugnant zeal, Hudson Lowe was dissatisfied. He often lost his temper with his orderly officers, blaming their timidity and lack of realism, and he shouted at Gorrequer that if he had his way 'he would have a hole bored through the ceiling, if he would not show, and set people there to peep through and watch him. His proposing to the Orderly Officer to sneak about the windows in the evening and put his ears to them and peep in at the crevices of the shutters!' And when the officers who received all this advice seemed shocked, he declared it was because 'people seemed to conceive these things as such matters of delicacy'.

✤   ✤   ✤

Under the direction of Hudson Lowe and his advisers, an absurdly large staff bustled about—there were enough of them to run an army of 30,000 men according to the French commissioner: nearly 500 officers and non-commissioned officers in all, ruling over 2,500 of the rank and file. 'What a lot of precautions to guard one man in the middle of the ocean!'*

The troops were commanded by General Sir George Ridout Bingham, K.C.B., who had been promoted soon after his arrival; he was a veteran of the Spanish and Portuguese campaigns, and had come out on the *Northumberland* with Napoleon. His relations with the Longwood party were satisfactory until the day when Hudson Lowe's interference made them impossible, but Bingham was always cordially received by the Emperor, especially when he came to introduce a party of officers who had just arrived in the island or were taking their leave.

* Chateaubriand, *Mémoires d'outre-tombe.*

His successor was less popular: he was General Pine-Coffin. ('What a name!' exclaimed the Emperor when he heard of the change.) To Gorrequer he was merely General Coffin, and he soon became the laughing-stock of the island by rearing and fattening animals so as to sell them to his subordinates as joints and legs for roasting like a village butcher. Under his command the garrison was always on manœuvres, in camp or on the watch, and often in a state of agitation. By day and night the guns were kept manned, the coast patrolled, and pickets and sentinels stationed; these were provided by the 53rd regiment (600 men), the 66th regiment (700 men), the St. Helena regiment (600 men), the four companies of the St. Helena artillery (300 men), a detachment of the Royal Artillery (60 men) and a troop of mounted dragoons (20 men). The 53rd were encamped at Deadwood under the very nose of the French; the 66th at Jamestown, and when one regiment relieved another, one of them remained close to Longwood and the other at Jamestown, a possible place of disembarkation. Detachments made up of different regiments were also stationed at Sandy Bay on the south of the island, and at Lemon Valley and Egg Island on the north and west, whence it was possible to communicate with ships at sea. Finally, to complete these formidable preparations for war, there were nearly 500 guns ready for action, while the mortars were kept in reserve, and the visual signalling was constantly in use to keep the Governor informed of any movements.

Besides this disposition of land forces, a naval force under the command of a rear-admiral was entrusted with the defence of the island by sea. Sir George Cockburn, its first commander, was succeeded by Admirals Sir Pulteney Malcolm, Robert Plampin and Robert Lambert. Of these only Malcolm was in favour at Longwood: presented to the Emperor on June 20, 1816, he at once made an excellent impression. 'There is a man with a countenance really pleasing, open, intelligent, frank and sincere,' he said delightedly to O'Meara. 'There is the face of an Englishman. His countenance bespeaks his good heart, and I am sure he is a good man. I never yet beheld a man of whom I so immediately formed a good opinion as of that fine soldier-like old man.' The handsome old man, who was born in 1768 and therefore very little older than Napoleon himself, belonged to a distinguished family, and having been an admiral since

1813 had every reason to consider himself the superior of Lowe, who was only a regular colonel with the local and temporary rank of lieutenant-general. His wife Clementine, eldest daughter of the Honourable William Elphinstone, came of an influential family; as niece of Lord Keith, the famous admiral, she had the highest connections in the navy, and was also *persona grata* in the world of the East India Company, of which her father was a director. Finally she had access to political salons through her cousin Margaret, the wife of Flahaut, natural son of Talleyrand, and Napoleon's aide-de-camp; and was a close friend of the Lansdownes, Hollands and Hobhouses —liberals who had championed the person and honour of the ex-Emperor of the French in Parliament and the press.

Five days after his first audience the Admiral took his wife to Longwood and Napoleon laid himself out to please her, sent his barouche for her, had her escorted by the Grand Marshal and made her sit beside him on the sofa. Lady Malcolm's journal reveals in every line the pleasure it gave the exile to talk to these two generous and frank people, so different from the middle-class individuals who held the reins of power at St. Helena. Like many English aristocrats the Malcolms felt sympathy for the liberalism spread through Europe by Napoleonic ideas. The Admiral's brother, Sir John, an intimate friend of Wellington's, did not conceal his Bonapartist opinions, and when he was present at the return of the Duchess of Angoulême to Paris, he could not help confiding to a friend: 'The joy which the people of this capital display makes me melancholy. I continue to think of what has passed.' Napoleon overwhelmed his visitors with questions, and talked about naval heroes, the battle of St. Vincent, Lord Keith, peace in Europe, and taxation.

'If you are Scotch,' he said smiling at Lady Malcolm, 'you must know Ossian's poems.'

And he went on to talk of the Scottish poet (*Durthula* was his favourite work). But had their authenticity been established, or was Macpherson really the author? The two French translations were bad; the Italian was better.

'It was I made them the fashion. I have been even accused of having my head filled with Ossian's clouds.'

Sir Pulteney always received a warm welcome and even if Napoleon was not dressed, he was invited to sit on the bedroom sofa;

their conversations lasted for hours, for this sailor who was also a man of the world liked to talk about anything, from history to politics, or naval matters to poetry. As for Lady Malcolm, in spite of her curious appearance—'a stunted little thing, a grotesque painted on a Chinese fan' Madame de Montholon called her, perhaps out of envy—in spite of her passion for gaudy finery, so common among fashionable Englishwomen, she enjoyed every consideration, rides in the barouche, compliments, and a parting present of one of the beautiful cups from the imperial coffee service.

'Admiral Malcolm is the favourite,' wrote the Russian commissioner; 'he is sought out and flattered, and an Emperor is alone with him for hours on end.'

'As for Lady Malcolm,' added the Englishman, 'she is prouder of taking an outing with Bonaparte than she would be of an invitation to share Princess Charlotte's barouche.'

But these pleasant meetings, reminding the Emperor of the time when the most discriminating intellects disputed for the honour of his company, did not make the Admiral forget his duties nor the fact that he was Sir Hudson Lowe's subordinate. The flagship *Newcastle*, with sixty guns, had to guard the port; a frigate kept watch on the other approach to the island, while two brigs cruised, one to leeward, one to windward, for weeks on end without dropping anchor. At sunset all the fishing boats had to be in harbour and under supervision: they must not put out to sea again until dawn. The current of sympathy that flowed between the pavilion of The Briars, where the Malcolms were lodged, and Longwood House, could not last, for in spite of Malcolm's loyalty, the Governor was very ready to take offence when he heard of these meetings and conversations: he could not bear to think of his policy being discussed, perhaps even criticised. The situation was becoming more inflammable when the Admiral, whose command included the naval station at the Cape, decided in September 1816 to proceed to South Africa, and to pay a farewell visit to Longwood before setting sail. Since Malcolm had witnessed the violent scene between Napoleon and Lowe in August, the Governor considered that he owed it to his own self-respect and authority to prevent this audience, and to show the island population that the Admiral was on the side of Plantation House and its policy. He therefore sent him a note implying that this meeting with

Bonaparte would be inopportune. His warning did not have the desired effect, however, and the Admiral wrote firmly but politely setting aside his objections: 'I regret that you do not see the visit of ceremony that I propose paying to Bonaparte in the same light I do. . . . I think, however, that although [the government] may order further restrictions, yet they will continue to desire that he may be treated with a certain regard. This conviction alone induces me to keep to the opinion that I expressed to you. My visit will most probably pass in ceremony.'* He then scored his point against the Governor by paying the visit in question, during which the Emperor showed great wisdom by carefully refraining from mentioning Sir Hudson Lowe's name. But in March 1817, the links between the Governor and the Admiral, Plantation House and The Briars were finally broken, rather it would seem as a result of their daily official contacts than because of meetings with the 'detained persons'. The relationship between the two men soon became embittered, although the Admiral scrupulously reported his conversations with Bonaparte, perhaps because Lowe disliked his subtle way of slipping in recommendations to be diplomatic. 'I never saw him so moderate,' said Malcolm, 'and judging from his manner I think any indulgence that may be shown will be acceptable.' There are none so deaf as those who won't hear, and in his large, angry, nervous handwriting Lowe began a pompous analysis of the Admiral's suggestions, with all his usual grandiloquence: 'The manner in which you expressed your opinion to General Bonaparte of the notice taken by Sir G. Cockburn and myself of the letters addressed to us by Counts Montholon and Bertrand will have impressed him with your disapprobation of their conduct: in this way you may have done some good.'

This criticism must have enraged a man like Malcolm, as anyone who understood the psychology of the senior service should have known. There was no real rupture, however, and no public scandal, but by the time the Malcolms finally left St. Helena in June 1817 at the termination of Sir Pulteney's command, a strong mutual dislike existed between the two. Years later, whenever Hudson Lowe came across the Admiral's name among his numerous papers, he always used to fulminate: 'The admiral had been the cause of all the difficulties and all the trouble he [Sir Hudson Lowe] had experienced in

*Lady Malcolm's Journal.

his relations with Bonaparte. He buoyed up their hopes, made him believe that Lords would take up their cause, that he would be supported at home. He came here in fact for that purpose, and as a spy, but he had done for himself, he would never be employed again. The Foreign commissioners would not have given trouble only for the admiral. . . . The admiral had done an incalculable deal of mischief and was sent out here for that purpose.'*

It is now definitely known, and perhaps Lowe was aware of it, that Admiral Malcolm would for some unknown reason have liked to be governor of St. Helena. Was it from a desire to soften the lot of the illustrious prisoner? Or from the ambition to have his name associated with an important historical episode? Or a wish to get the better of his adversary at Plantation House? Who can tell? In any case the Malcolms were warmly received in England: of course they had many relations, and the publicity they received came from the small élite of leading figures in politics, business and the press. The Liberal party also started a campaign to glorify Sir Pulteney's noble behaviour and circulate rumours as to his next post. There was talk of First Sea Lord, Governor of St. Helena. . . . When all this excitement died down, the Admiral completed his career without the desired interlude at St. Helena, which might have altered the Emperor's fate. Hudson Lowe could breathe again: he now had no serious adversary among the Englishmen on the island.

✤   ✤   ✤

Most of Sir Hudson's time was now occupied with the deployment of strong military forces, the spy network, the problems of provisioning Longwood, and relations with the army and navy: in his gloomy, damp little study in Plantation House, he received letters and bits of gossip, listened to or questioned colonels and private soldiers, valets and washerwomen, and spent whole days and evenings scrawling page after page of his reports to Lord Bathurst.

This task accomplished, and the fair copy having been entrusted to the faithful Gorrequer and his scribes, Hudson Lowe got astride his horse and took the vertiginously steep road over Ladder Hill to Jamestown, to the headquarters of the East India Company. Inside

*Major Gorrequer's Papers (unpublished).

the old castle, in his large office with its windows wide open to the sea, he found the members of the council, his assistants and advisers in the work of administration. There were Sir William Doveton, the treasurer; Robert Leech, the accountant; Thomas Brooke, the secretary, and Thomas Greentree, the storekeeper: a colourless chorus of obscure scriveners who could be transfixed with respectful terror by one word from Sir Hudson Lowe.

They met once a week in the council chamber, and were presided over by his Excellency Sir Hudson Lowe, K.C.B., Governor and commander-in-chief, to discuss the thousand and one details of the daily life of the colony—questions of lodging and provisions, law-suits, the upkeep of the Company's buildings, requests for leases and other petitions sent to the secretary during the previous week. In his administrative work, Lowe does not seem to have been so long-winded as he was in conducting military affairs: each question was usually briskly dealt with and settled, and every ship setting sail for England, or arriving thence, carried a packet of dispatches between the directors of the Company and the Governor. From 1816 to 1819 the general tone of this correspondence was friendly, Lowe's occasional self-important remarks were deliberately ignored in London. But in 1819, over the affair of farmer Breame, Lowe went too far and gave the board of directors a chance to tell him once and for all in round terms exactly what they thought of his administration, and of his conduct to those who owned land in the colony.

The affair can be briefly summed up as follows: Breame, the Company's farmer, was accused of corruption, irregularity in his accounts and fraudulent sales, and the Governor suspended him from his duties without waiting for the result of a long, complicated inquiry which did not absolutely prove his guilt. Breame at once left for England, where as might have been expected, he made a scene which somewhat shook the directors. On May 2, 1821, three days before the Emperor died, the directors wrote to Lowe and took him violently to task, with the apparent intention of both summarising and bringing to an end his administration. Their list of grievances was marked: 'Secret and Confidential':

'In the perusal of the letters from St. Helena dated in the last year, it has been impossible for us to pass unnoticed the Tone and Stile in which you have been betrayed not only in the letters coming immediately from yourself but occasionally also in the despatches from the Governor and Council.

Although we are persuaded that you were not influenced by intentional disrespect to the Court in what we have here alluded to, we are confident that on deliberately reflecting upon the exceptional matters which we are about to point out you will acknowledge that they are liable to such construction, and will not fail to admit their impropriety considering the relative situation in which you stand to the Court.... We cannot offer Ourselves to be thus dictated to as to the manner in which we may choose to seek for information relative to our affairs at St. Helena, or the persons to whom we may see proper to apply.... In the same despatch we have adverted to the right we possess of animadverting to all the Proceedings of your Government, and this right we cannot allow to be disputed or called in question on the ill-grounded apprehension that Our Orders may prove of hurtful example.... We shall pursue the subject no further. Enough has been said, we trust, to convince you, Sir, upon calm and dispassionate review of all circumstances to which we have here called your attention, that the view you have taken of Our Orders is not warranted by any fair construction of them, and that the Tone and Temper in which you have indulged in discussing them are as unsuitable to the relative situation in which you stand towards the Court.... We cannot suppose that you have intentionally shown Disrespect to that Authority in the several instances which we have pointed out, and if (as we cannot for a moment allow ourselves to doubt) you shall on mature reflection be convinced that you have been led into Error or Misconception, we would gladly hope that this unpleasant correspondence will here terminate.'

This brutal rebuff is extremely interesting: it puts the finishing touch to the psychological portrait of the gaoler of St. Helena. These criticisms came from Englishmen who signed themselves his 'affectionate friends', and they had nothing to do with the French prisoner. They cannot therefore be ascribed to that strong feeling that so often distorts the verdicts brought against the Governor by historians and writers. One thing plainly emerges: Hudson Lowe had tried to treat the directors, his chiefs, in the same domineering way as he did the 'detained persons' at Longwood and his own subordinates—that is to say with his customary high-handedness, arrogance and absolutism. Everything in the antique equipment of the East India Company that hindered or caused embarrassment to his 'mission' was in his eyes useless, open to criticism and futile. The authority he had been given by Lord Bathurst, the approval of the party in power in

England and its press, had so blinded him that he believed he could receive nothing but approval.

Sir Hudson Lowe's partisans have tried to represent his time of office at St. Helena as an enlightened proconsulship; they speak of the emancipation of slaves, plantation of forests, improvement of the water supply . . . and of the complete satisfaction of the East India Company. The invaluable document quoted above shows plainly enough that, in dealing with this intransigent governor, the board of directors found it as difficult to get their authority respected as the Emperor did to preserve his dignity.

8

IV

THE FOREIGN COMMISSIONERS

✛✛

The Allied Convention of 1815—The Marquis de
Montchenu—Baron von Stürmer—Count Balmain.

✛✛

Three very different, interesting and unusual characters drifting at
the mercy of events between the warders' and the exiles' camps,
drawn first one way and then another by greed or curiosity, anxious
to please the Governor and enjoy his hospitality on the one hand,
and to get close to the prisoner on the other, and write to their courts
'Bonaparte told me' or 'Bonaparte maintains'—such were the three
foreign commissioners, the Marquis de Montchenu representing
Louis XVIII, Count Balmain nominated by Tsar Alexander, and the
Baron von Stürmer chosen by Austria.

The Convention signed by the Allies in Paris on August 2, 1815,
laid down the following regulations for the Emperor's fate:

'His custody is especially entrusted to the British government. The choice
of the place and of the measures which can best secure the object of the
present stipulation is reserved to His Britannic Majesty. The imperial
courts of Austria and of Russia and the royal court of Prussia are to appoint
commissioners to proceed to and abide at the place which His Britannic
Majesty shall have assigned for the residence of Napoleon Bonaparte, and
who, without being responsible for his custody, will assure themselves of
his presence. His Most Christian Majesty is to be invited, in the name of
the four above-mentioned courts, to send in the like manner a French
commissioner to the place of detention of Napoleon Bonaparte.'

When the news of this clause of the treaty came to Napoleon's
ears, he based certain hopes on these envoys and the diplomatic
nature of their posts. 'After all,' he said to Las Cases, 'the Emperor
Francis is a religious man and I am his son. As for Alexander, we
were friends.' Here Napoleon revealed a weakness: born of the
people, he always remained 'of the people'; convinced of the sincere

feelings of such absolute rulers as Alexander and Francis, he held the bourgeois belief that personal alliances forged during his years of glory would remain unbroken in adversity as would happen in the families of prosperous commoners. He could not accept the idea that these sovereigns' protestations of friendship were political, and that once he had lost his imperial crown he was no longer 'the tender and affectionate son' of the Emperor of Austria, nor the Tsar's 'affectionate brother', but a rather embarrassing connection, whose existence they would try to forget by buying back the correspondence they had been foolish enough to address to him. As for the commissioners, they were given no special mission and no personal messages whatever from their sovereigns: this was another cruel disappointment for the Emperor.

Talleyrand's appointment of Claude Marin Henri, Marquis de Montchenu, as commissioner of the King of France, took place on September 22, 1815, just before he was himself disgraced and replaced at the head of the French cabinet by the Duc de Richelieu. Witnesses tell us that when he affixed his signature to the ministerial decision, the man the Emperor had created Prince of Benevento murmured maliciously: 'Montchenu is a c..t and a gossip. He will bore the prisoner to death.' Before making Napoleon die of boredom, the marquis first made the English die of laughing. From the day he landed on the island he created a sensation with his gold-trimmed general's uniform, his sword and powdered, pig-tailed wig. Small, rubicund and lively, very much a product of the Ancien Régime, he flung himself on a group of British officers who had come to watch the distinguished visitors land and be welcomed by a salute of thirteen guns from the island batteries. 'If any of you speak French, for the love of God tell me, for I do not understand a word of English. I have come to end my days on this rock and I cannot speak a word of the language.' History took note of this remark; it was repeated to Napoleon, who commented with a look and a smile that can easily be imagined: 'I know that Montchenu. He is an old fool, a gossip, an armchair general who has never smelt powder in his life. I won't receive him.' The Russian commissioner reported this remark to the Tsar, adding bitterly: 'The annoying thing is that the portrait is a good likeness: the marquis has grand ideas about his post—it's the only one he's ever had.'

A descendant of a family from the South of France which he pretended was related to the royal houses of France and Spain, the Comte de Montchenu decided one day to take the more resounding title of marquis: when he strutted on his high red heels among the English of St. Helena he never failed to remark on the age and importance of his lineage. Fifty-eight years old, he had entered the army at fifteen and had been a colonel since 1791. As an émigré he took refuge at Coblenz, where he made the impression of being 'a man of mediocre intelligence who was intriguing for a post that his past career in no way justified'. After a three months' voyage in his company his Austrian colleague Stürmer wrote to his court at Vienna about him: 'He has none of the qualities needed for the post entrusted to him. I believe him to be an honest man, but he has very little education and absolutely no tact. Having never been involved in affairs, he unfortunately has no notion of them, nor does he know how to put his ideas into effect. Boundless vanity is the motive force behind everything he does; he is not liked here and the ridiculous airs he gives himself have finally discredited him utterly.' His hatred of the Emperor was inexorable. While the other commissioners displayed almost diplomatic discretion, the marquis got on his high horse, banged on the door and shouted. If Bonaparte refused to show himself they must break the door down. If they would only give him a few guards as an escort he would soon see to that. Ever since he had returned to France, after having his name crossed off the list of those who had emigrated under the Empire thanks to the support of Lebrun and Cambacérès, he had intrigued ceaselessly against the 'usurper'. He took refuge at Lyons, making a living no one quite knew how, and used often to test the tolerance of the imperial policy by exclaiming: 'When that man falls from power I shall beg the king to make me his gaoler'. He kept his word, and did his best to get himself talked of in France and the rest of Europe by carrying out his duties with the utmost strictness, nor did he neglect to extract what financial gain he could from his terrible period of exile. His salary of 50,000 francs was worth £2,500 on St. Helena, a very comfortable income; but every batch of letters that left the island included some complaints of poverty, and he bored the minister to death with details of his valets' food, his horses' fodder, the price of candles and the scarcity of fish.

Accompanied by a young aide-de-camp and acting secretary called Jean Claude Gors, who had honoured his chief's ancient lineage by adopting the particle and becoming Captain de Gors, he set out in search of somewhere to live. This was hard to find, for all suitable houses had been taken over by the officers who had come to reinforce the island garrison. Finally he rented a furnished house in Jamestown for £360 a year, and soon began to pester his minister, the Duc de Richelieu: 'The laundry is amazingly costly; it would be incredible except for the enormous cost of fuel, the difficulty and expense of getting washerwomen; soap is also prohibitive; I think therefore I must allow £100 for it. As for fodder for the horses, I have made a contract with Bonaparte's purveyor at a charge of four shillings and twopence a day for each horse. These items together come to £988 before I have eaten a single piece of bread. Among foodstuffs the scarcest are beef, milk and butter, in fact all the most necessary.' A month later he returned to the charge: 'I am in the greatest possible distress and have to live from hand to mouth. My mode of existence is pathetic.'* What we know of the daily life of the good society of the island casts some doubt on all these expenses, so ceaselessly bewailed by the marquis; his meanness was proverbial, and, whatever he might say in his letters, he never gave dinners or receptions. On the other hand, no sooner did he get an invitation than he was riding off to demonstrate his hunger and thirst. It was said that one need not even invite him, he deliberately appeared at the right time for any party that was being held. His nickname was soon known all over the island: his colleagues and the educated English who understood French called him the marquis of 'Monte-chez-nous'; for the rest of the inhabitants he was 'Old Munch Enough'. For the manners of this scion of a noble house were far from irreproachable: everyone on the island talked about his drunken behaviour at Plantation House (one evening he dirtied several large towels in Lady Lowe's dressing-room), his amorous assaults on the person of his landlady, an elderly Englishwoman who defended herself by slapping his face, or how he made ardent declarations to Lady Lowe and loudly told everyone that 'if he were a bit younger he would make a cuckold of her husband'.

As soon as an approaching ship was sighted, everything else was

*Archives of the French Ministry of Foreign Affairs.

thrown over, and the impetuous commissioner sat down at his desk and wrote long letters, as confused and lacking in content as they were foolish and vulgar, which still repose in the files of the Quai d'Orsay.

'Monseigneur, everything is in the same state as when I last had the honour to write to Your Excellency on June 20 last. We have still not seen Bonaparte and it looks very much as if we should not see him until an order from the British government insists on it. . . .

'I have already had the honour to tell you what an influence Bonaparte has obtained over everyone; he makes much of the subalterns, who adore him, but he has quarrelled with the chief, who is afraid of him but still does his duty faithfully, and who becomes more of a nuisance the more Bonaparte keeps him at a distance. . . .

'Last Friday one of his chimneys caught fire during the night. It was put out with a great deal of difficulty, thanks to six hundred men from the camp, who arrived just in time, for everyone agrees that ten minutes later everything would have been burnt. The house is partly of wood and there is no water on that plateau. . . .

'Life is so monotonous that nothing very interesting ever happens in his house. However, here is a little story: I have already had the honour of speaking to you about Betsy Balcombe. Last Sunday several people were invited to the churching of Madame de Montholon. When they were gathered in her house, Bonaparte, who knew all about it, stood at a window which looked straight into the room they were in, and greeted everyone. He even said a few words and then went down into his garden where everyone joined him. He had not seen little Betsy for some time and disliked her too great familiarity, but he asked her if she was as naughty as ever. He remarked that she had grown a great deal, adding quickly: "Well, ill weeds grow apace". Somewhat piqued, the little girl remarked that he had not shaved that morning and that it was "very rude and horrid" to receive ladies with such a long beard. . . .

'There are forty servants, some French, some slaves, and they need fifty-one rations daily. There are also twelve horses and two carriages. . . .

'When he goes driving in his carriage, Gourgaud and the Polish officer ride beside the two doors, dressed in uniform. Although I still have no horses, as it is impossible to procure them here, I already know the island well. I have even visited some parts of it with the Governor, who sometimes lends me horses. The streams run into the sea at twenty-three places; however, there are only four where it would be possible to land a few men in a launch, and that only rarely because the breakers are too violent. All the same, they are all guarded and defended by batteries. Even if a few men were landed in one of these gorges, they would have to get out again, and this is physically impossible as the cliffs are vertical almost everywhere and bare of vegetation. If so much as a dog has been seen anywhere, at least one sentinel is stationed there. . . .

'We noticed a little cove, called Rupert's Bay, where a boat could come in to land and drop anchor. There is a path down the valley, and it would be possible to get out by it, though with great difficulty; there is a well-guarded fort opposite and one on each side with plenty of artillery. . . . However, I must say that it would only be possible to land in small boats and with water up to the armpits, because the cove is full of rocks, and a ship could only anchor within half a mile of the batteries, as the sea is so deep elsewhere. . . . There is also a fort, and even if it were taken it would be almost impossible to get out again: there is a frigate with 36 guns moored in this place. The plateau of Longwood is the only one in the island; it is very large, probably four miles in circumference.

'In this enclosure Bonaparte and his family, as they are called here, can walk about unaccompanied, but only during daylight. As soon as the sun sets the night guard goes on duty, making such a close cordon round his house at a distance of fifteen paces that the sentries can almost touch each other. . . .

'The Governor usually receives a report on his prisoner four times a day, and two wherever he may be. . . . It therefore seems as though escape were impossible, for even if the Governor failed to prevent it, the sea-coast has its own form of protection which makes it impracticable. All the signal stations are manned day and night. As soon as a ship is sighted, normally when sixty miles off, a shot is fired, and a piastre is given to the one who saw it first. Two brigs cruise round the island night and day; frigates are anchored at the two places where a landing is possible; for to reach Rupert's Bay it would be necessary to come under fire from the forts in the town and the new castle. At night, nothing can approach or leave land, and armed launches keep scrupulous watch until dawn. . . .

'A few days ago an American ship, prevented by bad weather from landing at the Cape made as if to enter the harbour; she was politely requested to go on her way. The captain was furious, pretended that he needed to rest, and tried to insist; he was politely told that his ship would be fired on, and he finally departed grumbling and very angry. Next day, a Portuguese warship was more fortunate; she had absolutely no water left; she was not allowed into the harbour but some was sent her. . . .

'After the retreat has been sounded, no one is allowed to circulate even in the centre of the island without giving the password, and this happens very rarely. . . .

'I can have it whenever I like by getting it myself or sending Monsieur de Gors. My two colleagues have to get it in person. . . . The Admiral often goes to see Bonaparte, and last week he talked to him for nearly three hours. They discussed Egypt, Waterloo and various British officers. Bonaparte spoke of us, and said: "I do not regard myself as a prisoner; I was never taken by you, I put my trust in English fair play; you have me in your power, true enough, but I do not regard myself as your prisoner. If I received these gentlemen as commissioners, I should admit that I was the prisoner of the powers they represent; therefore I will not receive them. If they want to see me I shall be delighted: they need only address themselves to Bertrand. And besides, what is that Austrian doing here? He has not come to bring me news of my wife and son. After all, he is my own son. I have seen his master at my feet twenty times. And that Russian? I have more than thirty letters from his Emperor, thanking me for all I have done for him. Does it enter his head to take an interest in me, and bring me some relief in my present unfortunate situation? I will show you all the letters I have received from sovereigns. In Louis XVIII's case I have nothing to complain of; that is different, I have never had any dealings with him". . . .

'He complained bitterly of the Governor. "Has England no other colonies to send me to?" The Admiral told him why no change was possible. "Then I must die here?" "Yes, I think so," replied the Admiral smiling. As Bonaparte was talking, he glanced up at the summit of a high mountain and saw a sentry posted there. "Well, really! What foolishness! What good is that sentry? Are they afraid I shall escape? Can I fly away like a bird? Why this prison? Why can they not let me go all over the island?" "You are free to do so." "Yes, if an officer comes with me; I realise they cannot let me go alone to the town, that would not be possible, but why not in the rest of the island? What is the point of that officer? I am always treated like a prisoner; I am not a prisoner; you have me in your power, but I am not a prisoner." . . .

'Here you have the explanation of his present conduct, Monsieur le Duc. I have had the honour to mention my need for horses and the difficulty of getting them here. I have decided to send Monsieur de Gors to the Cape, where some are to be found at a very high price. Besides which, he needs a change of air for his health's sake. This climate is much too highly praised in Europe; it is not unhealthy, but neither is it as good as we expected. I am not exactly ill but I do not feel well. I have no appetite. The heat is very great; even in mid-winter the thermometer does not fall below twenty degrees, even at night. The food that can be got here at a price is unwholesome for us. I will say no more about my lodgings; for lack of means I must put up with these four walls, and even if I find something better I shall have difficulty in obtaining what is essential. . . .

'I beg you to come quickly to my aid by sending a provisional credit, and within the next month I will send you a detailed statement so that you can fix the amount of my salary. . . .

'I have had the honour to inform you that Baron Stürmer and I have written to ask the Governor to receive us. Count Balmain's instructions make no mention of a report or of seeing the prisoner with his own eyes; he believes that a note in the Emperor's hand, requesting to be treated with the greatest respect, prevents his asking for something Napoleon is known to dislike. . . .

'We are told that some sort of manifesto is soon to appear. I am with respect, Monsieur le Duc, Your Excellency's very humble and obedient servant, Montchenu. . . .'*

Montchenu's relations with Governor Lowe were distinctly picturesque; it is harrowing to go through these files of letters and compare the Englishman's dry notes, written in fluent but uncertain French, with those of the Marquis—awkward, nebulous, and packed with defects of style and taste. Of course they did not deal with important political questions, and whereas one man was concerned with restraining an importunate chatter-box, the other was begging an invitation and apologising for a blunder. 'All I want is to spend two or three hours playing whist as many evenings as possible,' whined Montchenu, 'for I dislike any serious occupation after I leave the dinner table. My sole purpose is to kill time before it kills me.' Impossible to be more forthright or less elegant. Lowe had plenty of opportunity to get to know what his correspondent was like, without these ingenuous notes. However trifling the cause of any quarrel that might arise between the two men, the commissioner would be on his high horse in a moment, hurling phrases at the Governor's head which he believed to belong to the vocabulary of diplomacy: 'Our courts . . . my title . . . the rights of the people . . . the rights of nations . . . the dignity with which I have been invested'. The reply generally came back at once and the Englishman knew very well how to get the better of the old buffoon: 'This is the only explanation I am in a position to give you . . . the two notes you speak of have made no impression; the other was not couched in the tone or terms we are accustomed to.' After the note was sealed and delivered to 'Old Frog' by a dragoon, Hudson Lowe still went on fulminating against the King of France's commissioner, treating him as a worthless oaf, and his 'master' and his 'court' as little better. As Gorrequer noted one day: 'Sir Hudson Lowe saying before Admiral

*Archives of the French Ministry for Foreign Affairs.

Plampin that *Le Gros Cochon* (Louis XVIII) was a blockhead and a fool, and the old cringeing Admiral encoring in abject style and re-echoing what he said with reasoning of his own.' Two days later: 'Sir Hudson Lowe saying what a damned piece of impertinence it was of *Gros Cochon* (Louis XVIII), what a damned blockhead he and his ministers must be, to send such a letter to Frog (Montchenu). What damned stuff it is, did you ever see such nonsense?' The Marquis had taken it into his head to show Lowe dispatches from Paris, telling him to be present himself in person at Longwood and collect information about Bonaparte: 'When he told me of Balmain telling him Frog had orders "*de voir les choses de plus près*", his saying in his triumphant style "I wish he would dare write or speak to me on the subject. I'll settle him in a short time, I like that, his Court pressing to interfere in my views here or what I consider right or wrong. I would very soon put his Court right up that point. I shall take care neither his nor any other Court shall interfere with me here".'*

The Governor knew very well that all this sound and fury was a tidal wave, that would break up into tiny wavelets and die out on the gravel in front of Plantation House, and that a well-laid table and an appetising meal would make the quinquagenarian more prudent. 'While I was in Brazil,' wrote Balmain to the Court of St. Petersburg, 'Monsieur de Montchenu the French commissioner stayed at Plantation House, enjoying delicious meals and whist parties and taking no interest in anything else.' Thus, as rapprochements followed rows, Montchenu was for Lowe either 'a dirty schemer', an 'imbecile' and 'an ass', or else 'the only one of the commissioners one can be on terms with'. From such lips as his, both verdicts were equally harsh.

✣   ✣   ✣

Monsieur de Montchenu's Austrian colleague, Baron von Stürmers was a young professional diplomat, who had served under Prince Schwarzenberg, and was fresh from important missions at St. Petersburg, Paris and Florence. He had been chosen for St. Helena 'as a reward for good and loyal services'. Before going on board the *Orontes* he had hastily married a young Frenchwoman, Catherine Boutet, whom he had got to know when the Allies were encamped in

*Major Gorrequer's Papers (unpublished).

the capital. At Longwood there was delight at his arrival, for after searching his memory Las Cases told the Emperor: 'Two or three years ago a clerk in the War Office . . . came to my house to give my son lessons in writing and Latin. He had a daughter whom he hoped to place as a governess and asked us to recommend her. . . . Madame Las Cases sent for her; she was charming and most attractive in appearance. And now this young lady, our acquaintance, our friend, turns out to be the wife of one of the Allied commissioners. Your Majesty can judge of my astonishment. I sent my servant to meet the new arrival. He came back to say that the lady did not know what he was talking about.' Napoleon laughed and gave his crestfallen chamberlain a short sharp lecture on psychology: 'How little you understand the human heart. So her father taught your son, or something of the sort, and your wife befriended her when she was a nobody—and now she's a German baroness! But, my dear fellow, you're the one person on the island she is really afraid of.'*

According to the English, Stürmer 'belonged to Metternich's school, polished manners. calm demeanour, well-bred,' and the Baroness was 'a pretty Parisienne, nothing more'. Just as delighted to be Madame de Stürmer as the widow Johnson had been to become Lady Lowe, she had a passion for clothes and jewels but was short of both, and an English officer related that this little dressmaker caught up in the diplomatic world shamelessly made up to General Gourgaud to get a diamond-headed pin: 'You ought to give me a present in token of our friendship—a pin for instance: it's sharp, you know, but it fastens things too.' It did not take Hudson Lowe long to sum up Stürmer's natural suitability for his post. He was 'a true élève of Metternich's. No chameleon could change his hue more frequently than he has done on observing any desire or opinion he has ventured upon not meeting my assent.' The Governor seems in fact to have been on about as easy terms with the Austrian as with the Marquis, and there was no reason to think that the Emperor Francis's commissioner would interfere seriously in the administration. But alas! what sovereigns dare not or cannot do is often risked by their valets, and from Figaro onwards there is a long list of servants whom intrigue or the desire to please have seduced. The Stürmer affair can be briefly summarised: the Emperor of Austria,

*Las Cases, *Memorial of St. Helena*.

the lugubrious Francis, was a passionate botanist and had an interesting collection of plants and herbals at Vienna; the fact that a commissioner was being sent to St. Helena, where his son-in-law was
exiled, at once gave him an idea—not of establishing contact between
his daughter and her husband, but of sending an expert botanist to
the famous rock, to bring back specimens of the flora of St. Helena to
Schönbrunn. Philippe Welle, one of the assistants employed in the
imperial gardens, was chosen. If proof had been needed of the well-
known folly of Marie-Louise's father, this simple action would have
sufficed—this absurd craving to possess in his glass-houses (where
the ex-Empress of the French was sometimes seen with her lover) a
tropical plant labelled 'from St. Helena'. In any case, a correspondence began between Longwood and Vienna, by way of Paris and
London, not exactly at embassy level but through embassy servants.
The mother of Marchand, Napoleon's valet, was nurse to the little
King of Rome, now Prince of Parma, and she entrusted the botanist
with a small packet and a letter: the packet contained a lock of fair
hair, and the letter said briefly: 'I am sending you a lock of my hair.
If you get an opportunity to have yourself painted, send me your
portrait. Your mother.' This at least is the official version of the letter
given by historians. But in his Memoirs, not published it is true until
1842 and perhaps containing some errors, Marchand states: 'Inside
the envelope I found a carefully folded paper on which was written:
The King of Rome's hair. On another almost similar sheet was: To
my son. "This is yours," the Emperor said to me, "and this is mine."
After opening the packet and seeing his son's beautiful golden hair
he told me to put it in his dressing-case. I laid it beside a lock of the
Empress Josephine's hair which had been sent to him at Elba after
her death. These two locks of hair are now in my reliquary.' The
different versions of the message, and General Gourgaud's failure
to mention that his sister had sent him, by the same messenger, an embroidered handkerchief and a letter, are at first sight
surprising. It is in fact probable that some discretion was preserved
at Longwood in order not to embarrass the messenger and perhaps
make use of him to send some reply. This was reckoning without
Hudson Lowe's spies and the impossibility—even today—of going
into any house in St. Helena without being observed by more than
one pair of eyes. The Governor was furious when he heard that

Marchand had had an interview with the botanist. But when, a little later, he discovered that he had brought packets with him and handed them over, he had a violent quarrel with Baron Stürmer and even threatened to have him tried for having violated English law concerning the security of the colony. Stürmer defended his subordinate to the best of his ability, and in consideration of the fact that Welle had been sent by the Emperor of Austria in person, a worthy adversary for the English Governor, Lowe contented himself with expressing an anxiety quite disproportionate to the importance of the incident in his dispatches to Lord Bathurst, and suggesting stricter measures for guarding the Emperor: 'Your Lordship will judge from this circumstance of the real obstacles to the granting General Bonaparte a greater degree of personal liberty and more freedom of communication than he at present possesses, and I cannot avoid considering the residence of the commissioners as the principal hindrance to the enlargement of either.' Everything was grist to the mill of Hudson Lowe, gaoler and detective.

Welle got permission to botanise as he pleased all over the island, and only left after a stay of six months. As for the Baron, tired of the view from Jamestown and its stifling heat, he rented an attractive house called Rosemary Hall, and moved in with his wife and the Russian commissioner, who came to live with them. His salary of £1,200 was barely enough for the style of life suitable to his official status, but Stürmer conducted himself discreetly and reasonably, until the day in 1818 when a row with Lowe precipitated his recall.

✤   ✤   ✤

The Russian commissioner was without doubt the most attractive and trustworthy of the three envoys. His full name shows his complicated origins and explains his combination of dry Scottish humour with fantastic Russian imagination. Alexander Antonovitch Ramsay de Balmain was in fact descended from an old Scottish family, who had gone to France with James II and later settled in Russia. Wearing the sombre uniform and shaven head of the St. Petersburg Cadets, the young aristocrat had lively, inquiring eyes, which sometimes shone with malice. Born in 1779, he was twenty-one years old when he became a captain in the Guards in 1800, but having thus

reached a rank opening the way to a military career, he fell a victim
to a common sort of misfortune at the time: the young noblemen of
St. Petersburg were always thirsty and free with their fists and when
drunk often took it into their heads to fight the police. Balmain was
court-martialled after a scuffle with a policeman, and demoted to the
ranks, like Tolstoy's hero. In the reign of the Tsar Alexander, when
the army was being reorganised to meet the threat from Napoleon,
such a setback did not ruin a young man's career, and, disgusted
with the army, Alexander Antonovitch entered the diplomatic
service. In 1805 he was a counsellor at the College of Diplomacy,
and he was soon afterwards posted in Sardinia, at Naples, Vienna
and London. At the moment when Napoleon's army was making its
final onslaught on Holy Russia, Balmain rejoined the army—again
like Tolstoy's dashing young aristocrat whom he so strangely
resembled—and took part in the last campaigns of the Empire with
the rank of lieutenant-colonel under Bernadotte and Wellington,
carrying out various important missions. He received several distinc-
tions: the order of St. Vladimir, the Prussian Order of Merit, the
Swedish Order of the Sword. After peace was signed, his one desire
was to return to the embassy in London, where he had had a great
success; still a bachelor, he belonged to that Regency society where
Brummell, Byron and Hobhouse counted for more than Wellington,
to whom they secretly preferred Bonaparte—that strange romantic
figure who had inspired their god Byron. Balmain therefore did all
he could to get reappointed, and among the archives of the U.S.S.R.
there has come to light a letter from Count Lieven, Russian ambassador at the court of St. James, which finally decided the matter:
'I venture to remind your Imperial Majesty of the promise made to
the Grand Duchess Catherine when she was in London, to approve
Count Balmain's appointment to the embassy in London. He was
previously attached to it, and left to serve in the last war. He is a man
of great ability, intelligence and aptitude for work.'

His past career and the stars decorating the Russian commissioner's uniform made a great impression on Hudson Lowe, and as
soon as Balmain had arrived he wrote to his chief: 'The Russian
appears to laugh at the other two, and really seems to have much
more in him than either of them. He is descended from a Scottish
family.' In spite of a salary of £1,200, soon afterwards raised to

£2,000, together with an allowance of 1,600 ducats for setting up house, Balmain preferred Russia to St. Helena, and Jamestown did not make him forget London. His exile was the occasion for an observant letter written in classical French: 'It is the saddest place in the world, the most isolated and inaccessible, the most difficult to attack, the most unsociable, the poorest, the most expensive, and above all the most suitable for the use to which it is now being put.' To him, as to Tolstoy's Bezukhov, the prisoner at Longwood was the focus of interest: 'I was struck immediately on arrival by the tremendous hold this man, surrounded by guards, rocks and precipices, still has over people's minds. Everything at St. Helena shows the effect of his superiority, and Las Cases says: "My happiness consists in ceaseless contemplation of a hero, a prodigy." The British approach him timidly. The very men set to guard him court a glance, a conversation, a word from him. No one dares treat him as an equal. Having in his misfortune nothing noble to contemplate, his genius finds amusement in turning this state of affairs to account and perplexing them all. He excites the envy of some, and makes much of others.'

We are a long way from Montchenu's pretentious chatter! During the four years of his mission, even when his relations with Hudson Lowe changed to those of son-in-law and father-in-law, he never ceased sending detailed dispatches to St. Petersburg, all to be regularly laid on the Tsar's desk by the minister; as a diplomat and a gentleman, the Russian commissioner knew exactly how to reconcile his own admiration for Napoleon with his master's wishes, which had been clearly explained to him before he left. The long note of his instructions drawn up by a minor official, and still to be seen in the Soviet archives, must have been read through by Capo d'Istria or Nesselrode, who underlined the words, 'the personal respect due to him' in reference to the attitude to be adopted towards Napoleon. The commissioner was to endeavour to provide 'a detailed journal, carefully and regularly kept up, which would certainly provide historical material of the highest interest'. It was an absorbing occupation and a distraction from the spiteful mediocrity of social relationships and the consuming boredom. In October 1816 Capo d'Istria wrote to Balmain: 'Your reports numbers 3 and 4 have been sent us by Count Lieven. His Majesty has studied them and deigned to express his satisfaction both with the moderation of your conduct and the exact details you furnish. His Imperial Majesty instructs me to ask you to keep us informed of anything subsequently observed and not to be afraid of overloading your reports with your ideas: these are always of interest and will be appreciated as much as your recent communications.' And again: 'The different reports have been set before His Imperial Majesty, who has read them with great interest and instructs me to inform you of his complete satisfaction. The Emperor likes to receive reports straight from St. Helena of everything that goes on there.' To console him for a life of exile that was made more painful by enforced celibacy, this perfect courtier could enjoy the knowledge that all his reports were read with attention by his sovereign: arousing the interest of crowned heads is generally profitable, especially when the reader is the Tsar of all the Russias. And the reports from St. Helena—they have passed through my hands in Moscow—all bear a discreet pencil-mark identified by Soviet archivists as the signature of Alexander I.

But to make his reports conscientiously the commissioner needed evidence about the daily life of the prisoner, and Hudson Lowe was miserly with information. Balmain had to shift for himself, and since he was not lacking in discretion his relations with the Longwood party have the flavour of a spy story. He could not approach Napoleon in person and had to content himself with identifying that famous silhouette from afar through field-glasses, but he never missed a chance of a conversation with members of the suite. These began soon after his arrival: anxious to prove his respect for the prisoner he refused to associate himself with his colleagues' attempts to force the door of Longwood House without delay, so as to obtain material proof of Bonaparte's presence. In his report Balmain added adroitly: 'The noble and generous feelings of our Royal Master have been recognised, and Bonaparte himself was pleased by them. One of his suite came up to me in the town and said very politely: "The Emperor knows that you did not sign the note sent by the other commissioners and appreciates your honourable behaviour; he asked me to thank you".' By means of such diplomatic messages as these, it is plain that Balmain never missed a chance of paying court to the gentle and enlightened Alexander. 'Bonaparte has more than once said "If I were in the power of the Tsar my wishes would have been anticipated. He is a noble and generous prince".'

One day young Las Cases came to see the Russian and complained indignantly of the English, but he did not get the encouragement he hoped for. Next Gourgaud was sent to assure the Tsar's envoy that the Emperor was extremely anxious to meet him. 'He is most amicably disposed towards you. You will find him approachable and informal. You will give us all the greatest pleasure.' After the orderly officer, Montholon was sent: 'Why don't you come to Longwood and dissipate your boredom a little? You are invited . . . you will be warmly welcomed.' The final offensive was launched by the Grand Marshal himself: 'The Emperor Napoleon has a proud, noble character. He always speaks his mind frankly and as he has reason to complain of the Regent of Great Britain, he will not stoop to write to him. However, if the occasion arose, he would describe his sufferings to the Emperor Alexander. For he loves that prince. He is confident of his help, and recognises his fine qualities.' Balmain understood the message: 'Bertrand was insinuating that they would be glad to entrust me with a letter for our Royal Master, but I pretended not to guess at his meaning, and put him off the scent by my serious demeanour.' But Bertrand was only gathering strength for another attempt, and in April 1818 he put his cards on the table. 'During the last few days General Bertrand has made me a strange proposal. While speaking of Bonaparte's sufferings and misfortunes he suddenly said to me: "the Emperor is suffering from crushing boredom and from the inhuman way he is treated on this rock, abandoned by the whole world. He wishes to write to the Emperor Alexander, who is his only supporter. I beg you to let me entrust you with his letter." And he made a movement as if to take it from his pocket. "No," I replied, "that is impossible. I should be failing in my duty." "Not at all," he went on, "for the Emperor Napoleon has made important revelations to the Emperor Alexander. It is not merely a question of saving a great man from oppression, but of serving Russia. This letter will be read with pleasure, even eagerly; your master will be delighted. By refusing to send it to your court you would neglect and lose sight of his interests, or rather you would sacrifice them to the English. I will also tell you that you are described in it in such a way as will make your fortune." "I promise to report faithfully all you have said to my court; but I cannot take charge of any letter. I have not the right. And if I did, I should be repudiated."

9

"Nonsense!" he cried, "you might be repudiated for form's sake here in St. Helena, but you would be rewarded in Russia, I am sure of that. In any case, think about it".'

Was the letter already written? And if so, what was in it? It would be fascinating to know, but the Grand Marshal's papers are silent on the subject, although revealing that during April 1818 Napoleon and Bertrand had many long conversations about the Tsar of Russia.

These meetings between the Russian and the prisoners, and the remarks exchanged between them, were all reported to Hudson Lowe, who was so tormented by curiosity that he could not help questioning Balmain, and sometimes exceeding the limits of diplomacy or even mere politeness. 'You reproach me for my meetings with Gourgaud,' the Commissioner protested, 'but will you explain what are your desires and plans in this matter?' 'Clear your mind of any idea that I meant to reproach you,' was the Governor's smooth reply. 'You have behaved perfectly correctly, and Gourgaud is an excellent man and an honest soldier. He is not the man I am afraid of. But if you do not take care they will set Bertrand or Montholon on you, and I have not the same opinion of them: they are intriguers.' In June 1818, Balmain reported to his court the schemes that were threatening him: 'I have asked the Governor to write to us officially as follows: the commissioners of the Allied powers are requested not to pass inside the boundary of Longwood, nor to speak to any of the French party. "No," he cried in alarm, "I will not do it. I dare not even consider it".' A few days later Hudson Lowe was taking a more masterful tone: 'Your court has forbidden you to hold any opinion as to affairs at St. Helena, yet you report my behaviour to them.' And Balmain retorted: 'My court does not wish me to interfere in the affairs of St. Helena and I obey it implicitly. But any man who uses his intelligence must have an opinion about what is happening in front of his own eyes.' It seems that the Governor had guessed, even if he had no certain means of knowing it, that the Russian commentaries were not favourable. How furious he would have been if he had been able to read some passages from these dispatches!

'Hudson Lowe has a special gift for assuming an innocent expression or tone of voice when he has scored a point. . . . The empty, muddled, unbalanced brain of Hudson Lowe . . . in whom a bottomless pit of commonplace ideas, a cold suspicious character and an overbearing manner are

combined with the desire to be pleasant and a tyrannical fidelity to duty.
. . . Lowe shows his narrow-mindedness in everything; his responsibilities
suffocate him, make him tremble, he is frightened at the least thing, racks
his brains over trifles, and makes heavy weather and a great deal of fuss
over doing what others would do with ease. And then he has the failing of
losing his temper and flying into a rage, when he no longer knows what he
is saying or where he is, and loses his head completely.'

To make a temporary break in the writing of these terse reports,
and get away from a situation calling for continuous verbal acro-
batics, Balmain was encouraged by the Governor to take a holiday in
South America towards the middle of 1818. He eagerly took advantage of a ship going from St. Helena to Brazil, and turning his back
on the rock and Hudson Lowe's intrigues and suspicions, found a
country and a town that delighted him. Good spirits are the best
remedy, and the sick man was restored to health. For Balmain the
northerner, 'the Bear' as Gorrequer called him, had been ill ever since
coming to the tropics. 'As soon as I reached Jamestown I was seized
with inflammation of the mouth and throat.' The pain was so acute
that he rolled on the floor. Next it was his stomach and his liver, and
soon afterwards he began to go into a visible decline; it was probably
the beginning of scurvy after the long voyage, following on a series of
migraines. A year later, in 1817, the symptoms reappeared: 'My
health is bad; my nerves are upset and the climate makes them
worse. The island of St. Helena is really unhealthy.'

When he came back from Brazil his ailments had largely disappeared, and Balmain dazzled the English by describing his audience with the king of this youthful American state. But his journey
had no effect on his relations with Hudson Lowe. Hardly was he
back when the commissioner was so reckless as to ride in the direction of Longwood, and at once received a series of notes from Plantation House, which he forwarded to St. Petersburg with a spicy
commentary. The Governor quoted Major Gorrequer as evidence in
support of his allegations. Balmain wrote in pencil in the margin:

'Major Gorrequer owes everything to the Governor and it is not the first
time he has told lies to back him up. I have made him realise that it is
indecent to confront me with his aide-de-camp. . . . This letter is astonishing, incredible, unimaginable; I laughed till I cried over it. . . . Can one be
bothered with such rubbish! And this is the man to whom Napoleon has

been entrusted. . . . He invited me to dinner, I had a conversation with him. . . . He promised that he would send me no more notes through his aide-de-camp, nor cross-examine me like a criminal. In return, I gave up my visit to Madame de Montholon and our personal relations are better than ever.'*

But these relations were very soon to take an unexpected turn, owing to the fact that Lady Lowe wanted to make use of her husband's position to arrange suitable marriages for the two Miss Johnsons. She had in mind an officer in the army or navy, but it was the Russian diplomatist who carried the day. The very strange idyll between the forty-year-old commissioner and the English girl of eighteen delighted Hudson Lowe, who said cynically to his secretary in October 1819: 'The Russian no longer bothers about visiting Longwood. He spends his time elsewhere: going riding with his chosen heroine.'† The Tsar's officers were as gallant in ladies' drawing-rooms as on the battlefield, and conducted their manœuvres equally dashingly; on November 5, the following dispatch left for St. Petersburg:

'I was reduced to such an extreme state of weakness by continual violent attacks of nerves that I began to be afraid I should not be able to continue occupying the position Your Majesty deigned to entrust to me, with the zeal and activity I knew I am capable of; I was therefore obliged to ask to be recalled. . . . It is strictly true to say that it is on the advice of my doctors that I have given consideration, Sire, to the possibility of marriage . . . Sir Hudson Lowe's stepdaughter. . . . This young lady combines intelligence with the finest qualities of character. She is a model of grace and amiability. . . . Her parents have already given their consent to our union. To test her daughter's feelings, Lady Lowe made some objections concerning my age and unprepossessing appearance. She showed indifference in this respect, and said that she enjoyed my company.'

Besides permission to get married, Balmain begged for the special honour of being attached to the august person of the Tsar as his aide-de-camp. Permission was granted and the appointment promised; the marriage took place on April 26, 1820, in the library of Plantation House, and the couple left the island on May 3, after a series of brilliant balls and receptions which finally won over the Russian to the English camp and prompted him to soften the tone of

*Balmain's dispatches—unpublished manuscript notes.
†Major Gorrequer's Papers (unpublished).

his dispatches. He assured his minister Nesselrode with much satisfaction that he 'left on good terms with everyone'. 'You are going to be a widower now, Monsieur le Marquis,' he said ironically to Montchenu, who was from now on the only allied commissioner.

When he arrived in Russia Balmain began a regular correspondence with Lowe, but the tone of his letters was light, as was suitable to an absent son-in-law writing to a father-in-law who occupied an important office. Now that he was married, the Russian did not want to give up his post, and made efforts to be appointed permanently to St. Helena: he had to argue, write, implore and convince—for the Baron de Holland was about to go in his place—and finally received the appointment in June 1821, a few days before the tragic news arrived. 'Please help me,' Count Balmain groaned to his minister, 'Napoleon's death has reduced me to the last extremity. I was to leave next Sunday and I have had considerable expenses. Now I am penniless and in debt.' He was given several posts as commissioner until 1823, when we lose sight of Alexander Antonovitch, Count Ramsay de Balmain: his recollections of life in St. Helena in the days of the great Emperor, had he written them in his declining years when passions were cooled and witnesses dispersed, would certainly have been of enormous interest.

✤   ✤   ✤

Such were the three men whose duty it was to act as links between the prisoner and their sovereigns, one of whom was the prisoner's father-in-law, another his friend. In fact, they caused serious difficulties for the British. Bonaparte's suite might plot with the commissioners, wrote Lord Bathurst to Hudson Lowe, 'who will have too little to do not to be tempted to do a little mischief; on this principle also you will encourage them to amuse themselves by going to the Cape by way of change of scene, and engage to furnish them and their court with a regular account of the state of your prisoner.' As for the Prime Minister, Lord Liverpool, his pessimism equalled that of the Secretary of State: 'Living in a place where they have little to do, they will soon become bored, and quarrel among themselves, and their disputes might well become a serious inconvenience for those guarding the prisoner'. As an obedient public servant, Hudson Lowe

adopted his chief's opinions as his own, and did his utmost to tyran-
nise over the three envoys to the point of making even their daily
existence unbearable: by being friendly to one, quarrelling with the
second and despising the third, he succeeded in cutting them off
completely from Longwood and leaving them nothing to do, and
therefore predisposed to discontent, boredom, and above all desire
to get away from the accursed rock.

As for Napoleon, who had hoped that the commissioners would be
accredited to Longwood and enable him to maintain equality and
communication with the sovereigns, when the truth became obvious,
he reacted as the British had done: 'What folly to send commissioners here without duties or responsibilities! They will have
nothing to do but roam the streets and climb the rocks. The Prussian
government has been wiser, and saved money as well.'

As witnesses before the bar of history, all of them except Balmain
are without weight, without sense of proportion, without importance:
the marquis was only interested in the price of commodities, and
reminds one of Voltaire's good Abbé Trublet and his anxiety 'to be a
somebody', while the Austrian lacked both intelligence and judgement. Balmain was the only one who understood the position of the
fallen sovereign whose exile he had the honour of sharing, and was
able to infuse his observant dispatches with something of the strange
atmosphere of St. Helena.

V

DAILY LIFE IN THE ARMY

✤✤✤

The army—The camps—Rations—Receptions given
by the Governor and at Deadwood camp—The Royal
Navy—Relations between the French and British
sailors—Relations between Hudson Lowe and the
admirals—The soldiers—The climate of the island—
Women.

✤✤✤

The inhabitants of St. Helena, whether Europeans or natives,
civilians or military, lived through the same nightmare as Napoleon
himself from 1815 to 1821, because Hudson Lowe and his henchmen
persistently treated them with the same severity and suspicion as they
did the prisoner at Longwood. They had the advantage of relative
freedom it is true, but lack of supplies, overpopulation and security
measures had transformed their daily life into a form of military
fatigue-duty. Having no share, or merely a very remote one, in the
official policy controlling the relations between Plantation House and
Longwood House, they had to put up uncomplainingly—for everything was known and everything repeated—with shortages and
police control, passwords and domiciliary visits, rules and restrictions and the unpleasant atmosphere of a fortress where everything
must be subordinate to guarding the prisoners of State.

They were not all in the same boat, needless to say, and the colonel
did not see things with the same eyes as the private soldier, or the
island sage, Sir William Doveton, with those of the coolies who
carried out most of the manual labour. But each in his different way
reacted and suffered from the burden of physical and moral restrictions: fear makes men so taciturn that one must read through masses
of public and private papers, newspapers, letters and memoirs in
order to reconstruct the elements of the daily life of those who were

121

neither Hudson Lowe nor Napoleon—the only two people who could, each in his own way, defy constraint with impunity.

The society of the time seems to have spontaneously divided itself into clans: this tendency is seen in all small communities and also among soldiers who are leading family lives in a garrison. The days followed a different pattern according to whether one belonged to the army, the navy or the East India Company. Lower down in the scale there was no longer any question of social life, but merely of life itself: eating, working, feeling afraid and escaping a flogging.

From the first, the army lorded it over the rest: this was normal in an island where the governor wore epaulets and the prisoner was 'a general officer of the highest rank'; the navy, a privileged caste in England, did not take kindly to this supremacy, and the important inhabitants of the island, who were the higher ranking employees of the East India Company, were not at all pleased at being invaded by 1,500 Europeans, who fell upon provisions, conscripted the help of all able-bodied men, took possession of the best houses and offices, and in a word became masters and gave orders where they had once been received as guests. Everyone was discontented, and all the documents reveal the same lassitude, bitterness and mutinous feelings that develop in concentration camps.

✤   ✤   ✤

The troops disembarked from the *Northumberland* at the same time as Napoleon, and profited by their early arrival to install themselves as comfortably as possible. While the rank and file were divided between Lemon Valley, Francis Plain, Deadwood and Hutt's Gate, their commanding officer General Bingham took over Knollcombe, an enchanting house buried in a romantic valley five minutes away from Plantation House. The senior officers were mostly quartered in cottages round Deadwood camp, very close to Longwood, while the subalterns had to put up with barrack life. Families took the rank of their husbands, a custom which sometimes caused friction: the officers working under Hudson Lowe had made themselves unpopular by seizing the best lodgings. Sir Thomas Reade chose Alarm House, half-way between Longwood and Jamestown, where he shamelessly collected the best available furniture, to the great dismay of Gorrequer, who as a bachelor was fobbed off with the worst room in Plantation House. Colonel Wynyard and his young wife were at Rock Rose, surrounded by the astonishing scenery of Sandy Bay. The charming Lieutenant Jackson and his companion in work, Wortham, took possession of Rose Cottage. Later on, so that Jackson should be closer to the persons he had to watch, Lowe installed him at Longwood itself, in a cottage next door to the guard-room. Non-commissioned officers and private soldiers were massed together under canvas. Their lot was made far from enviable by the exposed position of Deadwood plain, which was lashed by a cold wind throughout the rainy season, and became a scorched desert in summer: not a tree, not a rock, no shelter. The conditions prevailing in the camps were such that the climate, food and hygiene combined to have disastrous results. 'The most prevalent complaints,' wrote O'Meara, 'are dysentery, inflammations of the bowels, liver affections and fevers, all of them generally of a violent form. . . . During the first twelve or thirteen months after its arrival at St. Helena, the second battalion of the 66th regiment lost, by these diseases, fifty-six men out of a strength of six hundred and thirty, being one in eleven.'

It was a heavy toll. It is distressing to read the names of all these young men, snatched from their homes in Ireland or Scotland, only to be laid side by side in the clayey soil of the cemetery at Plantation House, their names mingling in the parish register of deaths with those of colonists and natives. And during the first week of May 1821, the same copperplate hand was to write, beneath 'Napoleon Bonaparte, ex-Emperor of the French, died at Longwood House and buried on the property of Richard Torbett', the names of members of the British Army who had died 'without glory': the six soldiers William Hagerty, John Murphy, Hannah Ford, James Sister, Terence Cuningale and Michael English, who had not lost their lives in a 'just war' but in an unjust exile.

For the lives of the common soldiers were an infernal round of day duty and night duty, fatigues, hard work and route marches. 'There are sentries in the trees, among the flower-beds, at the windows,' wrote Balmain. 'Monsieur de Montholon told me that he could see at least thirty of them from his bedroom. It is only six miles from Longwood to Jamestown, and I counted nine posts manned by officers, three by non-commissioned officers, fifteen by sentries.

More than a third of the garrison do sentry duty. They are crammed into every hole, and since my arrival four or five have been blown over precipices by the wind.' Discipline had to be harsh to prevent boredom finding sudden outlet in subversion, to which the staff of the East India Company had always been prone. However, one morning in December 1820, Hudson Lowe found himself reading an anonymous letter protesting against the way the soldiers were treated: this was something he particularly dreaded and he made haste to put all the responsibility for the situation onto the commanding officer and the colonel of the regiment, before forwarding the letter to London.

✤   ✤   ✤

The daily ration was not designed to sustain the morale of the troops—that famous morale which always figured so largely in the discussions and decisions of the General Staff. It was reduced to bare subsistence level by the difficulty of getting supplies, and all the troops, whether officers or corporals, had to make do with a pound and a half of bread, one of fresh or salt meat, two ounces of rice and three pounds of wood a day. These figures were also subject to the uncertain times of arrival of supply ships, and in February 1818 a writer complains that 'Lowe is running to and fro trying to build defences against the Bonapartists of South America, and does not even trouble about provisioning his troops. For the last month, men have been on half-ration and there is no fodder left for the horses.' Of course officers were well enough off financially to add the fruit and vegetables necessary to a normal diet to their daily fare, but at what a cost! If their pay—a captain's was £350 a year—is set against the cost of food, it becomes obvious that it was not easy to 'keep the pot boiling' and that officers and rankers alike had to subsist on salt meat. Mutton cost two shillings a pound, a chicken from six to ten shillings, a cabbage from one to two shillings, and carrots a shilling a dozen. Eggs reached five or six shillings a dozen (three times the price of 1966) and the innkeepers of Jamestown fixed the daily pension at thirty shillings, or an adjutant's entire pay.

✤   ✤   ✤

There remained to the officers the inestimable delights of social life and those parties beloved of the English: the bachelors caroused in the mess at Deadwood, and married men with private means entertained at home. The most highly prized invitations were, of course, to receptions at Plantation house, since General Bonaparte did not keep open house. In the large official rooms on the ground floor, where crystal chandeliers sparkled and women in their provincial finery glided over the Chinese carpets, every captain, every agent of the East India Company seemed suddenly to be living through a few moments of royal splendour beneath the frozen gaze of the King and Queen in their picture-frames. The Governor is the representative of 'the Crown', as the English say, and it mattered little that in those years, from 1816 to 1821, the 'Crown' stood for a demented king, talking to the trees at Windsor, and the ridiculous and pathetic Prince Regent. The servants of the State, exiled on St. Helena, did not listen to scandal or the pamphlets going the rounds of the London streets; and to them England was not the florid, vicious and pretentious quadragenarian who ruled in his father's name, it was the heavy piece of jewellery that encircled the monarch's forehead, the lion and unicorn of the royal arms, the proud emblem of the Garter. England was a symbol, and symbols are without blemish. The Crown stood for the omnipotence of Great Britain and the Governor was its humble and proud representative: his presence was feared and his absence dreaded, his dangerous friendship was sought after and shunned at the same time; attending his receptions was an onerous duty.

The aides-de-camp received the guests in the flower-decked hall, and announced them to Sir Hudson and Lady Lowe who would be standing by the drawing-room door. The Governor took great care of his uniforms and often glanced down to see if the aiglets were in place. His secretary wrote of: 'Sir Hudson's ridiculous vain way of going on with his new paraphernalia from London, strutting about like a peacock, admiring himself . . . . , buttoning and unbuttoning his coat, strutting up and down and admiring the reflection of himself in mirrors . . . doing nothing else at dinner than buttoning and unbuttoning his coat and admiring the aiguillettes and asking Lady Lowe what she thought of it.'* The latter did her utmost

*Major Gorrequer's Papers (unpublished).

to appear a lady to her finger-tips. Lacking the true distinction of the British aristocracy, she was simply a middle-class woman who had been temporarily favoured by fortune; she was often lacking in restraint and dignity but she took trouble and exerted herself with all the ardour of a newcomer to the fashionable world, and even the Austrian, Stürmer, who had no special liking for her, freely admitted that 'she is a born hostess, loves entertaining and does it gracefully; she keeps open house at Plantation House where she receives sailors, officers, civil servants and any notable travellers. She is the life and soul of island society, always ready for riding parties or excursions to Diana Peak or Sandy Bay, for evening receptions or balls.' Las Cases, who was a man of the world accustomed to drawing-rooms and the most polished manners, saw her as 'beautiful, amiable and something of an actress'. Others added 'paints rather too much', 'tends to wear daringly low-cut dresses', or even 'a little too imperious'. The malicious Gorrequer was not taken in by her assumption of grand ladylike airs as he cantered beside the door of her phaeton. Backstairs gossip reached him and he noted it down with relish. Lady Lowe had a weakness for the bottle. Even that scapegrace Jackson observed that she stumbled over her words after drinking, and if she cut down on white wine she would fling herself on the sherry. And she seemed rather too fond of a certain Den Taafe, aide-de-camp to the Governor; he was invited to play whist with her and spent a lot of time at Plantation House.

As they arrived, the respectful, submissive crowd of guests spread out through the drawing-rooms and began conversing in subdued voices; with the help of sherry and gin tongues were loosened and soon the room was full of noise. Even if the wind was shaking the ancient trees behind the long silk curtains, even if the rain was streaming onto the stone terraces—the candles twinkling in their sconces brought forgetfulness of time, place, exile and boredom. When the time came, the major-domo bowed ceremoniously to Sir Hudson and announced that 'His Excellency's dinner is served'. The East India Company had provided Plantation House with an abundant supply of sumptuous silver, and the table was carefully arranged and looked very attractive under the enormous cut-glass chandelier. The Governor and Lady Lowe presided at opposite ends and the guests often—very often in fact—found Sir Hudson languid, nervous and remote. At the end of the table where the aides-de-camp, the younger officers and Lady Lowe's daughters were sitting, the atmosphere was frankly gay, and Gorrequer, who missed no detail of these receptions, is scandalised when he sees the enterprising Lieutenant Jackson calmly put his arm round the waist of Suzanne Johnson, the younger of the two girls. When the servants had cleared the table, the port was circulated and the last toast was drunk; with an all-embracing glance Sir Hudson Lowe made sure that he had the attention of all the guests, stood up—to be followed by the others—and raising his glass said in a loud voice: 'the King'. 'The King', repeated the company, *mezza voce*. They sat down and conversation began again until the ladies retired, after the English fashion 'to powder their noses', and settled in an adjoining room. The men sat over the table while the decanters of port ceaselessly went their rounds. This habit amused Napoleon very much, and he often questioned O'Meara and other Englishmen about it. 'If I were you,' he said to Mrs. Balcombe, 'I should be very angry at being turned out to wait for two or three hours whilst your husband and his friends were making themselves drunk. How different are Frenchmen, who think society cannot be agreeable without the presence of ladies!' This custom had become very fashionable since the Regency and this was the time for the famous smoking-room stories which would have been impossible in the presence of the lady guests. On this subject, Lady Lowe was adamant. 'She could not bear a story that was in the slightest degree improper to be told in her presence', declared Gorrequer, adding afterwards that 'this did not prevent her allowing fornication to be going on at Rock Cottage between Napoleon's valet and a woman'.* Napoleon was certainly exaggerating when he spoke of an absence of two or three hours: in fact the port session lasted about half an hour, just the time needed for the ladies to adjust any disorder in their dress, see to their make-up, and drink coffee in the drawing-room, where they were joined by the men. After coffee came liqueurs, followed by games, charades and gossip; Lady Lowe was an enthusiastic whist player and arranged tables for it. For the Governor this was a time of relaxation and also of work. He went from group to group, from armchair to sofa, asking questions and holding forth.

When the clock struck eleven, the wife of the guest of highest rank

*Major Gorrequer's Papers (unpublished).

gave the signal, and the company took leave of their hosts, bowing and shaking hands. While Major Gorrequer went back to his room in the deserted wing of the house, His Excellency and his lady were alone at last in their private apartments.

Regimental dinners and balls also attracted everyone of importance on the island. But what a journey it was along the rough dark road that led to the gloomy camp of Deadwood! To get to the plateau from the town, ladies used to pile into carts with seats, drawn by six horses or oxen—for the descent they were differently harnessed, with two animals in front and four behind to check their speed. The ladies wore their travelling clothes and carried their ball-dresses in boxes. With slow ponderous tread the animals hauled them aloft under the moon or in total darkness according to season, and when they got to Alarm House, rain, wind and mist would often beat against the canvas covers of the carts and extinguish the lanterns of the slaves who were leading them. The decor of Deadwood camp, with its hundreds of little lights, was certainly very different from that of the Prince Regent's parties at Carlton House. 'We got down from the carriage,' said one lady, 'into mud up to our knees in the damp darkness.' The young officers had done their best to make their barracks look pretty, though they were hardly better off than the Emperor at Longwood. The buildings were constructed of old wood, alive with rats, and the flat roofs made of laths and tar-lined paper had cracks here and there through which water poured on rainy nights. The St. Helena exiles, officers' wives and planters' daughters, in all their eighteen-year-old freshness and their middle-class inexperience, were unaware of the wretchedness of their surroundings, and danced like lunatics until the dawn cannon was fired, finding these interludes a means of defeating boredom, embarking on a romance or showing off their best clothes. Gourgaud, who did not appreciate such frivolity, and judged women with the disillusioned eye of a rake, has left a picturesque description of one of these garrison balls:

'The admiral asked me if I would dance if he found me a partner. I said yes. A moment later he told me that I was to dance the first quadrille with Mrs. Balcombe, the second with Betsy and the third with the Rosebud. I had not meant to dance with the Balcombes and here I was, caught. . . . One dances twice running with the same partner: it's a dreadful bore . . . I was told that I was to take Madame Defontaine, wife of one of the councillors, to supper. After the second dance we went into the dining-room. *Quid pro quo.* I sat down beside an old lady in a different place from the one assigned to me, and I did well, for with the insolent one must be insolent. . . . I could not go home until five in the morning because of my three, or rather six quadrilles. A rosy young lady made a terrible fart as she was dancing.'

Next day tongues used to wag for all they were worth, and the tiny incidents of the party provided conversation at morning tea-parties, given by the women in turn, and during which, for lack of a local news-sheet, news, scandal and other events were commented on, and characters torn to pieces. These gossips, dying of boredom amid their swarms of native servants, could find no occupation or relaxation in anything except backbiting, indiscretion and bickering; unfortunately Lady Lowe seems to have led her squadron into battle with considerable dash. 'La Donna* bursts out laughing,' notes Gorrequer, 'ridiculing in the most indecent way the appearance of Mrs. Wynyard the preceding day (which was the first of her appearance out at dinner since she had a baby), her dress, her looks, the manner in which her clothes and flowers on head were huddled upon her as if thrown at her, as if she really had been endeavouring to make herself look as ridiculous as she possibly could.' As a mother anxious to find husbands for her offspring, she never missed an opportunity of contrasting the abandon and bad taste of her guests with the tact, beauty and elegance of her two grown-up daughters.

❖   ❖   ❖

In this ingenuously commonplace yet tortuous little world, the officers of the Royal Navy seemed like noblemen among rustics; for, the men, young and old, who had just ruled a line of finality beneath the long list of the imperial wars were a rough lot—rough, but open, honest and usually sincere, from whom one would expect reasonable behaviour towards a proud but vanquished enemy. With very few exceptions, the sailors from top to bottom of the hierarchy were remarkable for their smartness and ability, and some went a considerable way in sympathising with Napoleon.

It is true that the four admirals who in turn occupied the ungrateful post of naval commander-in-chief between 1815 and 1821 were as different as they could possibly be: Cockburn was haughty but

*Major Gorrequer's nickname for Lady Lowe.

just and reasonable, Malcolm was an amiable and understanding aristocrat, Plampin a thick-set sea-dog, and Lambert a well-mannered eccentric. Moreover, with the exception of Cockburn, their contacts with the French were distant, officially at any rate. But as a whole their loyalties inclined them in favour of the exiles, and Napoleon, well aware which way the wind was blowing, always took a pleasure in the company of the Navy, kept on friendly terms with the officers and treated the sailors who worked for him humanely and with good humour. The conversations between the god of armies and the bluejackets of His Britannic Majesty's Navy must have been strange indeed. Perhaps they were to some extent inspired by the mute admiration Napoleon detected in his interlocutors, but certainly also by the effect produced on the prisoner of the *Bellerophon* by this admirable body of men, whose discipline and fine equipment had combined to save the British Isles from total invasion. As for the English, they kept their respect for the great man to themselves. Young George Home, midshipman of this same *Bellerophon*, referring to the Emperor's letter to the Regent ('I come like Themistocles') confided sadly to his journal: 'Alas poor Napoleon! The appeal was made to a heart more obdurate than the Persian Satrap. Castlereagh and his Holy Allies had no such ideas about generosity.' And another midshipman, scanning the roadsteads between the islands of Ré and Oléron for a sight of the ex-Emperor arriving in his boat, cried to the boatswain with a sixteen-year-old's enthusiasm: 'This is the proudest day of your life. You are this day to do the honours of the side to the greatest man the world ever produced, or ever will produce.'

Napoleon was received with royal honours on the *Bellerophon*, a ship that history has endowed with a sinister fame, and on the *Northumberland*, when the game was up and he was merely General Bonaparte, Admiral Cockburn (who had recently been appointed to take charge of him) and Captain Ross (who commanded the ship) showed as much courtesy as the strict instructions allowed towards the 'prisoner of State'. The Emperor presided at table, the regimental band played muted music as at official receptions; Cockburn, stiff and awkward in his role of admiral-warder, modestly took the seat on his passenger's right, and gave orders for fewer courses to be served when he was told how little the Emperor relished the pleasures of the table. The young officers vied with each other with adolescent eagerness for the honour of offering him their hand to help him over an obstacle on the slippery deck, or of exchanging a few words with him. All were thrilled by the Byronic hero's simple manner, and all—from admiral to midshipman—sent home more or less accurate but enthusiastic descriptions, for the Navy thought a good deal of itself, and was not at all averse to throwing dust in the eyes of landsmen, especially when this dust came from the gold braid of an emperor of France.

On arrival at St. Helena there were some complaints of the Admiral and his regulations, but when it became known that he was to be relieved by a certain Hudson Lowe Napoleon himself admitted that they might one day regret the sailor. In fact, though Cockburn was always a slave to the written orders he received—not to mention verbal instructions which have never been published—he was often the first to try and soften the lot of the exiles, and the surveillance established by him at The Briars was quite unlike the permanent state of readiness for action organised by Lowe at Longwood. As soon as the Emperor's residence had been definitely chosen, he ordered his ratings to perform prodigies so that the buildings could be enlarged and improved in three months. 'Every day,' says O'Meara, 'bodies of two or three hundred seamen were employed in carrying up from Jamestown timber and other materials for building.' If Napoleon expressed the wish to gallop as far as Sandy Bay, to visit Sir William Doveton, the most influential member of the council, Cockburn and his secretary would come forward, hat in hand, to escort him there, and spare him from being guarded by a junior officer. Next day Napoleon delightedly declared that he had 'won over' the sailor whom he had in a fit of rage described as a 'shark', but whom he recognised as a brave and irreproachable officer. 'We shall regret him,' he said, 'he is a man of honour; his bluntness is wounding but he is a truly brave soldier.'

This tendency to praise Admiral Sir George Cockburn increased when it became necessary to come to grips with Hudson Lowe, and it suited French policy to compare the latter's Prussian obstinacy with Cockburn's rough generosity. 'Your instructions are the same as Sir George Cockburn's,' Napoleon declared angrily to Lowe's face, 'he himself told me so; but you interpret them fifty times more harshly.'

10

Dr. O'Meara, as a doctor attached to the fleet, had much to do with the excellent relations between Longwood and the Navy, and this began at the very outset of Napoleon's captivity, and not only when O'Meara's hatred of the Governor, and the Emperor's material generosity, had drawn him into the opposite camp. He was an active ambassador, and brought to Longwood commanders, captains and other officers from ships in transit or laid up in the harbour all equally eager to be able to boast of having had an interview with Bonaparte. The French naturally delighted in these contacts, which relieved the monotonous passage of the weeks and also enabled them to construct a network for receiving information under the very nose of the Governor and his acolytes. As Montholon confided to Balmain: 'By handing over the profits from our writings to travellers, officers, merchants and captains of supply-ships, we manage to get everything through, to be printed in Europe.' This open door into the world caused serious uneasiness at Plantation House, and Hudson Lowe was often enraged with the bluejackets; he vented his feelings to Gorrequer, who was politely ironical, but once in his room with the door locked, hastened to note down his chief's unbridled remarks: 'O'Meara was the greatest scoundrel in the world. He never had said anything against Bonaparte ever since he came here. . . . He was the greatest scoundrel that ever existed. . . . Delighted at the admiral getting that letter from Balmain. Coming in quite pleased soon after he read it saying "why, that fellow is as great a rascal as Bertrand".'*

❖   ❖   ❖

The Navy privately condemned the Governor's policy and was disinclined to be associated with a mission having such a flavour of Botany Bay; this was crystal clear, but Lowe could not bring himself to admit it. He knew that opinions were openly expressed in the wardrooms, and that the Admiral himself had confidently declared that if he were given Lowe's place everything would be different. 'The whole navy do it,' fumed Sir Hudson, 'look at the Admiral the other day, he attempted to condemn the conduct of O'Meara but did he pass any remark on those matters after reading the correspond-

*Major Gorrequer's Papers (unpublished).

ence? It was all owing to that scoundrel and damn Admiral visiting and bowing at Bonaparte instead of marking in a proper manner the feeling he ought to have had after that conversation. . . . The fact is there is a feeling for Bonaparte throughout that ought not to be.'* Besides, Napoleon made much of the Admiral and his wife, and was constantly praising their elegance, high-mindedness, intelligence and aristocratic connections. The Bertrands were close friends with Captain Hamilton, of the *Havannah*, a ship of the St. Helena fleet, and it was said that the captain was not insensible to the charms and distress of the Countess. During the voyage on the *Northumberland* he was honoured with a place at the Emperor's table, and when he paid a visit to Longwood on April 21, 1816, the day before his ship set sail for Europe, Bertrand noted in his journal: 'Captain Hamilton dines with us; package handed over.' Sir Hudson Lowe therefore had more than enough reasons for mistrusting the sailors: letters were getting through in defiance of his authority and they were not likely to sing his praises.

The Bertrands also saw a good deal of Captain Dillon of the *Phaeton;* he was more than a friend to Madame Bertrand, he was a kinsman. Although Dillon certainly detested Napoleon, for he had languished in French prisons, it seems possible that he was willing to be entrusted with commissions and even correspondence. In 1816, Warden, the ship's doctor of the *Northumberland*, published his famous *Letters from the Cape*, and so produced a powerful current of sympathy for the exiles in Europe. When Napoleon was ill in 1819, Bertrand did not send for the artillery doctor—a satellite of Hudson Lowe's, but for Doctor Stokoe of the *Conqueror*, then in Jamestown harbour. The Balcombes were also on friendly terms with the sailors; William no longer wore a naval officer's uniform, but young Betsy was dying of love for the Honourable George Carstairs, and insisted on introducing him to Napoleon. The audience gave Napoleon pleasure and he openly declared that he had just seen one of the rare examples of aristocratic birth combined with an amiable character and lively intelligence. When he was told that this young beau, a favourite in the officers' ward-room and also with Admiral Malcolm, had proved himself as capable on land as on board ship, and had carried out with great ability the strange task of supervising and

*Major Gorrequer's Papers (unpublished).

exploiting one of the farms on the island, he added (so emphatically that his words reached the Governor's ears) that 'everything the British Navy undertook was done successfully'.

When reports of such remarks were laid on his table with a sly smile by Major Gorrequer, Lowe found them extremely provocative: his usual habit was to grow furious, shout, threaten, and end by taking a rather mean revenge. The Admiral wanted to move into the pavilion at The Briars, and when he asked for some furniture he was at once told rather curtly that it was not in the tradition of the administration to furnish premises completely and only a strict minimum would reluctantly be supplied. Whenever Malcolm went to Longwood, where he was always warmly welcomed, he was sure to receive one of the complicated notes that were Lowe's speciality: 'Your visit (to Longwood) at the present moment might do away with any impression made on his mind by your having abstained from seeing him ever since his late violent and revolting conduct, for no part of which any explanation has been offered. Whether this risk is of sufficient consequence to make you suspend your visit, I should wish to leave to your own judgement to determine upon.' No instructions to a subordinate could have been clearer, but Rear-Admiral Sir Pulteney Malcolm, G.C.B., G.C.M.G., refused to be treated like a midshipman: 'I have read with great attention your letter. . . . I regret . . . (that my convictions) alone induces me to keep to the opinion that I expressed to you.' Hudson Lowe's attacks on this obstinate gentleman always missed the mark.

There was another matter that ceaselessly tormented the Governor, and prejudiced him against the Admiral: it was the always irritating problem to a professional soldier of rank, seniority and precedence. Of course the old rule 'Office takes precedence over rank' set him above an admiral, but as everyone in the island knew well and often remarked, Hudson Lowe was only a major-general, with the temporary and local rank of lieutenant-general. Whereas Admirals Cockburn and Lambert had full right to their rank, and in a different place and circumstances their privileges as officers of the Royal Navy would have given them precedence. This knowledge gave all the naval flag officers considerable independence in regard to Sir Hudson Lowe, expressed in tangible form by the presence of the Admiral's flagship in Jamestown harbour. Invitations on board the ships were quite as much sought after as those to receptions at Plantation House. In his comfortable and luxuriously furnished ward-room, or on the scrubbed deck of his ship, the Admiral would be 'at home', wearing full dress uniform with his telescope under his arm, and surrounded by his smartly turned-out staff—and the Governor's satellites were not always invited. When the girls and the sub-lieutenants abandoned themselves to the frenzy of highland dances to the music of the bagpipes, under the paternal and amused eyes of Sir Pulteney and Lady Malcolm, they forgot for this all-too-brief evening the existence of the little sandy-haired man who had transformed the once gay colonial life into one of intolerable constraint.

On one occasion, however, in June 1817, Hudson Lowe scored a point against the Navy: it was the day that the *Conqueror*, flying the flag of Rear-Admiral Plampin, was driven into harbour by a south-east wind. Malcolm's successor was a man of fifty-five, who in spite of his excellent French made very few conquests at Longwood. Napoleon granted him an audience on arrival, but afterwards confided to O'Meara: 'Few men have so prepossessing an exterior and manner as Malcolm; but the other reminds me of one of those drunken little Dutch *schippers* that I have seen in Holland, sitting at a table with a pipe in his mouth, a cheese and a bottle of geneva before him.' The verdict was severe, but showed great perspicacity. 'The day we left England,' wrote an officer of the *Conqueror*, 'gave us a very unexpected passenger. Early in the morning a boat had been on shore to the Isle of Wight and while we were getting under way returned with a lady who, to the surprise of many, proved to be Mrs. Plampin. Her coming on board at that time, and not from Portsmouth, excited suspicions unfavourable to the lady, for none of us supposed that the Admiralty would have denied a passage to the wife of the Admiral. Our suspicions gained strength as we proceeded and were confirmed on our arrival at St. Helena.'

The arrival of a large ship was an important event in the little island, and the ship's officers were plagued with questions by the crowds who thronged the quays: what was the new admiral like? was he married? was his wife on board? The replies were evasive and the questioners got nothing for their pains. The Admiral came ashore alone for his ceremonial visit to the Governor: next day he called on Lady Lowe, who kept him in friendly conversation for a time. No mention of Mrs. Plampin. Not for a long while. In this community where the death of a sheep was news the incredible fact was soon public knowledge: the Admiral and the person in question were not united by any of the contracts that bind man and woman in respectable society. How shocking! The furies were unleashed against the unofficial wife. 'The storm burst forth,' notes one witness. 'Its fury was most severe at Plantation House. The ladies who formed the court of the queen of the island were unanimous in the opinion that the Admiral's conduct was the grossest insult that could possibly be offered them, considering that he was the second in rank in the island. They regarded it as the Governor's duty to punish him severely. The report soon spread from Plantation House that the lady would be immediately sent off the island, that the Admiral would be reported, and in all probability recalled. These rumours, no doubt, reached his ears, together with the curious fact that he had been preached at from the pulpit.' For the church had wasted no time, and the Reverend Boys, an arrogant and inquisitive clergyman and a stickler for morality, thought it his duty to reveal the Admiral's defiance of public morality from the pulpit. Furiously indignant, Plampin went to protest to Lowe, who while blaming the Admiral's conduct, saw in the irregularity of his liaison a means of rallying the new arrival to his side. Provocative sermons were forbidden, and the elderly sailor installed his mistress at The Briars and remained a zealous supporter of official policy during the rest of his command. The junior officers of the garrison stood their ground, however, and many of them 'refused to accept invitations to dine with Plampin and his old woman'; youth shows its courage in ways no longer practised by the middle-aged, and in matters of social prejudice it is often in the forefront of the battle.

In the light of these facts, one may well wonder what might have been the effect on Napoleon's existence and the daily life of the island, if the British government had given way to liberal pressure and agreed to replace Lowe by Malcolm. There was undoubtedly a question of it. This is proved by intercepted letters such as the following from Balcombe to O'Meara: 'Count Bertrand has assured me that, out of hatred of the Governor, many of the English have helped, are still helping and will always help Napoleon to communicate clandestinely with his friends in Europe.' It is said that among

the letters censored by Lowe there was another from the same corres-
spondent who added *in fine*: 'The two idiots will very soon be
recalled.' Such a cavalier expression startled the 'idiots' in question
—Lowe and Reade—and Gorrequer heard his chief say in threatening tones: 'They had better not remove me or I shall raise such a
clatter above their heads that will astonish them.' This threat of
Lowe's against his enemies, or perhaps his chiefs, seems to show his
haunting fear of disapproval and of being replaced by Cockburn or
Malcolm, but it also stresses an unexpected aspect of his character
and the nature of his mission. There must have been included in his
instructions certain 'considerations', details that might be used for
blackmail or public scandal, and he was threatening to make use of
them. . . . But he was not in fact replaced, and everything that can be
written on the subject must remain supposititious. Napoleon's relations with Admiral Malcolm being what they were, one may assume
that the appointment of the sailor as Governor would have turned a
sinister page in history—that of his dealings with Hudson Lowe; the
Admiral would have allowed the Emperor to live as he had hoped at
Longwood, as a gentleman farmer, able to move freely all over the
island, and make friends with the inhabitants, and a *modus
vivendi* would have been established between these two men of
honour which although it would not have changed the course of
history would certainly have considerably sweetened the exile's
last years.

✤   ✤   ✤

The background of this official life was peopled by a crowd of
soldiers and coloured workers, including a great many Chinese and
lascars: an undistinguished herd, who had no hand in politics and no
distractions or other object in life than performing their daily tasks
and serving their master or the Company. There is little document-
ary evidence about their way of life, not that the part they played was
unimportant. Among them were the sailors from the *Northumberland* who carted the stones used to enlarge Longwood House,
sometimes on their backs; there were the soldiers who kept a
constant vigilant watch on the exile; there were the Chinese

who trenched and dug and looked after the Emperor's gardens, under orders from his generals; and finally there were the slaves who toiled to keep the island supplied with vegetables and fish.

The two thousand soldiers belonged to the regular army and received harsh treatment from the officers who were all too ready with blows, and from dull-witted N.C.Os. Discipline, promotion and recruiting in the British army had often been the subject of Napoleon's acid comments; it was realised in London that far-reaching reforms were absolutely necessary, and in December 1820 a circular issued by the War Office called upon commanding officers never to lose sight of the fact that discipline and the hierarchy of rank could be most effectively preserved by suppressing all coarse, brutal and abusive remarks. Pay was wretched, and the daily ration had been reduced to a minimum of bread, salt or fresh meat, rice and wood; and the troops stationed in St. Helena had also to put up with the horrible isolation, the severity of the climate and the prevalence of disease.

For convenience' sake, some of the troops were stationed at Jamestown to keep guard over the town and port, others at Ladder Hill for defence against possible invasion, at Francis Plain to protect the west coast, and at Deadwood to provide pickets on the approach roads and sentries for Longwood itself. General Bertrand visited Deadwood camp in May 1816, and found 'the officers' and soldiers' barracks clean, well-ventilated and free from unpleasant smells; the soldiers slept in hammocks with mattresses and blankets'. This moderate and very British comfort did not make up for the spartan fare, a climate that undermined the health, and a lack of sanitary hygiene. A naval doctor has described how the six hundred and thirty men of the second battalion of the 66th regiment lost fifty of their number from dysentery. The same disease soon attacked the crews of the ships, who were even worse off in the stifling heat of the battery-decks at anchor. The flagship, the *Conqueror*, was to lose more than a hundred men out of six hundred in eighteen months, and a hundred and eight others had to be discharged as unfit and sent home to England. As for smaller ships, the exiguous proportions and promiscuity of the crew's quarters made them infallibly fall preys to the terrible tropical malady. *Mosquito* and *Racoon* each with a hundred men on their roll lost sixty and twenty-four respectively. *Leveret* committed eleven out of seventy-five sailors to the waves, and *Griffon* fifteen out of eighty-five.

✤   ✤   ✤

The climate was certainly appalling, but hygiene was deficient or even non-existent and colonial medicine in its infancy: St. Helena became the burial place of a large proportion of the young men who landed there in the prime of life, toughened though they were by the harsh climate of the British Isles. According to the experts the mortality figures recorded there exceed all those registered during the Royal Navy's campaigns in far-off places. It seems pertinent, therefore, to ask whether the climate of the island is noxious, or even deadly. Historians and journalists have embroidered this theme, but they have all been tempted to base their answers on the present state of things, when an efficient medical corps and a modern pharma-copœia have brought about a remarkable improvement in hygiene, and also on a special place—Jamestown—where the mists of the plateaux are unknown. As for those historians who have never been impelled to make a pilgrimage to the scene of the drama, they have endlessly elaborated the absurd assumptions of writers of the last century. Yet this large body of two thousand young men enables us to paint a complete and detailed picture, for their encampments were so placed as to be subjected to all the climates of the island from the harbour to the plateaux.

Above all, one must avoid trying to settle this controversial question by reference solely to the official reports, although the fact that they were severely censored by Hudson Lowe is in itself a crushing piece of evidence. Let us rather look at private diaries and letters; in this uneventful solitude, physical affliction and the severity of the weather occupy most of the writers' pages, and the details to be extracted from them have quite a different interest from those provided by official statements.

The Marquis de Montchenu saw the epidemics as a splendid opportunity to bewail his fate to his minister; but he could not con-ceal his genuine anxiety: 'We have two hospitals here, whose surg-eons get £1,200 a year. . . . Mortality has been the fashion for quite a time; the figures are pretty high but so long as Longwood remains immune I feel convinced I shall be spared. Congestion of the liver is the commonest disease; Count Balmain has already had it, but it was taken in time. Fever is very common also, and more dangerous, one is either dead or well again in four days; it is the disease of the moment and is also known as the "influenza". It is caused by the drought that has prevailed these last few months.' And Louis XVIII's envoy concludes by saying that his courage in continuing to live in this lazarette certainly deserves a salary of £3,000 a year: 'A speedy reply, I beg you, as my position is extremely distressing.'

Next year—we are now in April 1817—Gourgaud notes: 'Boredom reigns at Longwood, as also in camp, where four soldiers have died of dysentery in the last seven days,' while Baron von Stürmer informs his sister that 'a great many of the English are suffering from obstruction of the liver, and feverish diseases; not a day passes without a burial'. Commissioner Balmain, the first victim of the ills which attacked the inhabitants, has given us an excellent clinical picture: 'Not a day passes without my suffering either from my stomach or nerves, or from an incipient obstruction of the liver, and I am visibly fading away.' 'My health is bad, I suffer from nerves and they are weakened by this climate. The island of St. Helena is really unhealthy.' At this time he sent a report direct to Count Lieven, the Tsar's ambassador in London: 'My health is wretched and my doctor, Mr. Baxter, insists that I should return to Europe. . . . For the last six weeks I have hardly gone out at all, since I am subject to nervous attacks at any moment, spasms during which I see and hear nothing. Added to this, a permanent state of melancholy undermines and withers me, and no amount of thinking does it any good. Admiral and Lady Malcolm have a horror of this rock. They have both lost their usual high spirits. Except for the Governor, everyone has gone, and those who take their place will leave within a year, for it is impossible to stand it here longer. Beside the climate, which is quite different from what people say, the boredom kills one. It would be barbarous to leave anyone but a criminal here. My health is going from bad to worse. In particular, I am so crushed by hypochondria that, after trying all possible cures, the doctors have decided I must leave this horrible rock.' In 1819, when he had been there three months, he ended his report by repeating: 'Far from getting acclimatised to this horrible rock, I suffer constantly from my nerves. All the doctors admit that the excessive, unbearable heat of the tropics is harmful to my health and has already undermined it. . . . I was seriously ill last month and I suffer all the time from my nerves.' In August 1818 he went on holiday to Rio, and justified it to his minister by emphasising: 'Having again had nervous attacks and truly unbearable headaches, I decided after twenty-seven months of suffering to take a short holiday.'

The Russian's medical notes are invaluable; allowing for the exaggeration designed to impress his superiors, it seems that on arrival Balmain was suffering from an attack of scurvy (picturesquely described as 'inflamed throat' and due no doubt to the long voyage) and afterwards from nervous migraines caused by boredom, isolation and the heat—three factors peculiarly suited to cause a state of neurasthenia that could degenerate into neurosis.

General Gourgaud's journal provides us with abundant details, some very intimate, concerning the complaint everyone talked about —dysentery: the aide-de-camp was the first of the French party to succumb. In February 1816 he fell ill and was made to take medicine without much success, for he noted at the end of the month: 'Broke off this journal, having been seized with a violent bout of dysentery, which left me at death's door in the middle of March.' Hardly had he recovered when he met the Emperor, who asked with his usual brusqueness, and under the circumstances rather cruelly, why he was so depressed. Gourgaud replied that in fact he was feeling extremely ill, whereupon Napoleon shrugged his shoulders and admitted that he was unwell himself and tormented by pains in his intestines. 'Damned country!' he said, cutting short these disagreeable details. A little later, when the Emperor himself had been seized with violent attacks of colic, Gourgaud noted: 'There is a great deal of illness in the camp. Several soldiers have died. If only Hudson Lowe died it might have a good effect; instead we have this mortality among the rabble.' And in May it was Bertrand's turn to be seized with pain after a meal, and in October it was the Countess. In 1819 Marchand fell seriously ill with symptoms reminiscent of Cipriani's death: 'I was busy making some designs for embroidery at the request of the ladies, when I was seized with appalling colic and took to my bed.' He stayed there for three weeks under the usual treatment: mercury pills, which loosened his teeth and blistered his mouth. These famous blue pills were used as a providential panacea in the British Army during the nineteenth century, and probably owed their reputation to their effect on syphilis; they were made of mercury, honey, sugar and pulverised red roses. The Longwood party consumed them in great quantities.

Two doctors—O'Meara and Antommarchi—often commented on the sanitation of the island, and came to the same conclusions. They had the free run of the hospitals and had lived at Longwood three years and eighteen months respectively, a fact which lends a certain weight to their observations. After expanding the theme of the bad climate of the rock, O'Meara adds: 'It would thus appear that St. Helena, in addition to the general cause of insalubrity to Europeans ... has also local and peculiar causes for being particularly unhealthy, as the great mortality amply proves. The most trifling cold or irregularity is frequently succeeded by a violent attack of dysentery, inflammation of the bowels or fever proving fatal in a few days, if the most active and efficacious practice is not instantly followed. ... Dysenteries especially, and liver affections (which are indeed frequently combined) appear with the most concentrated and fatal symptoms, baffling the prompt exhibition of the most active and powerful remedies. .... Until the arrival of the State prisoner, very few Europeans resided for a continuance upon the island; and I can assert, from personal observations, that the greatest number of those now there, even of the officers, have suffered attacks more or less severe, either of dysentery or hepatitis, in which number I regret to say I was myself included; and that the opinion of the medical officers, who had the best opportunity of forming a correct opinion from actual experience of the island, is *that the climate is extremely unhealthy;* and especially that hepatitis and dysentery prevail to an extent and with a severity seldom to be paralleled.' And the Irishman goes on to refer to a thesis by Dr. Leigh, medical officer to the 66th regiment, based on his personal observations: *Medical dissertation on hepatitis and dysentery in St. Helena.*

Writing in 1819, Dr. Antommarchi was just as categorical and precise: 'I have found acute or chronic dysentery and hepatitis everywhere: no one escapes the effect of the climate.'

What was the nature of this disease that decimated the forces, attacked all Europeans and inspired an army doctor's thesis? Amoebic dysentery has been suggested—a terrible illness frequently complicated by abscess of the liver and prevalent in Africa and the Orient. It is an acceptable hypothesis in view of the fact that most of the 66th regiment had taken part in the Indian campaign, and that the five hundred Chinese employed by the Company were natives of a country where amoebic dysentery was endemic. Add to this that it can be transmitted, and the fact that the carrier micro-organism is extremely resistant, and it is easy to imagine thousands of possible sources of contamination: spring water polluted by infiltration, filth thrown into open irrigation canals, watering of vegetables, preparation of food. It is interesting to notice here that although amoebic dysentery has disappeared from St. Helena, the island still has a bad reputation for intestinal affections, and although the natives seem to have acquired immunity, Europeans often develop them.

These material conditions did not help to make the troops contented with their lot; nor did the oppressive restrictions enliven their spirits. The serving soldier could expect little satisfaction: strict severity was the rule among the officers and the slightest lapse on the part of subordinates was punished inflexibly. The worst off of all the troops were those in Deadwood camp charged with keeping guard on Longwood; more and more pickets were set up, often in places exposed to inclement weather. Their situation was tolerable by day, but during winter nights it was quite another matter. When the rain lashed the roads, forced its way through the branches of trees and flooded corners where a man might try to shelter, woe betide anyone who sought for a dry place in the deceptive darkness; he might be found one morning lying crushed or dead of starvation at the foot of a precipice. There were other problems by day: what the prisoners of State were allowed to do today might be forbidden tomorrow, boundaries laid down in the morning might be altered by evening, and the password could be somewhat mangled as it descended the hierarchic ladder from the Governor to a minor official. People understood each other with difficulty or not at all and one day a sentry fired on Napoleon and his party when they were out riding; another soldier took it upon himself to isolate the Grand Marshal's house and forbid him to communicate with anyone. When something of this sort happened, the unfortunate man concerned became involved in terrible scenes. Sent for by the Governor, he tremblingly penetrated the temple of power by the back door and was dragged before Hudson Lowe. Major Gorrequer used to sit in a corner taking notes of the evidence, and he has described for us how his chief excelled at the art of producing 'spontaneous confessions': the soldier withdrew after signing the declaration carefully prepared beforehand at Plantation House, ruing the day he had been marked out for the commander-in-chief's severity!

✤   ✤   ✤

It is impossible to speak of sailors and soldiers without adding a few words about women and drink, especially when the troops in question were stationed or billeted at St. Helena, where illicit unions were easily formed and brandy and beer flowed like water. The island had a well-founded reputation for sexual licence, and some writers have described it as the 'inn of the ocean', while others have replaced the word 'inn' by 'brothel'. It was certainly conveniently placed on that long, wearisome sea-voyage from Europe to Africa, and everyone who came on shore had passed through exhausting trials—the heat of the Equator or the storms of the Cape. Both sailors and passengers were eager to forget these unpleasant experiences and disembark on this hospitable rock, and during the era of sailing-ships a liaison with a sailor opened a dazzling prospect for a St. Helena girl, of life in Europe and a final good-bye to the boredom of her little community. There were no mercenary complications in these relationships: these were only introduced with the arrival of the troops in 1815.

This facile commerce naturally delighted unmarried privates and officers alike, not to mention the domestic staff at Longwood. Meanwhile married couples set the social tone, and Napoleon was often irritated to see 'protruding bellies' around him. The stern Hudson Lowe showed the same sacrificial ardour: married at forty-six— Napoleon was the same age, but declared that he was an old man and that the ladies need have no fear of him, for he could no longer hope 'to woo them successfully'—he lost no time in giving Lady Lowe children, though she was no longer in her first youth and far from delighted at the prospect of motherhood. Gorrequer reports: 'She says that she would never had married again if she had thought she would have got pickaninnies from a second husband'.* However, they were to have a girl and two boys, one of whom died soon after Napoleon in 1821. Madame Bertrand had five or six miscarriages both before and after the birth of young Arthur, and it was Madame de Montholon who so often had 'a protruding belly'; her daughter Napoléone was born at Longwood in 1817 and lived until 1907—the last of the 'witnesses from St. Helena'.

The Longwood bachelors, whether masters or servants, had a great many affairs with women, naturally involving some jealous quarrels; but the man who was watched and spied upon by everyone —Napoleon—preserved an imperial indifference to the surrounding licentiousness, born of too much leisure and laxity in morals. 'Some men of forty-eight still behave like young men,' purred Madame de Montholon, coquettishly making a bid for favour. 'Yes,' replied Napoleon, 'but they have not had so many sorrows to bear as I have.' The excuse was not entirely genuine: it was only in 1817, in the course of conversation with the Grand Marshal, that he let the cat out of the bag: 'It might get into the gazettes and do me some harm.' A little later, when he discovered that his valet Marchand was having an affair with a mulatto woman called Esther Vesey, daughter of an English sergeant, he ordered him to send her away, adding very convincingly that it would certainly be said in Europe that Esther's child was an imperial bastard, and had been attributed to his faithful valet according to court custom.

Faced with Europe's determination to forget, degrade and humiliate him, and the suppression of his name from official documents by the Austrian reigning house, he felt bound to maintain and affirm the Christian bond linking him to the proudest and most illustrious royal family in the world. Marie-Louise's dissolute way of life was not unknown to him, but it was of little importance beside the fact that she was before God and men, and according to protocol, the Empress, his wife and the mother of the King of Rome; he never failed to emphasise the fact in conversation when necessary. It was an effective way of affirming his son's position, his descent from two imperial houses and his rights of succession, and also of drawing attention to a relationship that embarrassed all the courts of Europe

*Major Gorrequer's Papers (unpublished).

and gave weight to what the English described as 'Bonaparte's mania to play the Emperor'. If Marie-Louise was still 'Her Majesty' according to the language of custom and court precedence, who could her husband be except 'His Majesty the Emperor and King'? To support this thesis and secure the rights of his little son, he expressed this constant concern in his will, by declaring quite near the beginning: 'I have always had reason to be pleased with my very dear wife Marie-Louise, and I retain the most tender sentiments for her to my last moments; I beg her to guard my son from the snares which surround him in his infancy.' This sentence had unfortunately been made all the more necessary by the fact that the young and blooming Empress had already given birth to two bastards by her lover General Neipperg, in 1817 and 1819, and when these lines of the will glorifying her for ever reached her ears she was already in labour of a third child.

If the Emperor had had a liaison while on St. Helena, preferably with a negress, it would have diverted the courts of Europe and provided material for the gazettes; the English, too, were comically eager to collect rumours and official gossip, among which that rare flower the truth might perhaps be hidden. One day, in the course of a lively argument with Hudson Lowe, Napoleon complained of the strict system of vigilance, and of sentinels popping up behind every bush; if he had a mistress he would not be able to receive her.

'But haven't you got one?' replied the Governor, both horrified and interested.

'I might have one,' retorted the Emperor in a bantering tone.

'Oh, I shall inform my government.'

This abrupt reply—a rude and involuntary reaction—clearly proves that Napoleon had broached a subject considered of importance by the British government; caricaturists would certainly have found a splendid theme in Napoleon at the feet of a slut. And what a godsend for the Viennese court! Knowing of the Vatican's refusal to recognise Josephine's divorce, and insistence that Marie-Louise's marriage was invalid, Vienna had been profoundly shaken by the death of the first Empress in June 1814, and the Pope's consequent offer to confirm the second marriage. The Emperor Francis and Metternich both refused to hear of it. As for Marie-Louise, if Méneval, Napoleon's ex-secretary, is to be believed: 'she swore that

she would not agree to a divorce, but she felt sure that he would consent to a friendly separation, and such a separation had now become
necessary'. The move from Rome was therefore extremely inopportune and had found the weak spot in their defences; even perhaps
such a great pope as Pius VII had a secret desire to remind the ex-
Empress and the daughter of the Austrian emperor of her duties as a
wife, mother and Christian. The Habsburg court were unable to get
out of the predicament caused by tangible proofs of adultery, and
there was a good deal of logic in the notion that any liaison of Napoleon's—as scandalous as possible—would have been grist to the
Austrian mill. Metternich could count on his English friends,
Castlereagh and Bathurst: they would do all they could to help. In
1819, Dr. Baxter, chief medical officer at St. Helena for three years,
returned to England, and at once received a note from Lord Bathurst
summoning him to the Colonial Office:

'On entering the room His Lordship came up to me and took me by the
hand familiarly, desiring me to be seated. His first question was how Bonaparte was. I said that as far as could be ascertained he was well at least. He
asked whether he went out or took any exercise. I replied that he had been
out in the evenings lately and that it was believed he took a great deal of
exercise in the billiard-room. He was anxious to know whether Bonaparte
had access to women and whether it was thought Mesdames Bertrand and
Montholon were condescending. I said I was not aware that anything of
the kind took place, but it was not unlikely that either of these ladies would
feel proud of any attention he might pay to them.'*

The stupid insinuations made by Gourgaud and Balmain, and
repeated by Montchenu and Stürmer, led to the Emperor's being
credited with a great many strange love-affairs: first of all there was
young Betsy Balcombe, a girl of fifteen; next the 'Nymph of the
Valley', the Miss Robinson who lived near Longwood with her
father; then 'the Rosebud', an English beauty who pursued Gourgaud; and finally Madame Bertrand and Madame de Montholon.
Gourgaud hated everything which took the Emperor away from his
daily commerce with his generals, and he filled his diary and his
conversation with invective. 'What right have you to complain of
Madame de Montholon visiting me?' said Napoleon furiously. 'You
said the other day that every Jack had his Jill . . . did you mean

*Lowe Papers.

Madame de Montholon?' But it was impossible to stem the torrent of the aide-de-camp's outpourings; he made such a to-do and stirred up so much mud that Napoleon blamed the mercury pills 'for having gone to his head'. The flood continued, however: 'La Montholon does her best to seem to dote on His Majesty: melting eyes, feet well to the fore, dress tightly nipped in at the waist, in fact she is trying to act the beauty—and that isn't easy.' And another day: 'While I am at St. Helena I will never consent to give precedence to M. de Montholon and even less to his wife. She can be a whore if she wants to, but I despise a man who lets himself be forcibly overborne by a woman, particularly a scheming, ugly one.' A few days later he noted sarcastically: 'His Majesty gives a friendly welcome to La Montholon, and pinches her. . . .'. These scandalous accusations were the point of departure for a furious quarrel between Gourgaud and Montholon, and afterwards between Gourgaud and the Emperor himself, when he tried to prevent a duel between the two generals.

Balmain's witticisms, designed to entertain the Tsar at the expense of the man who had once caused terror on the banks of the Neva, were even more crude and cruel: 'Madame de Montholon, old, dissipated and ugly though she is, is now the great man's mistress. She used to be merely his confidante and bring members of the fair sex to the imperial bed. By dint of taking trouble, persistence and simpering ways she managed to get there herself, and acquitted herself very well in her new situation. He is crazy about her, and gives her presents of dresses, jewels and other toilet accessories. Luncheon, dinner, getting up and going to bed all take place at whatever time she pleases. In fact the whole of Longwood is at her disposal.' Unfortunately for Balmain, this dispatch is dated March 16, 1818, and on March 14 Gourgaud had left St. Helena furiously angry and morbidly jealous of those who remained at their post beside the Emperor. The close agreement between the dates suggests a rapprochement, and it seems plain that since Balmain had no personal contacts with Napoleon's companions, and was therefore incapable of obtaining such detailed information, he had heard them from the aide-de-camp in person. Gourgaud must have relieved his feelings before he embarked, nor was he afraid of overdoing it later when he told the British ministers in London that the Emperor had a great many possible means of escape up his sleeve, that he was in regular correspondence with Europe and had vast secret funds at his disposal. His hatred of Montholon so blinded this brave soldier that he caused great distress to his late master by these erroneous statements, which induced the British to tighten the net round the prisoners of Longwood House. If we want to excuse his behaviour, we must think indulgently of the case of a young, active and courageous man, suddenly shut away in a tiny island, treated with disdain by the British, and supplanted in the Emperor's intimacy by practised courtiers. When he was removed from his military setting, this boisterous soldier, a man made all in one piece, became tiresomely demanding and wildly unstable. The dossier for the defence must also take account of the repression he had been subjected to during three years of exile: Gourgaud could not see a girl go by without staring at her and feeling violent desire for her; but such beauties as St. Helena could boast of hardly looked at this penniless exiled general, who was without prospects, a good talker, certainly, but rather too exuberant and unversed in the reserved ways of the English. His passion for Governor Wilks's daughter was only rewarded by a few pale smiles, and another English girl, Miss Churchill, who made a short stay on the island, was hardly more encouraging. The snobbishness of other women might have been gratified by his title of Baron, even of Baron of the Empire, but they probably changed their minds when they heard the dignified Mrs. Skelton, wife of the Lieutenant-Governor, tell the Frenchman: 'Your position here is so appalling!' So he had to fall back on less refined pleasures, and Gourgaud's journal is full of very crude references to his sexual adventures of one night only: 'I asked in the town for a negress . . . I picked up a pretty mulatto girl . . . I got a woman from the town to come here, went to bed with her and gave her six pounds . . . I met a pretty slave girl, asked her to come and see me and she said yes.' Even the austere Las Cases, who shared a small room with his son, was not afraid to make advances to coloured women. As for the servants, their love-affairs were innumerable, some legal, others temporary. Noverraz the Swiss married Josephine, Madame de Montholon's maid, and Ali Miss Mary Hall, governess to the Bertrand children; Archambault lived with a certain Mary Foss, and the gentle loyal valet Marchand had a child by Esther Vesey, a mulattress who had access to Longwood. The young Elban

Gentilini, seems to have been granted the favours of several soldiers' wives, and Gorrequer made a note of some of the edifying details: 'Gentilini is allowed to go to Wynyard's old abode for the avowed purpose of fornicating with Mrs. Snell, living there with her husband ... and the ladies frequenting the same on Sundays.'* This Mrs. Snell often visited Longwood, bringing her little girl: Napoleon sometimes played with the child, while the mother. ...

No chronicles have glorified the amorous adventures of the British soldiers and sailors employed at Longwood, but it would be an insult to their youthful virility to suppose that they remained aloof from such unions. At all events, the comings and goings were so noisy that the Montholons complained to Lowe, and sentries were doubled round the house, to the rage of Napoleon who angrily asked them: 'You say that whores are being brought in; if that is a scandal you could easily prevent it without calling in the English. You don't suppose this house is a convent?' It was all very well for him to talk: the attics above his room housed only the discreet Marchand and Ali; the Montholons were in the other part of the house and the wooden ceilings of their rooms were poor protection for their privacy!

These liaisons went on throughout the time of exile; and except for Noverraz and Ali, who took their wives to Europe, the others had mistresses of an extremely temporary sort. Marchand was the only one who took an interest in his son by his mistress, James Octave Vesey; before leaving the island in 1820 he deposited the round sum of £500 with an agent to provide for the child's keep. By a curious coincidence this money was profitably used to raise a mortgage on Alarm House, the home of Sir Thomas Reade. Young James Octave was rumoured to have been expelled from the island in 1840 for bad behaviour, just when his father was due to return with Napoleon's remains, and this unusual procedure in a British colony where birth gave the right of residence may have nourished the rumour about Napoleon's possible paternity. ...

At Plantation House love-affairs abounded, and officers, servants, corporals and sergeants all found their secrets quickly laid bare: they were living in a glass-house in an island of rumours. Major Gorrequer referred prudishly in his journals to an 'acquaintance', whom Lady Lowe refused to acknowledge at the races; since the young

*Major Gorrequer's Papers (unpublished).

woman was allowed into the enclosure, and the possibility of an introduction even arose, it follows that she must have been white, but we shall never know her name. The young major shows a weakness for laundresses, and Lady Lowe, who disliked hearing anything about the ancillary love-affairs that went on under her roof, kept a stern watch on the door, on the major and the attractive women servants. If Gorrequer is to be believed, the Governor's wife was extremely prudish and would not tolerate the slightest impropriety, even in conversation, which was carefully censored when she was present. But he tells us that this did not prevent some of the soldiers disporting themselves shamelessly with the negresses employed at Plantation House.

Admiral Plampin's disreputable situation was a public scandal, but for one officer thus publicly scorning the sacrament of marriage, a great many others happily carried on illegitimate affairs in secrecy. They had to defeat the curiosity of their spiteful companions, however—no easy matter, and one implying great discretion, the complicity of servants, and hypocrisy. One interesting adventure delighted the malicious: it has been curiously distorted by the historians who have confused Captain Piontkovski, a Polish officer in the Emperor's suite, with Captain Poppleton, one of the British orderly officers at Longwood. It was much like the affairs that come before French provisional courts. One fine morning in 1816, Lieutenant Nagle of the 53rd regiment issued a writ in his wife's name before the supreme court of St. Helena against Catherine Younghusband, wife of a captain in the same regiment. The documents set before the judges, Sir Hudson Lowe, Thomas Brooke and Sir George Bingham, were not without piquancy. Nagle accused Mrs. Younghusband of having passed on to the Balcombes and spread all over Deadwood camp the defamatory rumour that young Mrs. Nagle had been discovered by her husband in Captain Poppleton's room at Longwood at one o'clock in the morning. It was also alleged that a violent quarrel broke out between the husband and the lover, but that on the following day calm was restored, when Poppleton sent the deceived husband three deliciously spiced hams, which the island gossips immediately christened 'the hams of compensation'. Nagle presented his own case, and affirmed that Poppleton was an old and faithful friend of his family, and that since his duties often kept him

(Lieutenant Nagle) away from home, it was with his consent that his young wife spent the hours of waiting at Longwood with the orderly officer. Numerous witnesses were called but all were reticent; from the colonel commanding the regiment to young Betsy Balcombe, from Dr. O'Meara to the Captain's batman. A great deal of mud was stirred up by the attempt to disguise this very ordinary adventure, and preserve the officer's dignity and the reputation of the regiment. For failing in her duties as an Englishwoman and forcing a couple of whites to undergo the infamy of a trial, Catherine Younghusband was condemned to a fine of £250. The warning was taken to heart, and after 1816 the court never again had to concern itself with conjugal misfortunes.

THE DAILY LIFE OF THE INHABITANTS

Between the two groups in uniform, the army and the navy, the position of civilians was an unenviable one. They had in fact to manœuvre with the soldiers and alter course with the sailors: the former had control of promotion, funds and police, the latter the inestimable monopoly of communication with the free world. One can imagine what arrivals and departures of ships between St. Helena, the Cape and London must have meant to this isolated, poorly supplied colony, and what quantities of food and feminine fallals—from rose-water and bear's grease to Chinese fans—not to mention private correspondence, travelled in sea-chests and so escaped the censorship and slipped through the iron curtain Sir Hudson had stretched all round the rock.

The happiness or otherwise of the inhabitants under the new administration depended on the group they belonged to and the jobs they occupied; the daily existence of them all was upset, although of course these few whites, Africans and Asiatics thrown together on this desolate rock were divided into cliques corresponding to their social standing and the colour of their skins.

First there were the 'big' Whites, senior officials of the East India Company; then their subordinates, the 'small' Whites with whom they were on friendly terms and frequently intermarried. Circling round these were the officers of the St. Helena regiments: a handful of idle Englishmen, who were disinclined to face the foggy climate of Albion after their long service in the East, had put their rather rusty swords at the disposal of the Company, and ruled over the six hundred men making up the island's infantry and artillery. The members of the St. Helena militia, a body of volunteers recruited from the least privileged classes, rubbed along at a much humbler level. When Hudson Lowe arrived in May 1816, he reorganised this body in such a way as to make his radius of investigation embrace every house in the island; to increase the effectiveness of the militia he authorised each man to obtain from Company supplies one pound of salt meat a week at fourpence a pound, and three cottage loaves at fourpence each. This was hardly fare to sustain future field-marshals, and the militia does not seem to have distinguished itself either by its zeal or efficiency.

✦   ✦   ✦

The first group, the 'big' Whites, took a more active part in the daily life of the island: its members were in a position to defend their interests with a certain flexibility, and press forward into the front line. They were the descendants of English who had settled there during the last two hundred years, and as their families increased they schemed to acquire the most important posts for them. If the father-in-law was a judge, his son-in-law would be sheriff; when the elder brother was an apothecary, the younger would be a chemist, and if one daughter married a councillor, her elder sister would throw herself into the arms of the commanding officer of the St. Helena regiment. To prevent the island becoming too much of a family business, the Company adopted an immutable principle of entrusting the supreme position in the government to a retired Indian army officer, who presided in easy-going fashion over this handful of cousin-officials. Such was Governor Wilks, who was deprived of a comfortable sinecure by Napoleon's arrival in 1815 after passing many pleasant hours at Plantation House, embellishing the theme of his experiences in India in the chapters of an interesting book on that country. For the matters to be discussed in the Council and decided upon by the Governor were few and unimportant: the flogging of a slave, the imprisonment of a drunkard, the upkeep of buildings, agriculture and the pests it was subject to, and the very urgent question of supplies for the colony. The Company had never considered St. Helena as a 'paying proposition', but merely as a port of call on the way to the East; there had not therefore been any question of appointing an enterprising governor, a young, active or ambitious man, who might with small effort and expense have altered the fate of the whole community.

Napoleon's arrival, and the administrative changes that followed, created a violent upheaval in this pleasant creole society, sunk in idleness, used to short working hours relieved by gossip round the tea-table or glasses of brandy, living in large houses, with plenty of cheap servants. Of course they were disturbed by the French invasion. This little general in his cheap overcoat was going to be the cause of a great many inconveniences, the worst being the loss of the absolute power that had hitherto belonged to a few families and had rendered their existence in mid-Atlantic perfectly bearable.

These large landowners possessed the best houses: the Dovetons were at Mount Pleasant, the Hodsons at Maldivia House, the Brookes at Prospect House and more Brookes at Oaklands; these were all fine Georgian houses with tall airy rooms full of valuable well-kept furniture, and in the evenings the élite gathered there to exchange gossip and small talk. What comments and exclamations over glasses of punch were provoked by the landing of His Majesty's troops and its consequences in the form of requisitions, restrictions, decrees, passwords and curfew! All were eager to offer their services to the new Governor; it was important to keep their jobs, and profit from any advantages created by this unexpected situation. Sir William Doveton remained a member of the Council in the capacity of treasurer and paymaster; so did Robert Leech, accountant, Thomas Brooke, secretary, and Thomas Greentree, chief storekeeper. And it is not surprising to discover that Doveton had married his daughter to Greentree, that Brooke's wife had been Miss Wright, daughter of the colonel of the St. Helena regiment, that Leech's sister was married to the assistant secretary, and finally that these same men, Doveton, Leech, Brooke and Greentree, were judges and magistrates, and Doveton's son-in-law, Major Hodson, was advocate-general. Firmly entrenched in their posts, with an intimate knowledge of the country and its drawbacks, these large clans had free access to Hudson Lowe (who was not at all reluctant to leave the burden of civilian affairs to them) and received comfortable salaries of from £1,000 to £1,400 a year. It meant also that they were well placed on the lists of precedence drawn up by the aide-de-camp at Plantation House, so that they ranked before the colonels, in fact immediately after the Governor, the Admiral and the general in command of the army. When houses were requisitioned, the owners did well: Montchenu and Balmain mention having to pay the exorbitant rent of £400 a year.

The names of some of these colonists are linked with the Emperor's exile: particularly that of Doveton, whom Napoleon and his suite visited at Mount Pleasant in 1816 and 1820. The old man was knighted by the King in 1817, and had abandoned his official duties owing to his advanced age—he was nearly seventy—and retired to his house at Sandy Bay. He enjoyed a pension of £800 from the Company and was deeply conscious of his position as local patriarch. He might have been expected to be a dignified figure in the classic tradition of the English landed aristocracy—but alas the long time he had spent out of touch with current opinion had made Sir William somewhat simple-minded. He had made the journey to London to receive the accolade from the King, and spiteful gossips made fun of his artlessness. Had he not been so surprised by the London traffic that when he got out of the post-chaise he imagined a procession must be going on? His meeting with Napoleon produced comments of the same sort. The Emperor took his last outing on an October morning in 1820. Leaving Longwood by the gate where the sentries presented arms, he set off towards Sandy Bay, the place he had chosen for a picnic. The road was cut into the side of the mountain and wound its way towards the fertile, enchanted fairyland of Doveton's estate. Enormous ferns decorated the lower spurs of the chain running down from Diana's Peak, and the track was bordered by cabbage-trees, set on fire here and there by red patches of canna and the yellow of ginger plants. At Rock Rose Cottage, where Colonel Wynyard lived, there was a sudden blaze of camellias in flower, rippling against the vast blue tapestry of the sea. When they reached the gate of Doveton's property, Montholon went ahead to warn the old man of his august visitor's approach and ask permission to cross his land. The owner of Mount Pleasant added a personal impression to his report to the Governor: 'On reconnoitring them with my spy-glass, I perceived that they were the party from

Longwood. Count Montholon dismounted from his horse, and I went to the door to receive him; the Count informed me that the Emperor presented his compliments and requested he might come and rest himself.' He assured Montholon that his property was at the disposal of the riders: Bertrand and four servants were following a little way behind, and the party now dismounted in front of the steps of the house. Napoleon sat down on a sofa, invited Mrs. Greentree to sit on his right, complimented her on the healthy appearance of her children, and teased her about her husband's intemperance. She was extremely annoyed and replied shortly that she had not seen her husband drunk for at least a year. Breakfast was laid on the lawn under the great oak-trees, in front of a colourful and sparkling view: on the left was the green barrier of the mountains, in the centre the vast reddish crater of Sandy Bay with its pillars of rock, on the right the limitless horizon of the ocean, and everywhere myriads of brilliant tropical flowers—hibiscus, camellias, purple amaryllis, moon-lilies, crimson bougainvilleas. The Emperor's servants poured out champagne, while Sir William contributed one of those terrible home-brewed liqueurs, a species of rot-gut made of fruit fermented in alcohol. The meal provided by the Frenchmen seemed abundant to the islanders, though not to English taste: 'cold pie, potted meat, cold turkey, curried fowl. A ham, or pork, I could not tell which; coffee, dates, almonds, oranges, and a very fine salad.' As for Napoleon, the brave commanding officer of the St. Helena militia (as Doveton still was) found him 'as fat and round as a China pig'.

If he had not been so near his end and already feeling extremely ill (he flung himself into bed as soon as he got back to Longwood), Napoleon would perhaps have enjoyed the colonial atmosphere so reminiscent of *Paul and Virginia*, the innocence of the kindly old man, the health and beauty of the children, and the peace of the woods. But alas! it was a painful effort to hoist himself into the saddle after saying good-bye to his hosts for the day. Arrived at Hutt's Gate, half-way to Longwood, he dismounted and threw himself into his waiting carriage, and with eyes closed let himself be driven to the door of his house.

Another of Doveton's daughters was married to Major Hodson, who filled the post of advocate-general as well as being one of the officers of the garrison. He lived at Maldivia, an enchanting house buried in the valley between The Briars and Jamestown; its cool garden was shaded with cedars and rare conifers, and was watered by a little stream. One evening in November 1816, while the officers of his suite were getting ready for the Admiral's ball, Napoleon left the pavilion at The Briars for a walk with Las Cases. Seeing through his field-glasses this well-kept house surrounded by flowers and an impeccably cared-for garden, he descended the little path leading from the pavilion into Jamestown valley: it was a difficult track—Las Cases could hardly keep up with him—and the two visitors arrived panting at the door of Maldivia. The major and his wife did the honours of the house, and then of the garden, now lit by the diffuse rays of the setting sun. Napoleon remained there, paying them compliments, until the descent of darkness (always brutally sudden in the tropics) made their return by the path impossible, and the two men rode back to The Briars on Hodson's horses. The Emperor had taken an instantaneous liking to this six-foot-tall giant, whom he nicknamed Hercules; perhaps something about him reminded him hazily of the figures, bearing and eagerness of the young officers who had waited on him in his palaces in Europe or in camp—aides-de-camp, chamberlains or couriers. As a reward for their hospitality, the Hodsons were to have the special honour of being the only islanders to be invited to dine with the Emperor at Longwood. Of course the Balcombes were sometimes present, but they could hardly be counted among the 'yamstocks', as they had only been living in the island for eight years and were obviously still imbued with the European way of life and thought. They were very different from the simple-minded islanders who so greatly amused the Emperor. An affected lady asked one evening whether 'London and its streets were not rather melancholy since the departure of the Chinese fleet, like Jamestown after a schooner had got under way?' On another occasion, at an evening party at the Balcombes, a conversation was in progress about the latest novels, particularly Madame Cottin's *Mathilde*, when a fat Englishman with a moon face who was listening with all his ears, asked where Mathilde lived. 'Why, monsieur,' Napoleon replied calmly, 'she is dead and buried.' The *vacuum plenum*, as Las Cases called him, was on the verge of tears.

✤   ✤   ✤

The officers of the St. Helena regiments were natural allies of the great landowners: together they formed an opposition to the new order, but since the intruders could not be thrown back into the sea, they did their best by smiles and amiability to get on good terms with them and make up for their own humiliating loss of prestige. For beside the regulars on active service on His Majesty's behalf, the mercenaries of the East India Company made a rather drab impression. Whether they had been recruited from among retired members of the Indian army, or forces from the Cape, or families resident in St. Helena for the last century, these colonels, majors and captains did not shine in comparison with the regular soldiers covered in glory and decorations, veterans of the Napoleonic campaigns and others, who from now on controlled the fate of the colony. What a bitter blow for the old stagers—two colonels, two majors, thirteen captains, twenty lieutenants and eight sub-lieutenants—to be suddenly snatched from their peaceful rural life, put through their paces by the newcomers, forced to carry out fatigues they had hoped were forgotten, and often treated in an off-hand manner into the bargain! When a little difference arose between one of his officers, Major Powers, and some hefty artillery-man of the Company's regiments, Hudson Lowe flew into a rage: 'He wished he had known Major Powers was coming out before he left England. He would have got him the rank that he might have had the command of the whole bastards.'* What a shock for these harmless musical-comedy officers, who had gradually moved away from military to police functions, and then to the more restful and remunerative occupations of agriculture and stock-breeding. In 1815 poor Colonel Wright of the infantry and poor Colonel Smith of the artillery had been leading uneventful lives as rich landowners at Rural Retreat and Farm Lodge respectively! Bertrand was amazed when he had a look at Smith's property one day: 'He has twenty bullocks, sixty sheep and twenty-five slaves. He planted all the trees himself twenty-five years ago and is his own gardener. He has the best kitchen-garden on the island.'

The 'big' Whites and the officers of the Company's regiments had been solidly united by intermarriage, and those who gave orders found themselves sitting at the family dining-table with those who

*Major Gorrequer's Papers (unpublished).

carried them out, after the day's work was over. This explains the Creoles' extraordinary taste for gossip, criticism and back-biting: in the absence of a local newspaper or any contact with the outside world, all items of news concerning their professional life were discussed, interpreted and repeated indefinitely with innumerable variations, after first having been revealed to the home circle. In such conditions military discipline was lax, and an officer of the St. Helena regiment had to prove himself extremely incapable, intolerant or lazy for the Governor's thunderbolts to strike him. Something of this sort, however, brought Lieutenant William Fuller into the limelight in October 1815: he appeared before the Governor on the 17th and the result of his judgement is entered on the same page and in the same handwriting as the arrival of General Napoleon Bonaparte and certain other persons as prisoners of State. Fuller was placed under arrest for having been found in a shamefully drunken condition lying on the road to the fort, just after the general alarm had been sounded, and for having displayed insubordination and conduct unworthy of an officer while detained, as well as showing an intellectual standard incompatible with carrying out an officer's duties.

If the irruption of the regular army was a nuisance to most of that peaceable population, it was profitable to the staff of the East India Company, who were pleased to hear of an unexpected measure issued by the British military authorities: 'The Prince Regent has been pleased in the name and on behalf of His Majesty to approve of all the military officers of the Company's service on the Establishment of St. Helena receiving corresponding commissions from His Highness, with local rank on the Island of St. Helena.' A captain in His Majesty's army was now of equal rank with a captain in the Company's forces, and the Creole Onesiphorus Beale could hold his head as high as any English Marmaduke.

The officers of the Company had few contacts with the French party at Longwood on the whole, with the exception of Major Hodson, or 'Hercules', who was received with pleasure by the Emperor and figured on Madame Bertrand's list of guests. There was one of them, however, who was made welcome at Plantation House, for Sir Hudson, probably anxious to spy out the land among the chief local families, took as his assistant aide-de-camp Lieutenant Den Taafe, whose name was altered by Gorrequer to Damn Tuff, or Yam.

He must have been a handsome young man, for he attracted and held the languid interest of Lady Lowe, but with his Creole languor and a certain lack of polish (he 'puffed like a whale when eating'), he remained somewhat in the background, and seems to have been employed at Plantation House mainly as a red rag waved about by the Lowes to infuriate Major Gorrequer. The name of a certain Captain Bennet was also associated with the Emperor's at the time of the funeral in Geranium Valley. When the officers at Longwood asked for some mahogany to make the outer shell for the imperial coffin, they were told that this tree did not grow on the island and there was no means of supplying the wood required; Bennet then remembered a large dining-table in his possession and offered it to the carpenters. So that it is in mahogany from the dining-table of an officer of the St. Helena regiment that the Emperor now rests under the dome of the Invalides.

The relations of the regular army with this private force were never close or friendly, in spite of the equalisation of rank. The diary of Mrs. Shortt, wife of the doctor who succeeded Baxter at the head of the colony's medical department, gives us valuable evidence and much gossip about the social life of the officers. She rarely describes any evenings passed with the islanders, and when they occurred the arrangements were strange. 'Dined with the Admiral. A very pleasant party. Some of the native ladies came to tea and we danced afterwards.'

✤   ✤   ✤

The group of 'small' Whites melts into the shadows. This handful of minor officials of the Company, waiting in deadly idleness for a chance of bettering themselves whenever the occupants of more desirable posts should grow old or disappear, were relegated to an even lower grade when the intruders arrived in 1815. Descendants of the English, who had lived in the island since the last century, the Fountains, Kays, Seales, Porteous, Brabazons and Brodways had taken firm root and intermarried, and bore the picturesque titles of chief merchant, scribe, public auctioneer or harbour-master. In 1815 they had been influential subordinates sure of succeeding to the Dovetons, Greentrees or Brookes, many of whom were their relations, and they were chagrined to see this wave of soldiers and civilians invading the governmental machine and reducing them to the humble rank of employees.

The 'big' Whites were often in the Governor's company, but these less important families were only included in public and official life, and invited to the receptions that were the *ne plus ultra* of social life on some very special occasion, such as a ball given by the Governor on the Prince Regent's birthday. Oh that birthday celebration! What excitement it caused! It was held on August 12, and from the banks of the Thames to the furthest British outpost the colourful display went on. From the firing of salvoes at dawn until the time when fireworks exploded in the dark night sky, there was general rejoicing on behalf of His Royal Highness, who, bewigged, covered in medals and flattered by a group of courtiers, had not even the courage to show himself to the London public. The man derisively described by Lamb as 'the prince of Whales' had become a mere target for writers of pamphlets and epigrams:

> 'Not a fatter fish than he
> Flounders round the polar sea.
> See his blubbers—at his gills
> What a world of drink he swills.'

But what did it matter what sort of individual the monarch or his representative might be? In honour of these two dim figures, the old mad king at Windsor Castle and the buffoon of Carlton House, the rules of British protocol were meticulously respected wherever the Union Jack was flying. These salvoes and balls, held in England's honour even in remote regions of the Empire, did in fact show the prosperity of English trade. And the effect was enhanced when the batteries firing the salute were placed, as at St. Helena, under the windows of Bonaparte himself, whose preposterous figure could be seen silhouetted against Madame Bertrand's blinds. The evening before, the Governor had come to inform 'the general' that the guns would be fired on the following day to celebrate the birthday of His Royal Highness the Prince Regent, and to inquire what would be the response of the French to a possible invitation to the ball at Plantation House in honour of this extremely important event.

Next morning at sunrise the gun was fired and Deadwood camp

was under arms for a parade and review. The Governor arrived tightly encased in his splendid lieutenant-general's uniform, glittering with orders and followed by his staff. Directly he dismounted the band played God Save the King and a review of the troops followed, secretly watched by the Emperor from behind the Bertrand's window-curtains. A motley crowd was watching the spectacle: the 'big' Whites (from the best places), the clergy, 'small' Whites, slaves, shopkeepers and children all admiring the smooth movements, impeccably neat tunics and white belts.

That evening Sir Hudson and Lady Lowe held an official dinner in the Prince Regent's honour at Plantation House. The gilded invitation cards insisted on 'Decorations', and the men were buttoned into their grandest uniforms, while the women were decked in all their finery. They made their way to the dining-room in a procession, two by two, to the music of the regimental band. When dessert was served the Governor proposed His Highness's health and even the Marquis de Montchenu was unable to control his emotion. 'We have been celebrating the Prince Regent's birthday and the Governor entertained about fifty guests to a grand dinner. At the end of dinner he drank the prince's health which was greeted with loud cheers . . . . The health of the King (Louis XVIII) was accompanied by an uproar lasting nearly five minutes during which Henry IV's air was played.'

That night Deadwood camp was lit by innumerable lanterns, and carriages brought guests to the military ball from every corner of the island. When all were assembled, Sir Hudson Lowe arrived, followed by the Admiral and a crowd of officers, but without Lady Lowe; he opened the ball with the Admiral's wife who did the honours in the first lady's absence, and the strong wind that blew over Longwood went on echoing the music until the first light of dawn. Lady Lowe had no liking at all for noisy popular gatherings, and she remained at Plantation House, complaining to Gorrequer about the difficulties of her position: people had no manners, they showed no special politeness nor attentions to the Governor's wife. These mob rejoicings were in fact not very attractive; the general lack of restraint allowed every sort of promiscuity, and for every few agreeable and well-dressed guests one must put up with so much jostling and over-familiarity from people in hideous and shabby clothes! Even the

12

Austrian commissioner, who was no psychologist, was shocked: 'The men were coarse and uneducated, the women foolish and ugly, the people in general poverty-stricken.'

Next day, when the fairy lights had been extinguished and fine clothes put away, the crowds of unimportant people went back to work, some to the sale-rooms, some to the schools, some to their account-books, others to prison, for even the prison superintendent joined his betters on days of jollification. This small fry were as poor as church mice, for what amounted to absolute power was in the hands of a single man. And what a wretched fate for any middle-class Englishman to be deprived of the committees, meetings and parties he was so fond of and which added to his importance! So they hung on as best they could, and while important affairs remained in control of Plantation House, there were still small jobs available. And if the 'Governor in council' was rather too stuck up—Lowe went so far as to tell Gorrequer one day that his post at St. Helena was just as important as that of the Secretary of State for the Colonies—the president of the committee of weights and measures, the inspector of sheep and goats, the parish deacons and subdeacons would not allow their importance to be undervalued. So David Kay, Gabriel Doveton, Robert Leech, John Bagly and John Legg met every year and drew up a list of those inhabitants capable of carrying out the duties of sheriff, member of the church council, magistrate, inspector of sheep and goats and destroyer of worms in cattle! To give a little glamour to their meetings and satisfy their mania for order and detail they drew up long minutes such as the one I now have before me. 'The Committee elected in Vestry on the 13th instant consisting of the following members . . . met this day in conformity to the desire of the governor for the purpose of passing the inhabitants for the performance of the Parish and country duties and having duly considered the subjects are of opinion that the following lists consist of persons qualifying and suitable to execute the office of Sheriff, Church Warden, Constable, Bailiff, Inspector of sheep and goats and Wormer of cattle and that they should serve in the order of succession in which the names are placed. The Committee have made no list of Overseers of the Highways . . . but would recommend that no estate except those that exceed 10 acres should be liable to furnish an overseer. They are also of opinion that the Wormers of cattle should receive a fee of three pence for each worm from the proprietor of those cattle on which the worms may be found and think it advisable that to each person, on entering upon office, an oath should be administered, binding him to the faithful discharge of his duty.'

The near relations of the rich colonists shamelessly grabbed the best of these minor posts, particularly that of sheriff, a sort of municipal magistrate whose functions were vague, but who enjoyed the privilege of appearing at official ceremonies or sessions of the tribunal wearing a chain round his neck. Thus we find the names Fountain, Doveton, Leech and Seale on the list drawn up by the committee of those qualified. Other posts were less coveted, and the names of those entitled to them do not belong to any of the well-known figures of the period from 1815 to 1821. Porteous, in whose house the Emperor spent his first nights of exile at Jamestown, was a member of the church council, as also was Brabazon, the harbour-master; Saul Solomon, the Jewish owner of a shop in the town who supplied the ladies of Longwood and Plantation House with jewels and Chinese trinkets, was honorary rural policeman, while William Balcombe was inspector of sheep and goats. But no well-known name appears on the roll of honour of destroyers of worms in cattle!

This seedy local bourgeoisie, so self-satisfied yet so harsh to their slaves and pliant to those in power, were in fact a class of illiterates. The French were astounded by the gap between their actual condition and their pretensions: Gourgaud, who was enamoured of the Miss Robinson nicknamed 'the Nymph' by the Emperor, went off alone one evening to try his luck with his inamorata. 'Her house is poverty itself. Her father tells me that the Governor is a very good man and that he has harangued the three hundred militiamen and told them that, to show his appreciation of their services, he is going to give them fresh meat six times a year. This man thinks we are very fortunate to have enough to eat. He is a simple rustic.'

✧   ✧   ✧

The key word on the island was 'food'. From top to bottom of the social order, from Sir William Doveton in his estate at Mount Pleasant to the small farmer in Fisher's Valley, all were unanimous in their indignation with the French, who had been guzzling week after week while supplies were critically low. When Napoleon paid his unexpected call on old Doveton and invited him to share his picnic, what astounded the planter was not to find himself accepting hospitality from the most famous general in history, but the sight of the fare. 'The English were scandalised,' we are told by the Count Monthdon, 'to see us breakfasting at that hour on a great variety of cold meats, and—instead of tea—excellent wine and champagne in particular, black coffee and liqueurs.'

Even in less troubled times the food supplies of the island had always been a daily problem: at the present day the gift of a leg of mutton brought by a passing ship is still the making of a housewife's day. 'Bonaparte's arrival doubled the number of mouths to be fed, prevented foreign ships putting in to port and ended competition among suppliers. Everything, even fuel, came to us from England once a year, and the two ships that brought it were more impatiently awaited than the Cadiz galleons of long ago.'* The strict quarantine imposed by Lowe meant that ships were sent away that once used to exchange foodstuffs for a few casks of water; their captains now merely passed within sight of the island to verify their route, and then made off hastily, watched all the way by the boats of the naval station. 'And the famine is serious,' went on the Marquis de Montchenu. 'The Governor himself has been without any beef for the last fortnight, and in the hospitals they are making soup from salt meat. There has not been a single pound of butter to be had for love or money these last two months. Mutton is so scarce that we have to pay three shillings a pound for it. If this lasts I do not know what will become of us, for all the poultry will soon be gone. In spite of our penury, Longwood receives sixty pounds of beef and thirty of mutton every day. But they complain because without butter they cannot have pastry; what is necessary cannot be got, even for its weight in gold.'

The wastefulness that prevailed at Longwood naturally increased the general resentment: all the islanders knew that the British soldiers caroused every evening on wine sold them by Bonaparte's valets, and that the French servants were doing themselves proud. As Gourgaud admitted, 'We cannot possibly be drinking seventeen bottles of wine and eating ninety-eight pounds of meat and nine

*Report made by the Marquis de Montchenu.

chickens a day; that would be to lay ourselves open to attack.' The hot-headed, candid Gourgaud was right, for those of the inhabitants who were going short of everything hated Bonaparte more for eating their sheep and running through all their poultry than for bringing England to her knees by his blockade.

While the French were following Montholon's ill-judged advice and complaining in writing about the poor quality of the provisions supplied to Longwood, the islanders addressed a pathetic petition to the Governor concerning the food shortage. Security regulations established by the Admiral prevented boats going out at night to their usual fishing-grounds; fish had therefore become scarce and expensive. The contractors for the fishing trade, 'big' Whites such as Seale and Greentree, therefore begged the Governor to give permission for going out at night under the supervision of the navy. Characteristically Hudson Lowe evaded the question, and replied that the regulations had not been changed since Governor Wilks's departure, and that fishermen wanting to go out at night could do so on condition that they operated as a fleet, and obtained a special permit on every occasion from the competent naval authorities on board the Admiral's flagship. It was a clever device: the true owners of the boats refused to demean themselves by begging the necessary documents in person; and the slaves employed in humbler tasks and maintenance of equipment were not capable of dealing with the difficulties of approaching the Admiral's ship.

To stave off a possible famine, Hudson Lowe made up his mind one day to use the schooner *St. Helena* to get supplies from the African coast; fifty bullocks and thirty sheep could be brought back and landed on each trip, at a cost of seven to ten dollars a head; a good number died at sea from natural or other causes. But every positive measure this born policeman passed was accompanied by some countermove, some turn of the screw in an opposite direction: at the same time an act of council obliged all the inhabitants to make a declaration of all cattle of slaughterable age, under pain of a fine of two pounds, of which half was to go to the informer who had denounced the offender.

✢   ✢   ✢

Spiritual torments and bodily sufferings often go together, and when the islanders felt the pangs of hunger morality soon began to lose its hold on them. Since moral evils are the domain of the clergy, no chronicle of daily life on St. Helena at the beginning of the last century would be complete without a pilgrimage to holy sources, and a visit to the community's two priests in their parsonages at St. Paul and Jamestown.

God moves in a mysterious way, and it is impossible to explain the succession, uninterrupted for a century, of reverends who were for the most part rogues, crooks, fornicators and quarrel-mongers. Materially speaking, their benefices were of course miserable, as much because of their isolation as because of the small stipends, and it was not easy to find candidates. Hardly had they landed on the island, when these clergymen gave free rein to their evil instincts and quickly became trouble-makers or skinflints, and indulged in every sort of misdeed and subversive behaviour, so that a fierce rivalry soon began between the political authorities and these strange missionaries. When Napoleon arrived the position became even more delicate, for it was the beginning of a period of formidable power for the Anglican Church. The Reformed Church was at its zenith: after more than a century of strife and uncertainty—a century in which papism was eradicated and the nation achieved control over the spiritual domain—Anglicanism had finally been established. Linked to the government ever since Henry VIII's break with the Pope, and supported in its actions by the prime minister (who nominated bishops) the established Church authorised its representatives to speak out, criticise, blame and even condemn the great ones of the world. And if, even in England, the Church thus held a sword over the throne, it was no different in the far-off colonies where the devout still lived in a state of primitive innocence and helplessness. The ministers of their religion impressed the poor timid congregations with the idea of an authority that was both theological and political, uniting cross and sword. Everything was done in the name of the Holy Trinity and His Britannic Majesty, so that while the right hand was administering punishment, the left might rest upon the Bible. This close co-operation between Church and administration met with difficulties when governors and clergy, confined on an island of the size of St. Helena, turned out to have incompatible characters.

So it was that, in 1816, the confrontation of two figures such as Sir Hudson Lowe and the Reverend Richard Boys augured considerable troubles to come: in fact the sound of their quarrels reached the ears of the authorities in London and did not cease until the departure of the former in 1821.

At thirty, the Reverend Mr. Boys was the elder of the two priests, and had held his living since 1811. He officiated in the cathedral, a stone's throw from Plantation House; in fact an inconspicuous door connected their two gardens and permitted the Governor to go to Sunday morning services on foot, stick in hand, much like an English squire. Witnesses have described the minister as an honest and devout man, but stiff as a ramrod and fierce as a prophet suffering perpetual martyrdom, for he believed himself to be the butt of a malignant populace, 'persisting in their spiteful and wicked task of ridiculing God's representative'. Beside this he was tactless and narrow-minded, and backed by a cabal of bigots as cross-grained as himself. Finally, he was said to have a tiresome tendency to spy on people and denounce them and hold them up to obloquy from the pulpit, and he would stick at nothing in his pursuit of vice. This was something Sir Hudson could not put up with. When he found his way barred by the Governor's henchmen, the turbulent priest was left without redress except to pronounce anathemas from the pulpit and make hypocritical allusions to this 'abandoned and corrupted island', in the presence of the authorities and his few parishioners. Boys could never control himself; he unfailingly allowed free rein to his religious zeal, intolerance and ill-temper; if it served his purpose he did not hesitate to address petitions to 'the Governor in council'. The Jamestown archives are cluttered with his long letters, remonstrances and requests. In the month of June 1816 alone, perhaps with the idea of taking the new Governor's measure, he addressed a curt letter to the council, asking for an increase in schoolmasters' salaries, protesting against the bad condition of the cemetery, complaining of the poor distribution of books in schools, suggesting that a plaque should be put up in front of the church and that there should be changes in the working programmes of sacristans. Besides this the Reverend Mr. Boys fought somewhat cynically, but with just as much energy, for his own interests: although he had received compensation of £108 from the Company, he inundated the council with complaints because his town house had been requisitioned.

The Reverend Boys had adopted certain habits of behaviour towards the government ever since 1811; the Wilks, Doveton and Leech families were all devout church-goers, and thanks to them the Church, in the person of Boys, and as manifested in Holy Writ, took a lion's share in the government and administration of the island. It presided over the fate of schools, kept an eye on hospitals and barracks, fed the poor, taught the ignorant, defended the slaves, and even legislated on certain matters through the mediation of the Church council: its head could enjoy the intoxicating sensation of being at the helm of a ship. The arrival of Sir Hudson Lowe, and the occupation of the island by troops of the regular army, deprived him of this quota of power, added to his worries and challenged the supremacy of Christian principles.

Cruelly afflicted by this reduction in his importance, 'the prelate', as Lowe and his friends called him, made up for it on Sundays by slowly climbing the steps to his pulpit with half-closed eyes and flushed face, and delivering sermons whose fame was due less to his oratorical gifts than to the stormy reactions they aroused in the population. First there was the affair of Admiral Plampin: having discovered that the personage of second importance in the island was living in concubinage, Boys publicly protested against this abominable sin. Beginning with malicious insinuations, his campaign ended with a public denunciation and a demand that the Admiral should send away the guilty woman and return to the ways of God. The person most embarrassed was the Governor, who found himself obliged to cut the Gordian knot. If he supported the Admiral he would draw down upon himself the thunderbolts of the clergy and the enmity of the Reverend Mr. Boys, who would not fail to swamp the English religious press with his articles, while to fall into step with Boys would mean throwing the Admiral into the opposite camp, to the detriment of his own prestige and authority. Lowe chose the wiser part and remained impartial—officially at least, since no correspondence was exchanged on the subject. Perhaps he took action in the silence of his study, or had a stormy conversation with the priest? There is reason to think so, because the campaign suddenly stopped, and the Admiral was allowed to enjoy the earthly pleasures of the sins of the flesh in peace in the bucolic surroundings of The Briars.

But we must make no mistake about this strange missionary's character: his zeal was not purely religious, it bore the stamp of that intransigent absolutism commonly to be seen in a tiny community where mediocre minds quarrel over crumbs of power. The quarrels Boys had with Plantation House, with Longwood and the East India Company, show that even if the Church of St. Helena in the person of its doyen was prepared to hand over the unimportant trimmings of administrative life to the Governor, it was determined at all costs to keep control over social and family life, and remain at the helm of local politics. Hudson Lowe should look after his prisoners of State and leave his other cares to the Church—this was the Reverend Mr. Boys's absurd dream.

Let us now look at the man and his audience. His excellent portrait, now before me, contributes towards an understanding of the priest's tormented ambitions. The eyes are very small, half-closed and suspicious; the drooping mouth betrays bitterness and pride, while the plastered-down hair, stiff collar and severely cut coat show artificial compunction. He is a Dickensian priest, represented by a provincial actor. Let us watch Sunday service being celebrated in the sad, cold, damp church, according to the Anglican ritual. Sir Hudson and Lady Lowe are sitting in the front row beside Major Gorrequer and the aide-de-camp; behind them sit the members of the council and their wives; and further back still the senior employees of the Company, the underlings, the priest's family, the 'first' and 'second' class islanders, the servants from Plantation House and Sir Hudson Lowe's liveried domestics, respectable women of colour and their offspring, school children, and lastly soldiers in uniform and coloured men. This was the established order of precedence.

One Sunday Boys created a sensation: he shut his eyes, laid his large hands flat on the sculptured ornaments of the pulpit and began visibly searching for words: 'Verily I say unto you that the publicans and harlots go into the kingdom of God before you, for John came unto you in the way of righteousness and you believed him not, but the publicans and harlots both believed him.' The Governor started when he heard what followed: distinction, riches, rank, power, knowledge and science were all described as barriers preventing access to divine felicity. The humble, poor and unfortunate were forgiven their sins and praised for the sincerity of their beliefs. It was from among them that Our Lord chose his companions, and not from among the rich and powerful who refused to humble themselves before Him while the poor yielded to Him and enjoyed the favour of Heaven. Limiting himself no longer to publicans and harlots, the Reverend grew heated and declaimed a list of the wicked actions which did not prevent access to the Kingdom of God—a horrifying list which seemed to imply, as Sir Hudson wrote in his report to the directors, 'that there were individuals in the audience who had committed similar atrocities'. If Sir Hudson felt that he was being personally attacked, he must have been reassured when Boys went on to insinuate that these criminals would receive absolution and remission of their sins in preference to the rich and powerful, on condition that they had entered the sanctuary wherein these unexpected words were resounding, with the evident intention of repenting. And these words were addressed not only to publicans and harlots, but also to outlaws, those who profaned the sabbath, pimps, fornicators, adulterers, thieves, and assassins, for—added the preacher in a loud voice —'the most daring rebel is sure of salvation. What a comforting, consoling reflection! Every murderer who is seized by true repentance can be sure of being saved. Had you murdered your father or mother, nay, if you came at the present moment into this church with your hands reeking with the blood of the Son of God, you would by repentance be saved.'

This was the sort of pill that must be swallowed every Sunday by those of the island celebrities who submitted to religious practices and were guilty of the crime of *lèse-Boys:* this strange apostle envisaged his mission in terms of making the crucified Christ serve the ends of verbal incontinence and greed for power.

Since every insult is avenged, Hudson Lowe often had occasion to score points against the parish priest in this silent struggle. For instance, on March 25, 1819, a petition was laid on the Governor's desk in the Castle; it was signed by the names of most of the 'small' Whites—about a hundred in all—including Solomon, Seale, Hodson, Kay, Knipe, Harrington and Fountain. Their collective complaint is of interest; the tone was so violent, the means chosen to publicise the incident so official, and the result so unfortunate for the Reverend

Mr. Boys that it is difficult not to discern the white thread of the government police woven into the intrigue:

'We the undersigned inhabitants assembled at Vestry have observed with surprise and concern certain paragraphs in the *Morning Chronicle* of the 12th November 1818 where it is stated that a flagitious traffic in slaves has long been carried out here . . . the only traffic in slaves in this island is that of transferring or selling from one inhabitant to another, a necessity that must unavoidably continue whilst slavery does exist, even amongst the strongest advocates for its abolition. In the *Morning Chronicle* the sole merit for abolishing slavery on this island is strangely and unaccountably attributed to the Reverend Mr. Boys, senior chaplain, and our surprise is increased at neither having seen nor heard of any contradiction to the above paragraph being published either by Mr. Boys himself or any person on his part.'

When the text of this document reached the priest's ears there must have been a storm in the holy-water basin; unfortunately for this little story we have been unable to find any correspondence relating to this petition in Lowe's papers or the parish records.

The Reverend Mr. Vernon, who assisted Boys, was a young man of good family, twenty-five years old and of a peaceful disposition. So as to keep greater control over his senior, Hudson Lowe decided to follow the well-known adage, and gain power by dividing the opposition; he therefore made an alliance with Vernon against 'the old man', 'the prelate' or 'the archbishop' as he called him. More than once the two men were to be found deep in conversation at Plantation House concerning some complaint against Boys. What motives induced the young priest to form a coalition with his chief's enemies? Even accepting that Vernon, like most men, was neither wholly good nor wholly bad, it seems probable that his superior's suppressed bad humour annoyed him at least as much as the Governor's attentions flattered him. By condemning the former he was driven into the arms of the latter, and the pleasures of the table made up for the prickings of conscience.

Boys's passion for encroaching on the Governor's province naturally got him into trouble with Longwood, and so—indirectly—with Plantation House once more. In February 1818, Cipriani Franceschi, Napoleon's major-domo, succumbed to terrible internal pains only a few days after the death of a child of the Montholons' servant and a chambermaid of Madame Bertrand's; as the island had no Catholic priest, this thorough scoundrel of a Corsican valet was laid in the earth in the cemetery at Plantation House, to the sound of sad anthems sung from the Anglican church. It was the Reverend Boys who stood over the newly dug grave and pronounced the words: 'Man that is born of a woman is of few days and full of trouble'. No words of the Evangelist could have been more appropriate: Cipriani had had a short life and troubles had not spared him. The material arrangements for the funeral were entrusted, according to local custom, to the Jew Solomon, who hastened to present Montholon with the bill, amounting to nearly 1,400 gold francs, as soon as the candles were extinguished. The French exclaimed in horror, but paid up, and when Hudson Lowe was told of it he merely said laconically: 'If they choose to have him buried as a protestant, it is only what was done at every funeral.'* Wishing to make himself agreeable to the clergyman who had agreed to celebrate the service in spite of his well-known strictness, Napoleon sent him by Dr. O'Meara an engraved silver snuff-box and twenty-five pounds for the poor of his parish. His first impulse had been to send fifty pounds, but he decided to split the difference, with the unexpected result that the Governor was very much annoyed. 'It was a dirty thing also of Napoleon Bonaparte,' he declared, 'to give the poor only twenty-five pounds, and splitting the difference.'* Boys was delighted with the snuff-box, but was foolish and vain enough to show it to Vernon, who told Baxter, who told Reade, who informed Lowe. The priest had to return the object, not without some twinges of regret: in his old age Boys confessed to having brought back from St. Helena and sold at a profit, an egg-cup, a toast-rack, some plate, a cane and an armchair from Longwood, as well as some of the Emperor's uniform buttons, his autograph and a lock of his hair. It must be explained that Boys died in 1867, at a time when in the eyes of the court of St. James the outlaw of St. Helena had become by a turn of fortune's wheel 'his late Majesty the Emperor Napoleon', uncle of the Emperor of the French.

As for Vernon, his relations with the Longwood party were short-lived; all he did was to baptise the infants born to the exiles—the Bertrands, the Montholons and the servants—until the day when the

*Major Gorrequer's Papers (unpublished).

Abbés Buonavita and Vignali arrived from Rome, sent by Cardinal Fesch and Madame Mère.

The disagreements between the two priests grew greater, and after three years on the island, Vernon was on the verge of a nervous breakdown and openly sided with the Governor. The affair of the Emperor's snuff-box in 1818 in fact marked the beginning of an enmity which rapidly became aversion. In January 1821, Gorrequer writes: 'the Second chaplain coming to show some letters from the First chaplain, not before shown him. The second chaplain wanted to show there was little difference between what he had said and what he had written when he was attempting to stir up the Governor against the first chaplain.'* Hudson Lowe deserved little credit for dominating the clergy, and dissension flourished among them. 'The Reverend Boys would rue the day he went home,' he said sneeringly; 'he would not spare him; he had done for himself.'*

All things considered, and in spite of their difficult characters, the two Protestant priests were no more than small thorns in Hudson Lowe's flesh. They both behaved with the indifference bordering on contempt towards the French that was fashionable on St. Helena, with an undercurrent of curiosity about the exiles' private lives. The arrival of the two Catholic priests in 1819 ought to have had a calming effect: nothing of the sort—they went on until the last possible moment airing their grievances and insisting on the prior claim of their Church. On the day of the Emperor's funeral, Vernon tried to insist on conducting the funeral service alongside the Abbé Vignali, who refused outright. To make the ceremony a 'valid' one, the Englishman hurried ahead to Geranium Valley so as to consecrate the freshly dug grave before the funeral procession arrived: 'Oh Lord, be pleased to consecrate this earth to receive the body of Napoleon Bonaparte.'

✠   ✠   ✠

When Hudson Lowe arrived in 1816, St. Helena was the only country under British rule where slavery was still known, and the principle applied that every child of a female slave was born a slave. But in 1818, under pressure from the anti-slavery movement, the

*Major Gorrequer's Papers (unpublished).

question was raised in the island itself, and Hudson Lowe decided to call a meeting of colonists. After ten minutes discussion, the whites assured the Governor of their confidence among cheers, and left the task of drawing up a statement to a commission of thirteen. 'All children born of a slave woman, from and after Christmas Day 1818, are free but considered as apprentices to the proprietors of the mothers, if males, until the age of 18 years; and if females, until the age of 16 years; and masters and mistresses are to enforce the attendance of free-born children at church and Sunday school.'

All this looked very well, printed on the front page of the government gazette, and acted as well-founded and moving propaganda in favour of the Whites, but in 1823 the Reverend Boys was indignant to find sales of slaves still going on. He was told that there was no other means of disposing of the Blacks when their masters died or went away, and that these transactions were not illegal since they only took place between owners of slaves! The slaves living on the rock in Napoleon's time were still men without rights, without liberty and without power, in spite of the pompous declarations made by the government. They belonged to the same social category as the Chinese, and like them made up an anonymous horde of odd-job men and servants, the only difference being that the Blacks had been endowed by their owners with pompous and grotesque names such as Scipio, Augustus, Plato or Caesar, whereas the Chinese were only known by numbers.

The best known of the slaves was Toby, the Malay servant at The Briars. Bought from an English captain by the Balcombes, he reigned over the kitchen garden, and Napoleon sometimes addressed a few good-natured remarks to him or even gave him a gold coin. One day Betsy plucked up courage to go and speak to the Emperor about a plan she had set her heart on—the liberation of this good man. William Balcombe had refused. 'I cannot love my father because he has not kept his promise; but I shall love you very much if you will give Toby back to his poor children. Do you know he has a girl of my age, who is very like him?' Napoleon promised that he would give orders next day for Toby to be bought, and would afterwards arrange with the admiral to repatriate him. But Hudson Lowe expostulated, and retorted to O'Meara, who had acted as officious intermediary: 'You do not realise the importance of what you are asking; it is not

Toby alone that General Bonaparte wants to liberate so as to please Miss Balcombe, he wants to gain the gratitude of all the negroes on the island. . . . He wants to do the same here as at Santo Domingo. I would not do what you ask for anything in the world.'

So Toby the slave did not regain his freedom, but he at least had the consolation—a very slight one it must be admitted, for a slave and a Malay—of inspiring a great many sentimental engravings and pictures entitled *Napoleon and the Slave Toby* which were fashionable for a while during the romantic period.

After the Balcombes' slave, another coloured man, servant to Las Cases, was the most notable of the humbler islanders. James Scott was an enterprising mulatto, who had been engaged as a servant by Napoleon's chamberlain when Longwood was first occupied; his status as 'free mulatto' gained him certain privileges, and as he was allowed liberty to circulate in the island, his master at first used him to make contact with Madame de Stürmer, as we have already seen. The news of this event came to the ears of the Governor, who at once decided to send away the young man and give his duties to a soldier. Las Cases refused to accept a servant from the English, and those at Plantation House had to resign themselves to seeing James back at Longwood; meanwhile the young mulatto had been sent for and interrogated by Hudson Lowe. Only complete ignorance of native psychology could have failed to realise what importance this interrogation gave him: for a native of St. Helena an interview with the Governor was an ordeal in the strictest sense of the word; and besides, what had been said, what promise had His Excellency extracted from him? At all events, a week later Scott took advantage of the darkness and his knowledge of the locality to make his way into Longwood House one evening and go into Las Cases's room. He told him that he had been taken into the service of someone who was going back to England, and had come to offer to undertake any commissions. Next day, Napoleon and Las Cases discussed the possibilities of using devious methods to get notes and protests conveyed to Europe for publication there; the Emperor seems to have hesitated, however, and reached no decision. James Scott reappeared the next evening and repeated his offer to Las Cases, who, without obtaining the Emperor's consent got his son to copy a letter addressed to Lucien Bonaparte; for more convenient transmission it was written in minute script on a piece of white satin, which the mulatto was to sew into the lining of his waistcoat.

From now on events moved as swiftly as if the chamberlain had trodden on the greased plank of a trap: Scott showed the letter to his father who at once informed an officer of the garrison. The incriminating evidence was given to Sir Hudson Lowe, who ordered Las Cases to be arrested; he carried out this procedure in person, under Napoleon's nose. The prisoner and his son were confined in a cottage near Hutt's Gate until they could be deported.

It must be admitted that there was something mysterious about this adventure. Here was Las Cases falling into an obvious snare, and it is natural to wonder whether he was seizing the pretext to leave the island, in order to make the best of his collection of notes and publish his great *Mémorial*, because a few weeks later, when Lowe gave him the chance of resuming his duties at Longwood if he liked, he declined and chose to return to Europe. If the trap had been set by Lowe, why should he have offered the culprit the chance to return to Longwood? And what demon prompted Las Cases to adopt such a perilous way of transmitting a note which could easily have left Plantation House by the ordinary means? The actors in this drama have taken their secret to the tomb, but few historians have given sufficient study to the psychology of James Scott. Fear of the government was an obsession with the coloured inhabitants of St. Helena, and although the tortures of the preceding century may have been merely stories to frighten the children, even in 1818 a coloured man was more likely to receive the whip and hard labour than his freedom. For stealing two glasses of wine from Sir Thomas Reade, a slave received two years hard labour; whoever cut down a tree without permission was threatened with two hundred lashes. It is therefore easy to reconstruct the drama of this arrest as conceived by young James. The mulatto, who is described as 'cunning', a quality despised by the English, believed that an intrigue of this sort with the French, who were known to be rich, might bring him a small fortune; far from being shown the door, he was received by Las Cases, who was playing a double game when he gave him the letter. If the letter got through there would be the glory of its being published in Europe, if it were intercepted, it meant deportation and return to Europe, the publication of his valuable *Mémorial* and a martyr's halo into the bargain. When in fact Napoleon saw his favourite companion go, he repeatedly murmured over and over: 'Poor Las Cases!' Unfortunately this was reckoning without Scott's father, who found himself held up to obloquy by the government; after his son had fled he allowed fear to prevail over all other feelings and made haste to give the show away. He was thanked and congratulated, and his house was now free from the menacing—extremely menacing—threat of police reprisals.

✤   ✤   ✤

Only one of the Chinese inhabitants has been honoured by mention in the St. Helena chronicles, under the mysterious title of 'the Chinaman'. He is said to have been employed in the kitchens at Longwood, and he made use of his talent as a painter to produce on rice paper delicate landscapes of the island, views of the Emperor's tomb, and even a portrait of Napoleon on his death-bed, which seems to have been copied from one painted by J. W. Rubidge, an English artist who stopped at the island in 1821. These little pictures may well have been executed at a later date, perhaps around 1840, at the time of the return of the body, but it is probable that the artist was employed as a young man in the illustrious prisoner's household.

Negro slaves, Chinese and Indians all worked in identical material conditions, but while the Negroes belonged to the East India Company or white colonists, the Chinese were free, and as soon as they had saved up enough they invariably returned to their native land. They were relatively numerous. At the time when the decision to emancipate the slaves was passed by vote, the Company employed 97 slaves—53 men and 44 women—aged between twelve and sixty-five; the men worked as domestic servants, shepherds, gardeners and labourers, and the women were in charge of the linen, laundry, and the children of their masters. But the Company was not the largest owner of black and yellow man-power: the census of 1820 gives a total of 1,061 slaves, 481 Chinese, 613 freed slaves and 33 lascars.

The lot of these poor wretches in 1816 was of course not as bad as that of their unfortunate ancestors, and the threat of cruel repression and unimaginable tortures was now only a hideous memory; the

13

slave and his descendants had belonged to the same family for generations and they were subjected to a gentle paternal régime. Judicial power was now in the hands of the government, and even light corporal punishment was forbidden, which did not prevent the authorities turning a blind eye to well-deserved chastisement. Only major crimes were judged by the courts, and an accused man had very little chance of emerging safe and sound from such a procedure. Condemned to death, he would be executed by hanging at Rupert's Bay (which is still overshadowed by the atmosphere of the gallows) and the slave-owner was compensated for the loss he had suffered; but while a slave was currently worth the tidy sum of £100, the parish funds, from which damages came, only actually paid out about twenty pounds.

Wages were reduced to a simple formula: for washing church linen, vestments, surplices, albs and altar-cloths, the slave Martha received five pounds a year; but her medical treatment was free, and Dr. Kay, an unqualified quack who acted as apothecary, received twenty-one pounds a year for treating the slaves. Apart from the care of souls, the parish only undertook the expenses of burial on a basis of fifteen shillings a grave.

Food was on a corresponding scale: the yam, a tuberous root, was considered a treat for both slaves and pigs; there was sometimes rice, often fish. Their living quarters were in the basement, and one can still see a few of these cells with barred windows and a block of stone for a pillow.

The happiness of servants depended on that of their masters; in cheerful families, where there were laughing children and plenty of money, the slave shared in the general felicity and also in the left-overs of the numerous parties. The Balcombes showed great kindness to their slaves, and their descendants still possess affectionate letters from the master of the house to Sarah Tim, Betsy's nurse. On the other hand, modern applied psychology enables us to imagine the ill-treatment inflicted on their slaves by the small Whites: these sometimes cross-bred descendants of Europeans lived poorly themselves and were invariably the worst masters.

✤   ✤   ✤

The names of their Chinese servants were so impossible for English ears to retain that they were known by numbers. They were quartered in camps built by the Company, worked for a low wage, and were naturally popular for their skill and modesty, unfortunately combined with a tiresome tendency to drunkenness and theft. They were employed in all the improvements of the house and garden at Longwood, and on all irksome tasks; they constructed a magnificent aviary for the Emperor beside the ornamental water—it is now in the Bertrand museum at Châteauroux—also the Chinese pavilion surmounted by a dragon, and a painted grotto, while one of their less talented and fortunate compatriots had charge, under Marchand, of the night-stool. For a short while the Emperor had a Chinese cook, but the imperial palate was not tempted by his oriental confections and he was very soon dismissed.

The little yellow men worked all day long under the supervision of the French, carrying barrels of water, digging and raking the garden. The Emperor's presence was an encouragement, and they worked hard in the hopes of receiving a few gold pieces or a bottle of wine. As Ali noted: 'The Emperor has two Chinese servants: one who made the cage and the eagle surmounting it, as well as other things; such as the decorations in the grotto; the other, a carpenter, has been responsible for gates, drains and all sorts of similar work. The Emperor sent for him when something was to be made out of wood. This Chinaman was very intelligent and quickly understood what was wanted, with the help of a few English words and signs, if he was shown what was to be done on the site itself.'

Napoleon's sympathy and kindness to his black and yellow employees was noticed by the local ladies. People commented with amazement on the fact that one day at The Briars, when he was talking to two ladies in long sweeping dresses, he made them move aside to let a slave with a heavy load go past, and when his visitors showed surprise, he merely said: 'Make way for the load, mesdames'. At Longwood he always treated the sons of the Celestial Empire with respect, for he knew that politeness was highly valued in their distant country. One day he gave orders for a bottle of wine to be given to a Chinese gardener; one of his French servants threw the bottle on the ground, exclaiming, 'Hey, Chinaman!' Napoleon was indignant and at once explained to the blunderer: 'You destroy all the value of a present by giving it in such an unmannerly way'. The guilty man may perhaps have been Ali, who had hated the Chinese ever since Napoleon teased him about the birth of his first child. 'How is Miss Hall?' he said abruptly one day, when the lady in question—now Ali's wife—was on the point of giving birth. 'Very well, Sire.' 'You think the child will be yours? Don't you know that an ugly Chinaman has been making up to her every day when you were not with her?' 'Oh, Sire, I am not afraid of anything of that sort.' 'You'll be nicely caught, won't you, if she produces an ugly, dirty little Chinaman?'

When Napoleon dictated his will, on April 16, and had to make prodigious efforts with his failing memory to recall the dates, faces and names immortalised in it, some crumbs of the small fortune he disposed of on St. Helena found their way to his Chinese servants. A sum of 300,000 francs was to be shared among officers and servants' 'the remainder will be given in gratuities to the English physicians, Chinese servants and charity in the parish'. A few days later, during his final agony, witnesses heard him murmur: 'Who will look after my poor Chinese now?'

History has preserved no testimony written by these Orientals: they were all simple uneducated labourers. What reflections might have been inspired in a literate Chinese who had witnessed this solitary agony, or by the meeting between these sons of China and the Emperor of the West on this lonely rock!

VII

PLANS OF ESCAPE

Did Napoleon sometimes dream of escape, of eluding Lowe's vigilance as he had Campbell's on Elba, and reaching the United States
or trying to return to the Tuileries? The question has often been
asked, and answers unsupported by material proof have given rise to
the most fantastic theories. The escape from St. Helena has been
spoken of as a historical fact, some have supposed that a rifleman
called Roubeaud, the Emperor's double, was substituted for him in
1818. Others have declared that Napoleon died selling spectacles at
Verona, or digging his garden in Philadelphia, possibly even climbing
a wall to see his son in the park at Schönbrunn. It has been seriously
claimed that in 1840 he was ruling over a kingdom of Negroes. Leg-
pullers, historical yarn-spinners and propagandists for the ideals of
Bonapartism have all been intrigued by the same riddle. Did Napoleon escape? Did he even try to slip between his gaoler's fingers? To
accept it as certain that Napoleon deliberately chose to finish his days
in public at St. Helena rather than to sink into the anonymity of
America would seem to be underestimating his active and fertile
imagination. However, in his moments of deepest discouragement,
he sometimes uttered disillusioned remarks disowning any idea, any
plan of flight, and though his companions were more disposed than
their master to take part in a 'return from St. Helena', and sometimes slipped in some allusion to the idea, they met with no response.
Feelings ran high and cruel words were scribbled in notebooks.
'Montholon says His Majesty will never escape from here, that he is

183

too soft. . . . He might involve a lot of people, but by the time he reached the garden fence he would say he was too tired and didn't want to get shot.'* A year later Balmain was reassuring his court: 'Napoleon has no intention of escaping and creating confusion in Europe. He only asks, hopes and wishes for a change of governor and place of exile.' At first sight, on the evidence of Gourgaud, Montholon and Balmain, one may therefore admit that the man who had once ruled Europe and had been cast on this rock by the Allied powers had resigned himself to a glorious and public martyr's death —to being 'a living witness of his own death' to use Thiers's phrase. But there are a great many circumstances, words and actions which can be put together to construct a framework for certain possible tentatives aimed at ending an exile as melancholy as it was humiliating.

✤   ✤   ✤

We must begin with the history of a correspondence. According to British regulations, the French including Napoleon were obliged to send and receive their letters through the Governor, who assumed the right to open them and break their seals in the exercise of control. To avoid receiving letters from his relations, particularly his mother, from the hands of Hudson Lowe, Napoleon instructed the Grand Marshal or Las Cases to correspond with his family. This wretched manner of exchanging news caused the most sadistic and unworthy pleasure to his gaoler, and, in spite of hypocritical denials, he certainly commented on the letters in front of his subordinates.

'My old mother . . . wrote to say,' said Napoleon to Admiral Malcolm in Lowe's presence, 'that she would come to St. Helena and die with me. This was told round the island.'

'Not by me,' retorted the Governor.

The Admiral insisted that Sir Hudson would treat such a correspondence as sacred and secret, but this did not prevent Gorrequer recording remarks that make one's gorge rise. Las Cases, sent away from St. Helena by a plot originating from Plantation House, started trying to excite public sympathy for his exiled companions of yesterday as soon as he reached Europe, and particularly for the ailing and

*Gourgaud, *St. Helena Journal.*

abandoned Emperor. He seized every opportunity of letting Bertrand have the latest news of all the members of the imperial family, through the intermediary of the British Cabinet. These poor missives, reminding the son of his mother and bringing the father a smile from his son, all had to pass first across the Governor's desk. He sifted them at leisure and commented on them aloud to his companions: 'He takes the letters,' writes Gorrequer, 'which, after reading in a surly malicious tone and manner: "Look did you ever see such a damn sickening stuff, ridiculous fulsome trash as this is? The fool telling of "les membres de la famille impériale". Such a blackguard rascally set as they all are. Damn me if it does not make me sick in the stomach to read such damn trash as that." This was an exclamation at reading the effusion of Las Cases's feelings for the exile and his family.'*

A few days later a letter from Lady Holland arrived in London. The wife of the leader of the Liberal party offered to take the Grand Marshal's children into her house if they were to be educated in England, and added sympathetic messages intended for the Countess Fanny and her family. Lowe kept this letter for three weeks and only consented to send it on to Longwood at the instance of Lady Lowe. This arbitrary censorship of highly intimate secrets naturally prompted Napoleon to organise a safe and private network of communications. The chosen intermediaries were all officers and passengers on ships putting in to St. Helena on their way to the British Isles. It might seem surprising that the English should agree to act as accomplices of their recent enemies and infringe the regulations, but only to those who have no understanding of British currents of opinion. There were many on the other side of the channel who admired Napoleon's finest characteristics as a man of action and courage, his extraordinary human virtues and the military genius who had set the world spinning with a stroke of his hand. And the intellectuals of London, who were great travellers and readers, critical by nature and anxious to embarrass the melancholy Lord Liverpool's government, hastened to Bonaparte's defence. Their opinions were read in newspapers and books, and heard even in Parliament, where Lord Holland, backed by other holders of famous names—some of them connected with the throne—defended the dignity of the prisoner of St.

*Major Gorrequer's Papers (unpublished).

Helena, and where Byron threw the weight of his genius and generosity into the angry contest:

> 'Farewell to thee, France! when thy diadem crown'd me,
> I made thee the gem and the wonder of earth . . .
> Farewell to thee France! but when Liberty rallies
> Once more in thy regions, remember me then.'

An echo of this attitude was sometimes to be found among travellers and navigators, and friendly hands conveyed letters, packets and manifestoes to Europe unbeknown to the Governor and his jackals.

Some of the visitors to Longwood made themselves as useful as the disciples of the liberals and poets, merely because they saw this secret transmission of letters as an unexpected source of gain. As Montholon told the Russian commissioner one day, 'It is by giving up the profits from our narratives to travellers, officers, merchants and captains of store ships, that we get them to Europe to be published'; and he added quickly: 'At this very moment we have a valuable manuscript to be published. Would you like it? I'll be very glad to give it to you.' When Napoleon was camping at The Briars he received through Gourgaud a message from Captain Mackay of the *Minden*, a ship of seventy-four guns, offering to undertake commissions for Europe. The captain spoke French well and professed to be an admirer of the great man. Another sea-captain offered to take the Emperor on his ship, and so out on the high seas, for the sum of a thousand pounds, and as the officers of every class of ship putting in to port made a point of visiting Longwood and talking to the French, it is highly probable that other propositions were made, but for obvious reasons of security left unmentioned in journals and memoirs except in cryptic terms. Admiral Malcolm, who met all the sailors and their passengers, was alarmed by their behaviour. 'We should have to get rid of all the Company's ships,' he said, 'because all their captains are for the Emperor.'

The most surprising part of the whole thing was not the surreptitious traffic leaving St. Helena, nor the fact that the Emperor's companions had no difficulty in outwitting Hudson Lowe's undistinguished staff and police, but what went on at the English end. Here also there is a lack of conclusive documents, but we know from Bertrand, Gourgaud, Las Cases and Santini that letters, parcels and newspapers were sent to Longwood without being submitted to the Secretary of State for the Colonies, as the English censorship required. In May 1816 Bertrand refers to letters having been 'intercepted by the British government and not sent because they did not arrive by the usual route'.

The most sensational discovery of a secret correspondence was made by Lowe himself in 1818, and concerned letters from London to St. Helena; it only confirms the impression that active sympathy was felt for the exiles in the Governor's own native land. On September 19, 1818, the *Lusitania*, commanded by Captain Brash, arrived from England, bringing a case of books for Dr. O'Meara, sent by a certain William Holmes. At this time the Irish doctor was already on his way back to Europe, having been expelled from St. Helena by Hudson Lowe on August 2: naturally the Irishman spent most of the voyage planning a terrible revenge on the Governor, and whenever anyone questioned him he denounced the behaviour he was soon to expose publicly. A note from Admiral Plampin to Sir Hudson Lowe gives some idea of the battle between the Governor and the doctor, and the sort of arguments used:

'Young Blackwood, the son of the Admiral Sir Harry, who is a Midshipman of the *Favourite*, at present at The Briars for two or three days, tells me that the impudent vagabond O'Meara said publicly at Ascension that "had he obeyed your orders Napoleon Bonaparte would not then have been alive"—a precious rascal this to talk of prosecuting for defamation!'

An inquiry, insisted on by Lowe, produced an enormous dossier, signed by various officers, and proving irrefutably the material truth of the midshipman's assertions: O'Meara had given him to think that he had been approached with a view to poisoning Napoleon, or shortening his life by refusing all medical aid. This was only the first blow dealt the gaoler of St. Helena in a pitiless duel, and the first sign of a change of opinion, which, influenced by the 'voice from St. Helena', the clamorous statements of the Emperor's companions and the sarcasms of the Liberal Party, was to condemn the Governor and make him end his days in abominable notoriety. During his lifetime his name became a byword, and when the question of nominating a representative of the Crown in Ireland came up in Parliament, a peer said perhaps rather tactlessly: 'Now suppose the noble Marquis (of

Normanby) were to be succeeded in the government of Ireland by a Hudson Lowe!' Relegated to the company of Ganelon, Tartuffe, Shylock, Judas and other symbolic characters, Lowe paid a heavy price for his own errors and the guile of his chiefs.

The arrival of a case addressed to O'Meara excited the utmost curiosity. Lowe, who was born in Ireland, was well aware of the aggressive character of the inhabitants of the Emerald Isle, and was prepared for anything from the man who had refused to be his ally in order to devote himself to being his enemy. The captain of the *Lusitania* also brought with him a letter addressed to William Fowler, an associate of Balcombe's, to whom the books were to be entrusted. Aware that he was being watched, Fowler thought it wise to hand this letter to Sir Hudson, who opened it immediately, and found inside it a second envelope addressed to James Forbes, who was unknown on the island. This was doubly sealed and began: 'My dear O'Meara'. It was written by William Holmes and referred to the books he was sending—all of them in French, his visit to Paris on business with Laffitte, Napoleon's banker, and Balcombe's share in all this activity: 'He does not wish to appear active himself; he nevertheless acts in concert with me on all occasions'. Then Holmes expressed anxiety about the prisoner's health, 'if he shortens his life by refusing to take exercise he will only the more gratify the savage malignity of his foes'. But there was no need to despair, 'a change for the better will, sooner or later, take place and his great mind should not at this juncture forsake him. . . . I understand you are to draw for £1,800; you shall hear the issue . . . of my visit to Laffitte, and if your remittances are paid, trade of that kind can be carried to any extent.' But the fraud did not stop there: the case of books was eagerly searched and was found to contain more letters, one of them from Balcombe: 'My dear Barry . . . Holmes is indefatigable in his exertions in *your cause*, and all my friends, among the rest Sir George [Cockburn] and Sir P[ulteney Malcolm] are of the same opinion with us. All communications whatever must be sent to Holmes, as I mean to leave off any agency business in England except with him . . . no stone will be left unturned to serve our friends on the island . . . I am just going to the Secretary of State's office, where I have been twice before on your business . . . a change in the administration is expected.' Another envelope was addressed to Doctor Stokoe, who had replaced O'Meara as doctor to Napoleon; it was to be handed to General Bertrand; 'the 100,000 francs lent in 1816 are paid, likewise the 72,000 francs which complete the 395,000 francs mentioned in the note of the 15th March. . . . Remain quiet as to the funds placed; the farmers are good, and they will pay bills for the amount of the income, which must be calculated at the rate of four percent, commencing from 1816. . . . All other letters have been delivered. Holmes.'

When he reported this discovery to his minister Lord Bathurst, Lowe made no secret of his indignation at Balcombe's behaviour. He had been cross-questioned before he left, and had sworn that he had taken part in no transactions other than those personally authorised by the Governor; he had even added that he had not been entrusted with any messages, and would answer also for his wife and daughters.

✤   ✤   ✤

In Lowe's view, his regulations had been even more gravely infringed by the transmission of manuscripts to European publishers. We know that an astonishing number of books were written about the St. Helena episode, some dictated by the Emperor himself, read and corrected with his generals, and surreptitiously sent to Europe. *The Manuscript of St. Helena*, Santini's *Appeal*, Montholon's *Remonstrance*, and the *Observations on Lord Bathurst's Speech* were published in England as well as on the Continent. Later came *Letters from the Cape*, intended as a reply to the letters of Dr. Warden, medical officer of the *Northumberland*. Were the *Letters from St. Helena* and the *Manuscript of St. Helena* by Napoleon? He was a master of this form of literature; his jerky, brief, vivid style, his lively touches are marvellously effective and English firms were eager to publish. Bertrand notes in his journal: 'The *Letters from the Cape* were dictated by Napoleon in a few days at the end of March 1817.' They appeared in London in the same year, and O'Meara, attracted by the offer of £6,000, undertook to arrange for publication if he was at liberty. It is difficult to understand Lowe's annoyance when these manuscripts escaped his vigilance and inundated Europe: they presented no threat, there was no danger to be feared from them, since these publications only set before the public political considerations, judgements and sometimes prophecies. It was a very different matter when letters got through dealing with the prisoner's material condition and possible plans for escape. An earlier chapter has described the ruses adopted at Longwood to provide for the exile's expenses; anything connected with plans of escape is much more difficult to deal with, for there is very little definite evidence to go on. At both ends of a chain which undoubtedly existed great discretion was shown, and much patience is needed to single out a significant word, or allusion.

✢   ✢   ✢

There were two groups of individuals, in Europe and America, who were personally interested in attempts at escape, and also possessed the necessary funds: the members of the imperial family, and a few faithful French followers who dreamed of settling as farmers in America with Napoleon at their head, and are referred to by historians under the name of the 'Champ d'Asile'.

The Emperor's family had been through some difficult times, and his fortune had been greatly reduced by the defeats of 1814 and 1815. Madame Mère was of course ready to sacrifice all she possessed, but it was impossible at her age and in view of the vigilance of the European police for her to be head of a clandestine organisation. Her daughters, Elisa, Pauline and Caroline, existed on the remaining crumbs of their riches, while Jerome, Louis and Lucien had had to reduce their style of life. There remained Joseph, who as King of Spain and plenipotentiary had been in a good position to accumulate a huge pile; he had fled to the United States, out of reach of spies and supervision. All this is confirmed by a letter from Madame Mère, received by Napoleon in July 1815: 'Jerome is badly off financially . . . Caroline has no money at all . . . Pauline has not arranged matters with her husband . . . Joseph is in America, where his wife and children will join him.' Commenting on this letter to Bertrand, the Emperor said: 'Joseph is worth about twenty millions, for he possesses the Spanish diamonds; they have been searching for them for a long time. It was thought Murat had taken them, but it was Joseph, he told me so afterwards.' This question seems to have occupied his mind, because next day he raised the subject with the Grand Marshal. 'Joseph seems to be intending to found a town over there; there must be 300,000 French families. There are already more French in America than in any other foreign country. Besides those arriving from every direction, whose names are announced in the gazette, there are Regnault, Savary, Merlin, Chaptal, Grouchy, Lefebvre among our friends. . . . What country can boast of such a society?'*

Was he trying to convince himself that he ought to risk a similar adventure? Did he hope to get the Grand Marshal to consider such a plan? If the conversation had taken place later, say in 1819 or 1820, it would have been absurd to suppose anything of the sort; physically diminished, dulled by years of inactivity, prematurely aged, he could no longer have felt equal to risking such a dangerous expedition. But in 1816 and 1817 he was a different man. Witnesses describe him as surprisingly energetic, and as active as when he sat on the throne of the Tuileries; he had recovered from the prostration following Waterloo and he could have undertaken a peaceful campaign in the United States with all his old enthusiasm; this was the period of his conversations about Joseph and America, and as Napoleon's daily comments were often concerned with events and information extracted from his reading of the day before, we are entitled to wonder whether at the beginning of 1816 Joseph may not have tried to get into touch with Longwood.

In October 1817 there was a fresh discussion on the same subject: 'It was a serious error to come among the English and be sent to St. Helena, for if I were in America all would be well. Everything is very bad here. It was a great mistake.' The hope or possibility of settling on the other side of the Atlantic was therefore still alive during the years 1816 and 1817, and on his birthday, August 15, 1817, Napoleon again expressed the hope not to be on St. Helena when the time came to celebrate his forty-ninth year. What plans, what hopes, well founded or no, could justify these words? In the absence of glaring proof we must regretfully base our argument on slight indications, and reason from hypotheses.

When Napoleon was preparing to say good-bye to Joseph at Rochefort in July 1815, he entrusted his brother with some very precious objects, obviously in the hope of seeing him again one day:

*General Bertrand, *Cahiers de Sainte-Hélène*.

letters received during his reign from allied sovereigns—which he kept in proud remembrance of having been one of the 'family' of crowned heads—and also a large sum of money, estimated at eight millions, though this was denied by Joseph after his brother's death. Was this money definitely intended to establish an imperial colony in America? It is impossible to say, because no trace of communication in writing between Napoleon and Joseph remains, but there are two facts of major significance. Although his other brothers were much attached to him, he made only small gifts to them, of a few hundred thousand francs, while the brother who had made up his mind to reach the land of freedom at all costs was entrusted with archives, money and valuables, all of which seems definitely to imply some intention of getting back these treasures by rejoining the eldest of the Bonapartes on the other side of the Atlantic. At this hour of final confidences and vital decisions, it seems that Napoleon put immense trust in Joseph; he had always recognised that this somewhat lazy but able and discriminating brother of his possessed a great aptitude for negotiation and intrigue—inseparable elements in diplomacy— and he was confident that the ex-king of Spain would easily establish himself on American soil. He was right, and in spite of opposition from the unamiable President Madison, Joseph was received with open arms, after a miraculous escape from the British. His success was astonishing, but it must be remembered that under the titles of His Majesty Joseph Napoleon, King of Spain, Grand Elector of the Empire, he had been and still remained a Grand Master of the Grand Orient of France, and that he had had masonic protection from the time he left the Charente, where he had been given help and shelter by a freemason from Royan, until his arrival in the country of Benjamin Franklin, where lodges were influential in the government.

How is it possible, then, to believe that communications had been broken off between the two brothers, at a time when the means of rescuing the one who languished on his rock existed on the further side of the ocean? Apart from material considerations, we must not forget the solidarity of this Corsican clan, a clan that had been so often separated by success and miraculously reunited by adversity. With Napoleon in the hands of his most inveterate enemies, Joseph must have felt upon his own shoulders the weight of responsibility as head of the family and the protector of the Bonapartes. His letters from America have been published, and show him taking a close interest in marriages and inheritance, and defending his family's good name and his brother's renown. How is it possible to accept the idea of a complete breach between Philadelphia, where Joseph was installed, and the little island? And it is significant that the editors of the ex-king of Spain's letters mention that there are gaps in those published, particularly between 1815 and 1825, the period during which the restored Bourbons were all-powerful, with ambassadors in Washington and London, and therefore when it would be necessary to destroy any compromising documents. It was the same on St. Helena; the evidence of members of the Emperor's suite often refer to letters dictated by Napoleon to be sent to Madame Mère, Lucien and Pauline—but Joseph's name never occurs!

Amongst so much discretion, it is difficult to capture the truth in some word or phrase, and definitely establish the fact of contact between the two brothers. There are two useful indications, however: in his *Account of Napoleon's captivity on St. Helena*, Montholon states that on February 16, 1816, Napoleon received news raising 'hopes of better things', and in the first edition of his *Journal*, Gourgaud slipped in a phrase which has disappeared from recent versions: 'It was dated July. He asked for news of him. Hope. Written in Δ.' This brief reference concerns the arrival of a letter from Joseph.

Another surprising piece of evidence is to be found in articles published in 1816 and 1817 by the London weekly *The Anti-Gallican*, edited by the pamphleteer Lewis Goldsmith. This paper clamoured with indecent urgency for the man conquered at Waterloo to be given some exemplary punishment, an idea initiated by the editor, who was an extremely complicated character. Since the beginning of the Consulate, he had ceaselessly published savage attacks on the First Consul, and then the Emperor, but there were those who said that he was secretly on the side of the prisoner of St. Helena: it was whispered at Longwood that Cipriani had handed the Emperor a letter written by this same man on August 15, 1817. A few months later announcements in cypher began appearing in the columns of his paper. On November 24: 'the news of your sale of silver has created a great sensation here. It was a serious blunder on your part. You cannot possibly have been pressed for money, since Joseph promised us to provide for your needs. We have received satisfactory letters from Vienna; B...y is still there; in two months' time we will try again.' On January 6, 1817: '*The Anti-Gallican* has just arrived here. It is vexatious that the editor has sent a letter to you. That has aroused suspicion; it will be a nuisance if one cannot communicate with you by means of his paper, because I believe the others will not want to insert notices in code. So it is not necessary to reply to him. Harel has left for America. Funds have been sent to your brother Joseph. Lucien has become very shabby. Hortense is always in the best of humours. The army will be increased by 500,000 men. Russia is working up the army. Davout has been sounded by Pozzo di Borgo. Carnot is altogether Russian. If the English government makes any proposition to you, say nothing of it to Stürmer. Although Metternich has promised his help, it is not necessary for you to confide in him. In any case take the advice you have been given: do not sleep at night.'

As far as is known, these incoherent messages remained unanswered and without result, and their true origin has never been established; but they gave the ministers of Europe many a headache. The code was deciphered in Metternich's cabinet, and the resulting messages were at once passed on to London and Paris where they cast a chill. The messages to be inserted had been posted in different towns, from which the secret police concluded that Napoleon had agents in various countries and even in London, and that his confederates knew the code and were on the watch. Some historians have taken these messages to be the work of a journalist trying to attract interest in a paper with a small circulation, and to arouse the curiosity of the public: others have treated them as a practical joke. Neither of these two theories corresponds with the known character of Goldsmith, twice a double spy and an expert blackmailer. He was an English Jew, who had formerly supported the French Revolution, and knew Europe like the back of his hand. Expelled from Germany, where he took refuge in 1792, he reached Poland (where he was secretary to Kosciuszko), and then Holland (where he published a pamphlet attacking the enemies of France and of the great Revolution). His zeal gained him a warm welcome from Talleyrand (then Minister for Foreign Affairs), who introduced him to the First Consul. The new ruler of France offered Lewis Goldsmith the editorship of an anti-English paper, and (after this had produced

Le Maréchal de Camp Baron
Gourgaud

Le Comte Emmanuel Auguste
Dieudonné de Las Cases

Marchand, valet de chambre

Dr. Francesco Antommarchi

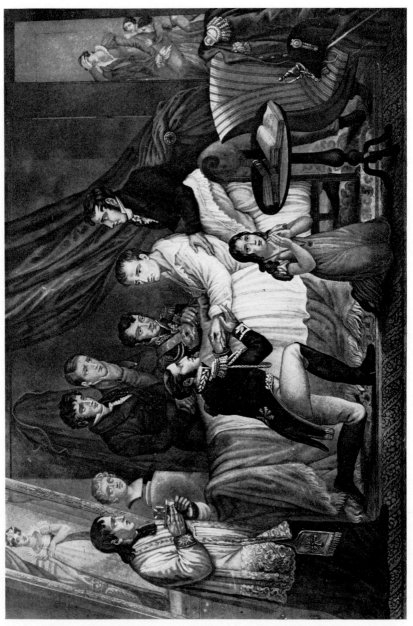

The last moments of Napoleon

convincing results) the enormous sum of two million francs to undertake a secret mission to Germany. He must have been both clever
and persuasive, for Bonaparte was a good judge of men and careful of
his money. He appears to have fallen from grace at the same time as
Talleyrand, probably about 1808 or 1809, and tried to get to the
United States, but was arrested at Dover and put in prison. He was
only set free in exchange for agreeing to embark on a campaign of
sordid anti-Napoleonic propaganda with money supplied by the
English. *The Secret History of Napoleon Bonaparte's Cabinet* was a
best-seller and proves that the journalist had information worth
English guineas.

Once these facts are known, and the man's character gauged, it is
quite possible to believe that overtures might have been made by the
one-time spy to his ex-master, with the sole motive of making money.
But what money? Perhaps Talleyrand was concerned, or English
spies. What a convenient and safe way of discovering the plans being
hatched at Longwood! It was also one that could have been used by
those most interested in the Emperor's captivity being absolutely
secure: Talleyrand and Louis XVIII—the king made use of Goldsmith after 1815—or the British Cabinet. But as spies seldom leave
their papers to the archives, even in London, we shall never know
what master Goldsmith served, or what diabolic hand drafted the
messages in *The Anti-Gallican*.

✦   ✦   ✦

The possibility of escape haunted Sir Hudson Lowe, day and
night without pause; the net he had taken such trouble to weave
around Longwood was fine-meshed, but it never seemed to him
completely effective, and from the evidence of both English and
French writers we can picture him always on the look-out, prying,
watching, controlling, having a tree cut down because its branches
overhung the surrounding ditch, or worrying about the camouflage
of sentinels. And, in spite of military and naval precautions on a vast
scale, batteries on the coast, sailing-boats, pickets, daily reports from
the police, he pressed his vigilance ever closer, and introduced among
those immediately surrounding the Emperor a few British soldiers,
who wore the green and gold livery but were in his pay. 'They were

employed confidentially at Longwood', admitted Sir Thomas Reade, head of the police. This gives some idea of the exact nature of their task.

Only at such a cost could the punctilious Governor achieve peace of mind—a peace of mind he had lost ever since his arrival at St. Helena, not without injurious effect on his nerves. His secretary tells us about his constant explosions of rage, his shouting, reproaches, fears and indecision; a day's work was a day in hell, meals were miserable ordeals. No one was spared his ill humour, and even Lady Lowe had to put up with biting comments, reproaches and rebuffs. 'She wondered his liking anything natural,'* she told him warmly one day; on another occasion she was feverishly packing her trunks to get away from the unbreathable atmosphere of Plantation House.

What had Lowe to fear from this man who was safely locked up at Longwood, with no army, no money and no family, and who was sinking every day into a state of the most paralytic boredom? Against such unequal odds, Napoleon seemed as if besieged by encircling troops, and having to rely for victory solely on the supreme resources of military genius and intelligence. Genius, intelligence—they were the Emperor's master cards against his gaoler's military deployment. His logic, his inimitable manner of analysing a problem and his infallible judgement showed no signs of age; visitors to Longwood as well as his regular companions marvelled at the clearness, logic and lucidity of his reasoning powers. 'You cannot imagine what Bonaparte is like,' Hudson Lowe complained in the presence of the Russian commissioner. 'His mind is tireless, he turns everything to account, tries everything, leaves no stone unturned to attain his purpose, and does nothing unintentionally. I could name several outstanding men who have been his tools without suspecting the fact.' And he went on to suggest that the work of guarding him would be a great deal easier if the victim would accept his fate. 'You know all our difficulties are his doing. It is unfortunate that I am not on good terms with him; it is not my fault I assure you; no one has ever behaved to a man worse than he has behaved to me. He has treated me like a pig.' Finding himself unable to establish those friendly relations with the prisoner which might have led to the relaxation of the police guard, and convinced that even the

*Major Gorrequer's Papers (unpublished).

strictest measures might be ineffective before that impetuous intelligence, Hudson Lowe refused to believe those who told him escape was impossible. In vain did O'Meara declare that a secret get-away would be a miracle, or Ali that one must be weak in the wits to imagine it possible, he—the Governor and commander-in-chief, who was marked out for blame should a catastrophe occur—was convinced that the little man who had commanded armies, won battles, treated with kings, put new life into the troops and moulded Europe in his plump hands, was cherishing more definite and realistic views on this important subject than any of the chatter-boxes surrounding him.

His suspicions were always directed against the navy and its hated officers. His instincts were not at fault, for during 1816 and 1817—the years when his prisoner was most active—a considerable number of naval men presented themselves at Longwood. It is not easy to reconstruct their conversations, because Bertrand, Gourgaud and Las Cases were very discreet witnesses and hardly seemed to have noticed what impression the august prisoner made on his guests. Is it likely they would have dared trust to paper any notes referring to possible escape? They were, as they well knew, at the mercy of arbitrary arrest or a house-to-house search. Gourgaud went so far as to put his papers inside a bottle and bury it in the park, while Bertrand used a special system of writing. Montholon, at work on his memoirs in 1845 out of reach of Sir Hudson's claws and the threats of the agents of the Bourbons, was the only one who could quietly raise a corner of the curtain and throw light into the dark corners. He tells us that on May 15, 1816, Las Cases submitted a plan of escape to Napoleon and that it was approved of by Gourgaud. But what plan could this have been? It is known that Las Cases spoke English well, galloped all over the island and made many friends there; besides this, two important events took place in May 1816 which make the discussion of escape plans plausible. Early in May, a fortnight after taking possession of Plantation House, Hudson Lowe made an unexpected scene with Bertrand. The orderly officer, whose task it was to make sure of Napoleon's presence twice a day, had not seen the shadow of his famous cocked hat for forty-eight hours. The Governor walked up and down the general's small sitting-room and suddenly lost his temper: 'It is essential for him to be seen by an

Englishman. Napoleon does not seem to understand his position, or else he is deceiving himself. An order has been given and he must carry it out.' Such virulence from a man who had only just come on the scene, and a manner of talking so redolent of gaols and warders, might well have inspired a desire in the French to get away from the tyranny they seemed to foreshadow. Just before the middle of May several ships put in at St. Helena, one of which was the *Cornwallis*, under Captain Toussaint, bound for China and thence due to return to Europe by the same route in January 1818. According to Bertrand's notes, it was at this time that Admiral Malcolm permitted himself to murmur that Napoleon could escape whenever he liked. All he needed was three sailors; he must not trust merchants, not even Balcombe. Of course he had no money, but that did not matter; everyone knew that if he signed a bill for four millions it would be honoured, and finally that the Company must get rid of all their ships, as all the captains were for the Emperor. . . .

These acidulated comments were repeated to the Governor by Sir Thomas Reade's police, and resulted in redoubled vigilance and increased restrictive measures. Towards the end of September 1816, he received a dispatch from his minister, dated July, along with some mysterious messages sent to a London businessman called Menet and posted in Milan. The first, dated May, was extremely alarming: 'Your government is deceived. Napoleon has won over a person at St. Helena. If you are a true Englishman, profit by this information, which is given you by a sincere countryman, and advise your Government to be upon its guard.' Menet took this letter to the London police who suggested that he write to Milan acknowledging it and asking for further details. Confirmation soon arrived: 'Perfect confirmation. We cannot give the details, but the fact is positive. Keep your eyes open; watch the slightest movements and take away certain powerful means that always succeed in corrupting, (gold). Burn this.' When he sent copies of these messages, the Secretary of State took the opportunity of raising the question of money, which had been preoccupying his own and other courts: cabinets of all countries were convinced that Napoleon had hundreds of millions of francs somewhere in Europe, destined when the time came to finance a change of situation: 'As it appears both from these letters and from your Despatches that General Bonaparte has money at command, which he disposes of at his own pleasure, I have to express my earnest desire that you would adopt some means of ascertaining the nature and amount of the funds at his disposal, and of preventing his receiving any further pecuniary supply without your perfect knowledge and acquiescence'.

✤ ✤ ✤

At the very moment when Lord Bathurst was writing these lines, Longwood was discussing the possibilities of escape: Montholon had just passed on the offer made by an English captain to help Napoleon to slip between the fingers of his guards, and transport him to the United States, 'for a million, to be paid on landing'. A discussion followed, in which Gourgaud took part, around a map spread on the table. 'It could be assumed that I was remaining in my room. The Governor is used to my staying indoors for several days on end. We could send one of our ladies, or perhaps both of them, to call at Plantation House: O'Meara would go into the town, and while Lady Lowe was making polite conversation about me in her drawing-room, we should leave this accursed place.' But Napoleon rejected this tempting vision with a shake of the head: 'It is a very seductive picture, but alas it would be madness. I must either die here or France must come and get me.' According to Gourgaud, the conversation was more audacious still: 'Through the town in broad daylight would be best. Going along the coast, we could easily get the better of an outpost of ten men with our rifles.' 'Why, yes, or twenty', said someone, improving on this. 'Ah, if only the Governor knew what we were talking about . . . I will pretend to be confined to my room. Only Marchand will know that I am not there; we will send Madame Bertrand to Plantation House and O'Meara to the town. I still have fifteen years of life before me.'

Perhaps these last words reveal more clearly than any others the state of mind of this man of forty-eight, in full possession of his physical strength and intellectual faculties. Believing as he did that he could count on another fifteen years, how could he possibly resign himself to utter annihilation, to slow asphyxia on this rock, and to the mediocrity of his daily existence? Why should he not calmly and logically admit that as he turned the pages of this book of boredom that

was Longwood, the chatter of his companions and the rough cruelty
of his guards, his hopes were focused across the ocean on what was
his true vocation: work, conflict and action? The evidence that this
thought tormented him night and day comes once again, from
Gourgaud; a few days after this conversation he increased Napoleon's ill humour by continuously harping on the boredom of his lot.
'We are on a battlefield here,' the Emperor said curtly, 'and anyone
who leaves a battle because his luck has run out is a coward.' Gourgaud knew that escape was in the air, and he flared up: he believed
that the plans were being kept from him, and his recriminations and
reproaches against the Emperor continued until he was brutally
interrupted: 'You must not suppose we are scheming behind your
back; try and harden your feelings, do not go into everything, do not
attempt to uncover what is being hidden from you.' What *was* being
hidden from the first aide-de-camp? He gives us the answer himself
a week later: 'I have not seen His Majesty for four days, and unless
he has escaped, I refuse to be treated like this!'

✤   ✤   ✤

Equally interesting in this connection are the commissions entrusted by Napoleon to Santini, Rousseau and Archambault, at the
end of 1816. After the humiliating scene over the Longwood expenses
in August, the Governor adopted the solution advocated by his
minister, and economised by sending Captain Piontkowski and the
three servants back to Europe.

Deeply mistrustful of the Pole, whom he had often suspected of
being a British spy, Napoleon instructed the Grand Marshal to give
him a simple *satisfecit* and a fairly large bonus, but refused to see him
before he left. But the three servants had all served him faithfully
for a long time, and he entrusted them all with important commissions. The bushy-haired Corsican, Santini, whose final job was to be
guardian of the tomb in the Invalides under Napoleon III, received
a copy of the *Remonstrance*, a long protest against the treatment of
the French at St. Helena, signed by Montholon. For greater security
it had been copied onto a piece of material cut from one of Madame
de Montholon's dresses and sewn into the Corsican's coat. Santini
also had to learn this text by heart, in case it was seized on the way,

as was probable. 'If you reach London,' Napoleon told him, 'get it printed. You will find a lot of good men in England; some of them do not at all approve of the way their government has treated me. Go and seek them out, they will help you.'

As for the younger of the Archambault brothers, the groom, and Rousseau, who looked after the silver, they intended to go to the United States and enter the service of King Joseph. Why was this? Was it their own idea, or did the Emperor suggest it? If Santini, the most simple-minded of the three and almost an illiterate, was given charge of the precious manuscript, it would seem probable that the other two, who had served the Emperor for years and were better educated and more intelligent, were being held in reserve for some special task. The four men set sail on October 19, 1816, but did not arrive in England until February 15, 1817, after being subjected to quarantine by the British authorities at the Cape. They lost no time, and Santini hurried to London, where his manuscript was printed, thanks to Lord Holland, leader of the Liberal Party. That Archambault and Rousseau embarked for America with all haste is clear from the fact that on May 21, 1817, Hyde de Neuville, Louis XVIII's minister at Washington, informed his Foreign Office: 'It seems that two members of Bonaparte's suite have just arrived from St. Helena by way of England. They are said to have met Bonaparte's zealous partisans, whose hopes have been greatly encouraged since this event.' A few weeks later the diplomat sent a further report: 'The arrival of the two emissaries from St. Helena is an established fact. Absurd rumours have been circulating ever since; they go so far as to announce Bonaparte's escape. The most probable explanation seems to be that these two individuals have been given a mission with this end in view, and have been sent to make arrangements with Joseph and the leaders of the party.' On August 4 another dispatch arrived in Paris: 'I am in a state of the most acute anxiety; the fact that my conjectures are confirmed by some circumstances while others seem to disprove them, has given me grounds for alarm, for even if the exact nature of the danger is obscure everything goes to prove that it exists. I do not yet know the situation of the fire but the heat proves there is one, and if it is not put out it will become a conflagration.'

Although this statement cannot be confirmed, it has been suggested that Rousseau and his companion brought the ex-king of

Spain a map of St. Helena annotated by Napoleon himself. It would seem likely enough in the light of the one fact that is certainly known —namely, that the mission entrusted to the two men was undoubtedly to give the eldest of the Bonapartes news of his brother, and after his frequent rides about the island during the year 1816, Napoleon may have thought it useful to annotate a map with a view to some possible future action, and give it to his messengers.

A link between the arrival of the servants and American plans concerning St. Helena has still to be established. Such plans undoubtedly existed, for Hudson Lowe mentioned in his memoirs that on his journey East in 1825 to take command of a regiment in Ceylon, he stopped at Vienna and had a long conversation with Prince Metternich. The Austrian minister told him that he had met General Bertrand in Paris, and that he had honestly admitted having no complaints to make of Sir Hudson: 'He did what he could to make the French comfortable, but the island was an intolerable place to live in. The French had little chance of being removed from the island as a result of their complaints, and their only hope (long before Napoleon's illness) had lain in an American plan to carry off the prisoner.' What was this plan? First of all it was noteworthy that, according to Bertrand, there was only one, which invalidates the numerous accounts of fantastic enterprises such as were seriously collected in July 1816 by Sir Charles Stuart, British Ambassador in Paris: 'The French Government have received intelligence that a person named Carpenter, who is a citizen of the United States of America, is equipping a fast sailing vessel on the Hudson River, for the express purpose of facilitating the escape of Bonaparte from St. Helena'. The ambassador explained that he did not know the date fixed for this exploit but that the word of the Duc de Richelieu, minister to the King of France, gave sufficient weight to the news to justify insistence on exceptional precautions being taken by the Governor of the island.

✣   ✣   ✣

Relying only on Bertrand's reference to the plan for escape having been in existence 'long before Napoleon's illness', we can bear in mind the years 1817 and 1818, and link his words with the strange episode of the Champ d'Asile—strange, for it is surrounded with a certain mystery making it difficult at this distance to analyse it in a few pages, even from the point of view that interests us, namely its connection with St. Helena. General Lallemand, a veteran of the wars of the Revolution and the Empire who had been taken prisoner at Waterloo and condemned to death in his absence by the King's courts, was granted permission in May 1816, after internment in Malta, to emigrate to the United States. At the same time several French soldiers of Napoleon's army who had gathered round King Joseph at Philadelphia founded a society called the Society of French Agriculture and Industry, with the object of exploiting a region in the Southern States on the borders of Alabama. Lallemand was the president—the very same Lallemand who, when the farewells were being said on board the *Bellerophon*, had failed to get the special honour of accompanying the defeated Emperor into exile; he had not lost his old enthusiasm. His younger brother Henri had emigrated with him, and married the daughter of Stephen Girard, a French immigrant who owned an important bank in Philadelphia, had an immense influence on public affairs, and had given help to the American government at various times.

Supported, it is said, by a society of freemasons (this may well have appealed to Joseph as ex-Grand Master of the Grand Lodge of France) and given approval in France by Benjamin Constant, this splendid plan for the development of virgin territory in the New World 'in the French manner', by the heroic survivors of the Grande Armée received the noble title of Champ d'Asile. That the more advanced and fanatical elements among the Bonapartists should have wished to found a French settlement and help to deliver their ex-Emperor, as well as commercialising American resources, is proved by numerous writings. An ex-major in the imperial army, called Persat, decorated by Napoleon, described in his memoirs how he got wind of several plans to help the exile about 1817; he at once went and offered his sword and his money to Joseph. 'The king welcomed me with that graciousness he always showed to Frenchmen. He assured me in touching terms that he had been ready to give his life and fortune to deliver the Emperor, but that he had been obliged to give up this plan because of definite information from London about the barbarous orders issued by the British government. These were to put the Emperor to death, if any serious attack was made on the 4,000 gaolers who kept watch on him.'

As it is hardly possible to doubt Joseph's word, and he was surrounded by such men as the Lallemands, Girard, Grouchy, Vandamme, Lefebvre-Desnouettes (cousin of Napoleon through the Ramolino family), who would certainly have censored his remarks, we must conclude that the plan was prepared between the month of October 1816, when Rousseau and Archambault arrived in Philadelphia, and August 1817, when Persat rallied to the conspirators. Why was it abandoned or never put into execution? It is impossible to be certain; perhaps Joseph hesitated, his financial resources being limited, at the thought of the enormous expense and risk of a failure which might leave him ruined in a foreign country, or felt afraid of arousing the disapproval of the American government, who had shown him no great friendliness.

But his remarks to Major Persat were made in August 1817, and make it possible to assert with confidence that the plans for escape which aroused the hopes of the exiles, and were mentioned by Metternich after Napoleon's death, were certainly those organised by the leaders of the Champ d'Asile.

The only other enterprise worthy of attention was that of Latapie, Brayer and Cochrane, and took place later. Brayer was a general commanding a division and Count of the Empire who took refuge in North America and afterwards in Buenos Aires. Like Latapie, a cavalry officer who had escaped from Louis XVIII's police, he was an ardent Bonapartist, while Lord Cochrane, a distinguished British admiral who had defeated the French fleet in Aix roads in 1809, was a renegade from Britain. Elected to Parliament after leaving the navy, while in opposition to Lord Liverpool whose government he attacked, he was suddenly accused of fraud, imprisoned and fined; this was too much for the future tenth Earl of Dundonald, and he took off his coat, again put on an admiral's uniform and went to South America, where he offered his help and prestige to the insurgents of Chile and Peru. At the end of 1817 this trio—Brayer, Latapie and Cochrane—were the subjects of many dispatches, and the French Embassy in London at once alerted the Consul-General in Brazil concerning what was known in London of the doings of the two Frenchmen, who were suspected of planning to seize the island of

Fernando de Noronha and collect mercenaries there to make an assault upon the rock-prison in the southern Atlantic. The Minister for the Navy, Comte Molé, and his colleague the Minister for War, Marshal Gouvion-St.-Cyr, did not turn a hair when they received orders to study and forestall these attempts to rescue their one-time sovereign, and in September Molé was able to inform the Premier, the Duc de Richelieu, that 'two armed schooners of three hundred tons, and a vessel of seventy-four tons equipped by Lord Cochrane, were to make up this expedition, which would be manned by eighty French officers and seven hundred men recruited in the United States; Fernando de Noronha was their rallying point.' Asked to give an opinion on the possibility of French ships blockading the shores of the United States, Molé became reticent: 'The coast is very extensive; there are innumerable ports and anchorages, and if close watch were to be kept on them all an immense number of ships would be needed. . . . Also since the suspected ships would be perfectly disguised as French cruisers, it is questionable whether the apparent correctness of the equipment and the flag under which they were sailing would make it possible for His Majesty's ships to waylay these vessels, force them to return to port, and attack or capture them. Yet this would be necessary to achieve the desired end: these are political questions of the utmost gravity.'

Early in 1818, the Marquis de Montchenu, Louis XVIII's commissioner on St. Helena, received detailed information about this expedition from the French chargé d'affaires at Rio. The arrival of the ship bringing these dispatches caused great excitement and agitation in the little island and gave rise to many rumours. 'It is a Brazilian ship,' Gourgaud notes, 'or else from England, bringing dispatches which have been sent up here at once; there was one for the Governor and one for the Admiral countersigned by Lord Bathurst; no one knows what they contain; this is obviously important but mysterious.' A few days later it was the sole subject of conversation, and Gourgaud adds: 'Bertrand said in the drawing-room that according to the Russian commissioner there was great agitation in the town. What is the reason for it? The Governor is behaving mysteriously. It is said that Joseph is now on the throne of Mexico, and that Clauzel has collected a large force of soldiers or sailors, perhaps to make an attempt on St. Helena. "Have you passed this on to the Russian?" asked the Emperor. "Yes, Sir," said Bertrand, "while my wife was talking to the surgeon of the 66th".'

A great deal of fuss about very little, as it seems in the last analysis, for the only sails that appeared on the horizon off St. Helena were those of merchant vessels in search of water. Were Brayer and Latapie intercepted like Lallemand and his associates, or did they merely become discouraged? At present we have no means of knowing the exact truth. There is one echo only: the Emperor's will. High up in the long list of beneficiaries, immediately after his few faithful followers at Longwood, are the names of Generals Brayer and Lefebvre-Desnouettes, who are to receive considerable legacies, doubtless to reward them for services that still remain unknown to us, however unusual they may have been.

✣   ✣   ✣

It would be illogical to study the problem of escape without concerning ourselves with the principal figure concerned, and asking the question: did Napoleon wish or hope to give Sir Hudson Lowe the slip? It is certain that from the first days of his exile he never believed that he would end his days on the plateau of Longwood: banishment is an essentially political measure, and only lasts as long as temporary hatred and the need for alliances. Riding with Gourgaud, one day in 1815, he tried to indulge in hope: 'The Prince Regent will yield to public opinion and get us brought back to England; it is also fortunate for us that when Princess Charlotte comes to the throne she will want to have us back.' Even if it was useless to expect mercy from the buffoon who was reigning in the name of George III, he placed all his hopes on the young and pretty Charlotte, whose strength of character was revealed by her brusque behaviour. Daughter of the drunken Prince Regent and the fantastic Caroline of Brunswick, the princess enjoyed a boisterous popularity very displeasing to her father and his cabinet; married in 1816 to Prince Leopold of Saxe-Coburg-Gotha, who had once sought the favour of being aide-de-camp to the Emperor of the French, she seemed to promise a reign of liberty, joy and generosity which might efface the memory of her father's scandalous behaviour. Her premature death in 1817 was a disappointment to the English and put an end to Napoleon's earliest illusions.

Perhaps the Emperor and his companions were counting on a political change in France itself, after the violence of the White Terror? Now that order was restored in Europe, people must be tired of murder, banishment and humiliation. 'Within three years the King will be dead: there will be a respite. . . . We must wait patiently; I still have a great many years to live; my career is not finished.'

✣   ✣   ✣

Although they were logical from a political point of view, these reasonable hopes of a return to Europe, either to enjoy the *pax britannica* under an assumed name or to defend the Crown against the uprising of the people, depended on too many unrealisable hypotheses. After two years of waiting, Napoleon had to bow his head and admit his impotence and his complete isolation. 'People feed me with illusions, they are wrong. The awakening is too painful. If during the two years I have been here I had not hoped for a return of my luck, I should have made up my mind and have created a life for myself as a rich colonist.' There and then he stopped dreaming of a second return, and taking off the conqueror's tunic, put on the prisoner's dress. His illusions abandoned, chimeras cast aside, he could now devote himself to the roles of historian and prophet. Leaving the King reigning in Paris and the Prince Regent dancing in London, forgotten by his friends, persecuted by his enemies, but rich in the glories of the past, he pondered the 'great events of his reign' and his century, with disillusionment and detachment amongst the absurd trivialities of daily life in St. Helena.

VIII

WHAT DID NAPOLEON DIE OF?

All the journals kept by Napoleon's companions—whether English or French—make it strikingly clear that the events and conditions of his daily life had a great effect on his health. In fact these documents, together with the comments of his doctors, enable us to draw up an exact clinical record and establish the relationship between cause and effect.

During the sixty-seven months of his captivity he was in the hands of five physicians: the Irishman, Dr. O'Meara of the Royal Navy, looked after him from July 1815 to July 1818; Dr. Stokoe, an Englishman and also a naval doctor, was sent for to see him five times between July 1818 and September 1819. Dr. Antommarchi was a Corsican sent by Madame Mère and Cardinal Fesch; he was attached to Longwood from September 1819 to the end, and was assisted during the last months by Dr. Arnott of the 20th regiment. O'Meara had the easiest task, medically speaking at least, for politically it ended by his expulsion. But during 1816 Napoleon suffered from nothing worse than a few sore throats, migraines, feverish aches of an influenzal sort, and a violent attack of dysentery in October, caused it was thought by the poor quality of the wine. Gourgaud arranged for an analysis, and when a large amount of colouring matter and litharge was discovered, the trouble was attributed to lead poisoning.

Early in 1817 Napoleon had another attack of dysentery, described in detail by Marchand: 'Although he was by temperament robust, the Emperor was seized with an attack of dysentery violent enough to alarm us all'. Then, about March or April, his legs swelled a good deal, especially at the ankles, and there was a return of dysentery, with shivering fits and abdominal pains. This was followed by a state of general exhaustion, noticed by all his companions. 'Napoleon is not well, he has not eaten his dinner.' 'He slept badly, has been very poorly and does not look well. He is depressed and tired.' 'He is sleeping badly and has not come to dinner for the last week.' 'The

208

Emperor fell asleep over the chessboard; he did not finish the game, dropped asleep and went to his rooms at nine o'clock.' 'He sighed: "My dear Gourgaud, I can't walk any more".' September is one of the worst and deadliest months at St. Helena, with rain, wind, fogs, damp cold, and on September 7, 1817, O'Meara noted:

'Napoleon complained of rheumatic pains and slight headache, which he attributed, and with reason, to the dampness of the climate and the house. "Every evening," said he, "when I leave my little sitting-room, where there is a fire, and enter my sleeping-room, where there is none, I experience a sensation as if I were going into a damp cellar".'

But towards the end of the same month the first symptoms of a more serious trouble made their appearance:

'Saw Napoleon at nine o'clock. He complained of a sensation of soreness in the lower extremities. His legs, especially the left, swelled, and the ankles pitted upon pressure. Appetite deficient. Some nausea at times.'

At the beginning of October, O'Meara made a more exact diagnosis:

'He complained of a dull pain in the right hypochondriac region, immediately under the cartilages of the ribs, which he said he experienced yesterday morning for the first time. Sensation in the right shoulder, which he described to be more of numbness than of pain. Slight inclination to cough. Want of rest at night. He said that he felt as if he wanted to lean or press his side against something. Gums spongy, and his legs a little swelled. Pulse 68. Appetite tolerable. Said he felt something in the right side which never was there before. Told him that it might probably be owing to costiveness and recommended a dose of physic, which I said would also be proper if it were the commencement of liver complaint, the prevailing disease of the island. That if it increased, and were accompanied by other symptoms, there could not be a doubt of its being hepatitis.'

From this time the Emperor's troubles steadily increased and his state of health deteriorated.

On October 5, O'Meara made a thorough medical examination, and recorded that the patient's right side was harder to the touch than the left, that it was visibly swollen and painful under pressure. Napoleon admitted that he had noticed this himself two months earlier but had put down the swelling to obesity. O'Meara then prescribed the remedies in use at the time: calomel, friction of the extremities, hot salt-water baths, antiscorbutics, gargles and rides on horseback. Napoleon complained of pains in his legs and of great lassitude; on October 15 he was restless and was made very irritable by a sharp pain in the right shoulder. By the 27th, he was melancholy and discouraged.

His illness developed slowly and in an unspectacular fashion, and since there were no serious crises between November 1817 and March 1818 his companions confined themselves to stressing the Emperor's irritability and languor, but in March even O'Meara was forced to admit: 'The progress of the disease in the Emperor continues to advance a little, though slowly.' This was the moment chosen by Hudson Lowe, as we shall see later, to send away the Irish doctor, accusing him of complicity with the French. Only a few days before he got his dismissal from the Governor, O'Meara scribbled in his diary: 'Napoleon much affected by a severe catarrhal affection, caused by the extreme humidity of his rooms.' It was now June, the season of heaviest rains and humidity.

The doctor's dismissal was so sudden that he had not even the time to make up some medicine for his illustrious patient, who found himself abandoned in the middle of an attack with nothing but a few mercury pills, purgative salts and an embrocation for his legs. He sent an alarming memorandum to the Grand Marshal, giving a precise and realistic picture of the Emperor's health in the month of July 1818, in which he speaks among other things of anxiety and almost total lack of sleep. 'Two years of inactivity, a murderous climate . . . isolation, desertion, everything to dismay the soul, all combined together. . . . If there is anything surprising, it is that the disease has not made more rapid progress. This is due merely to the invalid's strength of mind and excellent constitution.'*

Like all his colleagues of the period, O'Meara was quite ignorant of psychosomatic medicine, yet he had put his finger on the spot. It has often been suggested that Napoleon worried himself to death, but it was not until 1944 that the famous experiments of Wolf and Wolff in England proved the direct action of the nervous system on the functioning of the stomach. Their researches have made it possible to define the psychological conditions that may cause digestive troubles: during periods of anxiety, conflict or violent frustration,

*Marchand, *Mémoires*.

Napoleon's Funeral Cortège, May 9, 1821

Plantation House, Residence of Sir Hudson Lowe

View from Napoleon's bedroom

the mucus of the stomach changes its appearance and thickens. This discovery clearly shows that nervous dyspepsia may very easily result in a temperament subject to worry, irritation, hostility and other mental troubles, and that secondary organic changes, particularly ulcers, may be caused and aggravated by constant nervous tension alone, even to the point of haemorrhage and perforation.

In January 1819, Napoleon had a sudden attack of vertigo, and a naval surgeon, Dr. John Stokoe, who had put in to Jamestown on board the *Conqueror*, was urgently summoned by Bertrand. He could do no more than confirm O'Meara's diagnosis: obstinate constipation, hepatitis, and imminent danger of a fresh attack, which could only be staved off by bleeding. Enemas and purgative salts should also relieve the situation. In his report he added: 'The more alarming symptom is that which was experienced on the night of the 16th, a recurrence of which may soon prove fatal, particularly if medical assistance is not at hand.' The confirmation of the diagnosis of hepatitis—a disease which could be attributed to the climate of the island—was naturally displeasing to the Governor, and after four visits to Longwood Stokoe was ordered to return to his ship, and later went back to England, only to be immediately ordered back to St. Helena, where he was court-martialled and his name struck off the list of naval surgeons.

The fates of O'Meara and Stokoe would certainly have provided a salutary lesson for their successor, if he had been in His Britannic Majesty's service; but fortunately for the independence of his diagnosis he was a Frenchman and a Corsican. Unfortunately for Napoleon, however, his terrifying ignorance soon induced regrets for the common sense and honest proficiency of the two English doctors. 'Up to the present,' Antommarchi admitted, 'I have only had corpses to deal with'; and this ex-assistant in the dissecting room, engaged for a small fee by Cardinal Fesch, now began to subject his famous patient to the most preposterous treatment in an incredibly casual manner.

Between Stokoe's departure in January and the arrival of the Corsican in September 1819, the disease had of course made an unobtrusive progress, and Bertrand daily set down details of his master's decline. 'He is weak and in pain', 'he is uncomfortable', 'his stomach is over-loaded', 'he has a pain in his side', 'he is liverish'.

15

After a thorough examination of the sick man, Antommarchi advised that psychological remedies should first be tried for the pains in the abdomen and the region of the liver. According to him, the Emperor should no longer shut himself in his room and lie for hours on his chaise-longue; he must go out, talk, ride and take exercise. By way of medical treatment the patient should be given frequent hot baths and enemas, and also mercury pills, which he refused to take. Three weeks later Antommarchi confirmed his predecessor's diagnosis and informed Sir Hudson Lowe that Napoleon was suffering from chronic hepatitis.

In accordance with his new doctor's advice, Napoleon did for several months take an interest in his garden, and gave orders for the bare plateau to be ornamented with sunken paths, ponds, shrubberies, and formal flower-beds in the French style. Some of his energy returned, even some of his cheerfulness, and from early morning he could be seen, wearing planter's dress and leaning on a cane or a billiard cue, as he summoned everyone to take part— generals, doctor, priests, servants and Chinamen were enlisted to take part in the exhausting work of clearing the ground, digging and watering.

Suddenly, in about July 1820, the cruel symptoms of some really serious malady made their appearance: nausea, pains in the region of the stomach after meals, the clinical evidence of violent dyspepsia and of the ineluctable progress of the disease so well described by O'Meara, aggravated by the worries of daily life, quarrels with Hudson Lowe, discord among his suite, Gourgaud's stormy departure, that of Madame de Montholon, and the murderous climate. The July crisis came on after a sharp brush with the British; Lowe threatened to expel Bertrand, and Napoleon was shattered by the news, for although he had seemed to neglect the Bertrands in favour of Montholon, the Grand Marshal was still an officer of the Crown, and the star among the little court of exiles. The sick man went down with a high fever, pains in the liver and discomfort in the joints, and Antommarchi declared that his digestive and biliary systems were disordered. In fact Napoleon was at this time already under sentence of death from an illness which his doctor was unable to diagnose, nor was it to be fully understood and analysed until many years after his death. He put up a fight, it is true, ate, still went out in the carriage or on foot, but when he got back to Longwood, worn out by his efforts, it was always the same complaint: a razor-sharp pain in his side. Antommarchi then ordered enemas and more enemas, and even blistering on the arm although the trouble was in his stomach. Worn out by the struggle between his robust organism and the slow corrosion of disease, Napoleon longed only for the shadows and silence of his room. 'How good bed is, doctor! I would not exchange its pleasures for all the thrones in the world.' By January 1821 his stomach was rejecting all solid foods and he was being nourished on soup and meat jelly; anorexia, vomiting, flatulence, epigastric pain, constipation and increasing weakness combined to provide glaring proof of the existence of some gastric affection. Ignorant as Generals Bertrand and Montholon were of medical matters, they could not fail to notice the patient's physical and moral decline. 'He cannot possibly last long,' Montholon wrote to his wife. 'Our doctor claims that a change of climate would save him. I hope this is true, but hardly believe it for I have never seen anyone look more like a corpse than he does at the present moment.' What Montholon saw on the dying man's face was undoubtedly the stigmata of cancer: greyish colour, sunken eyes, and strained expression caused by anxiety and pain.

In March there was abundant vomiting. Antommarchi began talking of remittent gastric fever and then ordered two doses of emetic—two doses of tartaric emetic for a stomach already damaged and corroded by disease. Napoleon suffered a thousand deaths, rolled on the floor, and thenceforth obstinately refused all medicine prescribed by the Corsican. This was the moment chosen by Hudson Lowe to engage on one of his clumsiest operations: the British orderly officer had not seen the sick man for several days—how could it have been otherwise since Napoleon was confined to bed?— and the Governor insisted on being reassured as to his presence. If 'the General' refused to show himself, the door would be forced. In consternation, Montholon and Bertrand conceived the idea of calling in an English doctor as a consultant, with the dual aim of reassuring Hudson Lowe and assisting Dr. Antommarchi in his difficult task. Their choice fell on Dr. Arnott, surgeon to the 20th regiment, who made an examination of the patient, but with scientific caution and political sagacity decided not to commit himself definitely, and made a qualified diagnosis. His responsibility for the Emperor's end was grave, for he was as ignorant as Antommarchi but more malevolent. To get into the Governor's good graces he talked ceaselessly of hypochondria, and of the illness being more mental than physical. On April 5 he stated that he had never found him, during any of his visits, in the state described by Antommarchi. He believed that the illness was not serious. He even told General Bertrand that he thought there was no danger and he had advised Napoleon to get up and shave himself. The Governor was well satisfied, 'Sir Hudson Lowe laying it down that it was a disease of the mind, not the body, the reflection of his impolite conduct here, and his behaviour to him (and how differently he would play his game if he had to play it over again!), that he was now suffering from, and added with the grin of a tyrant: "If a person was to go in there and make a great clamour it would be the most likely thing to revive him".'* This shock treatment, already held to be beneficial in mental illness, was certainly a strange one for a patient who was slowly being destroyed by an internal disease. A fortnight later, Arnott had to alter his opinion in a hurry: 'After leaving His Majesty, he examined the black substance vomited, and by its nature decided that there was ulceration of the stomach.' In agreement with Antommarchi, the Englishman at once ordered pills to 'open the bowels, and concoctions of quinine to give strength and reduce the fever', a witch-doctor's remedy at a stage of illness when persistent vomiting and the fact that food eaten the evening before was regularly rejected next morning indicated an affection of the pylorus. When on April 25 Arnott discovered traces of blood in the vomit, he was still reluctant to talk of a serious or mortal disease, and referred to 'a disturbance of the digestive organs'.

With greater lucidity than was possessed by these 'specialists', Napoleon went straight to the point as usual, and attacked Arnott that same day on his views of the illness:

'How many openings are there in the stomach? How does the pylorus close? My father had a scirrhus of the pylorus, is it possible to recover from this, if it forms?'

He got the doctor to feel his side: 'Is this the pylorus?'

'No, it is the liver.'

'Could you tell if something was wrong with the pylorus?'

*Major Gorrequer's Papers (unpublished).

'No, it would be impossible: it is underneath the liver.'

The Englishman clearly saw that the purpose behind this running fire of questions was 'to sift the facts so as to find out if the trouble was in the pylorus, for the Montpellier doctors had declared it to be a hereditary disease'. While the doctors hesitated, groped their way, and deceived the invalid, the sick man himself was thinking all the time of the last illness of his father, Charles Bonaparte, who died in the prime of life of a scirrhus in the stomach in spite of the skill of members of the celebrated medical faculty of Montpellier; he knew very well that it was all up with him, and had already taken steps accordingly. On April 10 he discussed the terms of his will, and on the 12th he got Montholon to take down a draft of his bequests from dictation. A whole book, or at least a chapter, would be needed to analyse his will, dated 'Longwood, Island of St. Helena, April 16', for emotion and policy, nobility and simplicity, royal generosity and bourgeois attention to details have all left their mark on it.

On April 27 there was a violent vomiting in the presence of both doctors, and Arnott at last informed Hudson Lowe of the extreme gravity of the illness. From this moment until the patient's deliverance on May 5, the illness presented a long list of sordid details: vomiting of a brownish substance with the consistency of coffee-grounds, hiccups, difficult breathing, rapid and irregular pulse, falling temperature. On May 1, Napoleon fainted, on May 3 he received the sacraments, and on the same day two other doctors were called in, and the four medical men decided to administer ten grains of calomel.

'Desperate diseases need desperate remedies,' said Hippocrates. The unusually enormous dose of this unsuitable drug caused a terrible intestinal upheaval, with loss of consciousness, difficulty in breathing, cold in the extremities, and all the signs of a haemorrhage in the gastro-intestinal system, possibly provoked by this reckless medication.

A solution of ether and opium produced a restful period until the following day, on which date this extraordinary man at last gave up the struggle, saw life slipping away from him and quietly entered the eternal kingdom. The only sign of life still remaining in the body that had once been animated with such superhuman energy was his slow and difficult breathing. 'Eaten away by an inner sore made poisonous by grief—a sore which he had carried in his days of prosperity; it was the sole inheritance he had received from his father. The rest had come from God's munificence.'*

✤   ✤   ✤

No account of Napoleon's life at St. Helena would be complete without a few notes on the premature death of the greatest conqueror of modern times. The death of such an extraordinary man, powerless in the hands of his most implacable enemy as a result of military defeat as Napoleon was at Longwood, after his personality—and sometimes even his name alone—had convulsed a large part of the civilised world, was bound to arouse a tempest of feeling, set up opposing opinions and give rise to every possible suspicion.

Writers have not so much attempted to solve the medical problem by brooding over those cold remains, as to distribute the historical responsibilities, to prove that the most versatile genius of his century had succumbed to unjust persecution and deprivation of liberty, or else to emphasise that he had been a victim of a hereditary disease which would have struck him on the throne of the Tuileries just as it did on this rock.

The obstacles to a methodical investigation of the Emperor's medical dossier are innumerable: the doctors called in to care for him in his last illness were notable for the mediocrity of their skill, the remedies current at the time were inadequate, the pharmacopœia was primitive; and to make the problem even more troublesome and practically insoluble, the clinical picture resulting from diaries, letters and memoirs can only be a partisan one.

In the eyes of the French, their Emperor fell ill as a result of inactivity, confinement and the inhuman climate of the plateau of Longwood, as well as the incessant vexations caused by Sir Hudson Lowe.

The English took his slow decline merely as a trick, designed to arouse indignation in Europe against the man who represented Lord Liverpool's government; so much so, that when the condemned man tried to get the better of his sufferings and boredom in December

*Chateaubriand, *Mémoires d'outre-tombe.*

1820, by getting a breath of what he sadly described as 'God's good air', and when as a result of the jolting of his wretched vehicle he was overcome by nausea and deathly pallor, it was made the occasion for brutal mockery: 'Oh, it's a damned trick. It was all done on purpose to show off. Nothing but a trick, so that his pale face might be seen! All pretence to make people believe he is ill. . . . It was all for effect. Depend upon it, he took an emetic in order to make him sick in the carriage and that he might be seen by the English grooms vomiting,' exclaimed Reade.

The recent publication of the journals of the Grand Marshal, General Count Bertrand, and of the valet, Louis Marchand, have thrown valuable light on the crises that marked the stages of their master's last illness from 1820 until May 5, 1821, and the stubborn fight put up by a man still in his prime against a pitiless disease. Neither of them was sufficiently versed in medical knowledge to 'invent' out of partiality, and both of them—the Grand Marshal with the detachment of a Court official kept at the bedside of the dying man by duties of his function, and the young valet preparing tisanes, enemas and potions in the dark closet and warming his Majesty's flannel vests—have provided the scientists of this century with material for a voluminous clinical dossier to supplement the notes of Dr. Antommarchi and Dr. Arnott.

The symptoms prove the existence of an organic lesion of the stomach: pain in the epigastric region spreading to the right side, exhaustion, loss of appetite, feverish attacks and—towards the end—vomiting of blood.

The autopsy showed an affection of the gastric mucous membrane, a perforation the size of a little finger in the wall of the stomach blocked by the adhesion of the concave surface of the liver, a hardening of the edges of this perforation, and some hypertrophy of the liver.

The symptoms and post-mortem findings have made specialists hesitate between a scirrhous ulcer and cancer. Since a historian must venture cautiously into the domain of medicine, I have adopted the conclusions of my eminent friend Dr. R. Turner, pathologist and director of a laboratory, who has made a speciality of famous medical cases in his spare time, and I have pleasure in quoting his argument, which closely follows my own opinion:

'The description of the extensive scirrhous infiltration of the sub-mucosa certainly suggests a malignant linitis plastica. There was, however, no enlargement noted of the draining lymph glands and no metastases were observed in the liver. The body was also very well nourished. More important is that the clinical history was not that of a steadily progressive and continuous gastric process associated with anorexia, but of intermittent periods of exacerbation over a number of years. These facts throw very definite doubts on the diagnosis of cancer.

'The description of the ulcer itself, with its penetration of the gastric walls and with firm adhesion to the liver surface, is very characteristic of a chronic peptic ulcer. The Emperor's build and impulsive character, his hearty appetite, his habit of rapid eating, the long history of gastric pain and vomiting occurring in bouts at irregular intervals, the absence of enlarged lymph glands and second-ary deposits are all in full keeping with the diagnosis of peptic ulcer and the scirrhous infiltration may well have been inflammatory in origin.

'It has been reported that a French surgeon, Lieutenant-General R. Brice, has suggested that the gastric ulcer may have been due to an amoebic abscess of the liver which had ruptured into the stomach. Such an abscess would have been large and left an obvious and char-acteristic cavity in the liver and it is difficult to believe that the medical officers present would miss such a gross lesion particularly when, according to the accounts, a careful dissection was carried out. True the British doctors present may not have been expert patholo-gists but the dissection was carried out by Antommarchi who, though he may not have been a sound physician, had been an assistant to the famed Mascagni of Florence and had carried out many post-mortem examinations at the hospital of Sta. Maria Novella. He thus should have been an expert dissector, able to recognise gross pathological changes. In support of his theory Brice has suggested that the "bloody spittle" staining the Emperor's vest at the time of his death, and noted by Bertrand, may have been due to agonal vomiting of detritus from the ruptured abscess. The pus discharged from such an abscess is thick, rather like chocolate, whereas a thin sanguine discharge from the mouth and the nostrils, due to fluid emanating from the congested lungs, is not an uncommon agonal feature in death from a large number of varied causes and therefore is of very little significance as to the cause of death.

'Finally Rutledge, in a more detailed account of the post-mortem findings, has stated that in the area where the ulcer was adherent, the liver was indurated to the depth of a quarter-inch. This observation definitely rules out the possibility of a ruptured amoebic abscess and is exactly what one would expect to find in the case of an adherent peptic ulcer.

'Therefore, in my opinion, the available evidence (pathological and clinical) indicates that the Emperor's ulcer was most probably peptic in origin but possibly cancerous and was certainly not due to a ruptured amoebic abscess.

✢   ✢   ✢

'The next important question is: "Was the ulcer the true cause of the Emperor's death?"

'If it was a cancer he certainly did not die from gastric obstruction, nor malignant cachexia, for he was well nourished and no secondary deposits were present. If it was a peptic ulcer, how did it kill? Though coffee-grounds were found in the stomach there is no history of a frank haematemesis or massive melaena and the ulcer did not perforate into the peritoneal cavity and cause a septic peritonitis.

'It appears therefore that the gastric ulcer, whether malignant or peptic, was not the final and full cause of the Emperor's death as it does not, by itself, satisfactorily explain the death. The ulcer would thus appear to be a concomitant finding or a contributory cause to the death.

'If the Emperor's death was not entirely due to the ulcer what could be the other possible factors in its causation?

'What of the Emperor's liver condition and could disease of this organ also have contributed to his death? The unreliable Barry O'Meara had originally diagnosed that he was suffering from chronic hepatitis. The unfortunate Stokoe, who was introduced to the Emperor by O'Meara, was also of this opinion. Antommarchi, when he took over the medical care of the Emperor, agreed with this diagnosis, and Shortt, from the clinical history, held a similar opinion though Arnott, who helped attend him during his final illness, disagreed.

'There are many types of hepatitis, but it is clear, from their descriptions and conclusions, that the Emperor's medical attendants only considered an amoebic hepatitis, which they alleged he had contracted from the prevailing adverse climatic conditions of this "tropical island". Other forms of hepatitis, i.e., infective viral hepatitis, would not agree with the clinical picture. Also an acute hepatitis of this type, if it had led to chronic changes, which ultimately resulted in the Emperor's death, would have been manifested at autopsy by gross and obvious changes: nodules, hyperplasia or cirrhosis.

'True, many of the symptoms of possible amoebic hepatitis were exhibited by the Emperor, i.e., febrile attacks, associated with abdominal pain and pains in the right shoulder, but no enlargement of the liver was ever conclusively shown by O'Meara or the other doctors, with the exception of Antommarchi who is not convincing on this point. We now also know, from the post-mortem findings, that the abdominal pain can be readily explained by the gastric ulcer and the shoulder pain by the adhesions between the liver and the right dome of the diaphragm; thus the two most suggestive signs of hepatitis are explained away.

'An amoebic hepatitis also does not manifest itself simply by generalised enlargement of the liver, but by producing localised necrosis of liver cells which shows as a localised abscess. I have no doubt that if such an abscess had been present in the liver it would have been demonstrated by Antommarchi who, even after he returned to France and gave a more detailed account of the findings, does not suggest such a lesion but states that the consistency of the liver was normal, even though he thought a hepatitis was present. Whether or not the liver showed some generalised enlargement is a moot point but, if enlargement was present, it would appear that it was due to fatty degeneration or passive venous congestion, either of which under the circumstances would appear to be a very logical explanation.

'Finally if the Emperor did acquire an amoebic infection, he was unlikely to have acquired it on the island, as amoebiasis was not endemic there, though imported cases did occur when the island was the half-way house between England and India. I think therefore that an amoebic hepatitis can definitely be ruled out.

'The question of a possible amoebic infection has, however, been recently revived by a letter from Dr. Carandias to the *Lancet*. According to this letter, Lord Moynihan, in 1927, showed certain specimens of intestine to Professor Leriche and claimed that they had come from the Emperor. These specimens, which, according to Dr. Carandias, showed a dysenteric perforating ulcer of the bowel, have since been destroyed by a bombing raid on London which damaged the Museum of the Royal College of Surgeons. It is true that this Museum possessed specimens of intestine alleged to have come from the Emperor. According to the records these specimens were originally presented to Astley Cooper by O'Meara, who had obtained them from Antommarchi when the latter visited London after the Emperor's death. How had Antommarchi obtained those specimens? It would appear that with the presence of the British doctors he would have had no opportunity to steal them at the actual autopsy, and that, afterwards, the body was closely guarded by Rutledge. Nevertheless the possibility of this witty Corsican having surreptitiously obtained the specimens cannot be definitely excluded. Why, however, did not Antommarchi, in his later description of the post-mortem findings, after his safe return to France, mention them? Because of the way in which they are supposed to have been obtained and because of the unreliable character of O'Meara, there is definite doubt as to whether these specimens are authentic. When, in 1944, I was in Florence, I met Dr. Joan Ross, who was then Curator of the Museum of the Royal College of Surgeons. She mentioned these specimens to me and that there was grave doubt as to whether they originally came from the body of the Emperor. In 1913 Professor Keith, in a lecture, exhibited these specimens and described them. He made no mention of a perforation and histological studies had proved that they were not amoebic ulcer but hyperplastic Peyer's patches. Moreover if the Emperor had died from a perforated dysenteric ulcer of the bowel he would have died with the classical signs of peritonitis and perforation, and certainly the consequent septic peritonitis would have been evident at the post-mortem examination.

'The story of these specimens therefore helps very little in elucidating the cause of the Emperor's death. Even if these specimens originally came from the Emperor, they merely indicate that he probably had some generalised lymphatic hyperplasia, which is consistent with his constitution and the type of life that he led in latter days. They do not materially help in solving the riddle of his cause of death.

'It appears, from his medical history, that whilst on the island the Emperor suffered periodically from febrile disturbances. The first of these attacks occurred about October 1816 and was observed by O'Meara. From the clinical description these first attacks appear to have been typical of acute tonsillitis, associated with dental sepsis. Subsequent attacks were associated with headache and cough and may well have been due to recurrent sinusitis. Freischman has suggested that the Emperor's febrile illnesses may have been due to a melitensis infection but the evidence, I think, is far from convincing. The febrile disturbances appear to have been too slight, no enlarged spleen described, the history is unduly long, particularly as this infection was not endemic on the island and that, if it did occur, it was probably contracted at Elba. Finally the post-mortem examination does not appear, because of the absence of splenomegaly, to substantiate such a diagnosis.

❖   ❖   ❖

'Recently a new suggestion has been made. A tuft of hair, claimed to have been obtained from the Emperor, has been analysed by a new technique at the Medico-Legal Department of the University of Glasgow. This analysis has shown 10·38 p.p.m. of arsenic in the hair. The analysis, however, did not reveal whether this arsenic was concentrated at one or more sections of the hair or was evenly distributed. This finding of course immediately raises the question as to whether arsenical poisoning was a factor in the Emperor's death.

'The first questions that arise are:

'Is the hair authentic?

'When was it taken from the Emperor?

'How did it reach Glasgow for analysis, some 140 years after his death?

'In this connection it appears worthy of note that some three years prior to his death the Emperor presented to Captain Poppleton, who was the first orderly officer attached to Longwood, a golden snuff-box and a lock of hair to celebrate the occasion of the captain's promotion to major and his consequent removal from the island. The snuff-box was long preserved by the descendants of this gallant officer, and may not the tuft of hair been likewise to appear ultimately in the medico-legal department of Glasgow University? If so, this lock of hair was obtained too long before the Emperor's death to throw any light on the actual cause of the death.

'Arsenic is not a normal constituent of the human body, but traces of arsenic in innocuous amounts may innocently reach the body via various agencies, by natural contamination of foodstuff, water, etc., thus small traces of arsenic may be recovered from human tissues in cases in which there is no question of arsenic poisoning having occurred. In consequence harmless amounts of arsenic may be found in the tissues of persons who eat sea-food (as such traces of arsenic may be found in sea creatures). Also faint traces may be found in vegetables grown in arsenically contaminated soils. Salts used to preserve food may also contain traces of arsenic, especially in the old days before modern refinements in chemical purity of salt were introduced. As a result of these findings it has been arbitrarily agreed that up to 10 p.p.m. of arsenic in human tissues may be regarded as "normal". The finding of 10·38 p.p.m. of arsenic in a tuft of hair may therefore be of no significance as regards poisoning. There is also another explanation of why traces of arsenic may have been found in a specimen of the Emperor's hair obtained about the time of his death. Antommarchi prescribed a number of drugs which the Emperor was very loath to take and, at least on five occasions, shortly before the death, he prescribed tartar emetic, which is an antimony salt. Because of their frequent occurrences together in nature, antimony salts are frequently contaminated with arsenic and in the Emperor's day such salts would not have been chemically purified. Traces of arsenic in the Emperor's hair may thus have resulted from medical treatment. The proof of the pudding lies in the eating and the important question is not whether faint traces of arsenic were present in the Emperor's hair (as such may have an innocent interpretation) but whether he exhibited signs of arsenic poisoning.

'There are three main forms of this poisoning, viz. :

'The algid form, in which a large dose of arsenic, in a soluble form, is rapidly absorbed. In these cases there are no gastro-intestinal symptoms but there is rapid circulatory failure, with death in a few hours and no time for the arsenic to reach the hair. The Emperor certainly did not die this type of death.

'The acute form, which arises from a single dose of arsenic. In this form the dominating signs are those of acute gastro-intestinal irritation, as evidenced by vomiting, abdominal pain, violent purging and collapse with death, usually within a few days, or recovery if the subject survives to a week. The Emperor's final illness certainly does not fit in with this picture. It lasted too long and there was no purging.

'The subacute to chronic form. The predominant clinical picture of this form is periphrenal neuritis, chiefly affecting the legs with paraesthesia, paresis and rapid wasting of muscles associated with hyperkeratosis and skin pigmentation. The picture of the Emperor's final illness does not fit in with this classical description. The clinical picture thus, in my mind, excludes the possibility of arsenic poisoning.

'The only other evidence to support the diagnosis is the fact that when the Emperor's body was exhumed, in 1840, it was noted that the body was in a remarkable state of preservation. It has been alleged that persons who die from arsenical poisoning resist putrefaction, presumably due to the antiseptic effect of the arsenic on the putrefying micro-organisms. This, however, is not correct. The amounts of arsenic present in the bodies of these cases are too small to affect the growth of bacteria, and critical experience in recent years has clearly shown that bodies of persons who die from arsenical poisoning decompose just as rapidly as those of persons who die from other causes, provided that the bodies are placed under similar circumstances. It has, however, been well proved that bodies buried in airtight coffins may remain remarkably well preserved for very many years. The Emperor's body was first placed in a soldered tin coffin; around this was an inner wood coffin, then a lead coffin and finally an outer wood coffin and his grave was surrounded by cemented stone. There is nothing remarkable about the fact that when the coffin was opened, nearly twenty years later, the body was found to be extremely well preserved. There is thus no necessity to suggest that it was due to arsenic.

'Despite the toxicological findings recently made, I see no definite evidence to indicate that the Emperor died from arsenical poisoning.

✤   ✤   ✤

'Apart from the ulcer what then could other factors have been in the causation of the Emperor's death?

'When he arrived at St. Helena he appeared to be in sound health and for a while after his arrival he enjoyed a certain amount of exercise. Thus whilst at The Briars he often went walking with Las Cases. After his removal to Longwood he began to lead a physically very inactive life. He took less and less exercise, and spent longer and longer periods in bed. According to Montholon sometimes he would only get up for two or three hours per day and then he would spend most of the time reclining on a sofa. He took prolonged hot baths, which are very enervating, all this would help to account for his fainting and giddy spells. He, however, ate well and he grew new fat and appears to have developed dropsy of the legs. At times, towards the end, he was very depressed and often hardly spoke. True, at times, he made some attempt to rally and thus, after Antommarchi's arrival, he took an active interest in the garden and restarted horse-riding and even made an excursion to the Dovetons, at Mount Pleasant. But he soon resumed his inactivity.

'Also not only did he spend long periods cooped up indoors but, according to O'Meara, he kept all the windows closed and even had fires in the rooms in midsummer. So stuffy was the atmosphere that O'Meara complained that it made him feel faint. Naturally such a type of life must have caused marked physical deterioration and the resultant debility may well have been an important factor in contributing to his death.

'The Emperor was a remarkable man. He had risen to be Emperor of the French and conqueror and dictator of Europe. He was thus a man of intense vitality, with superhuman drive and energy. He was very definitely a man of decision and action, and not only was he a great soldier but an even greater administrator. He was unique. He also had terrific resilience: after the Egyptian campaign, with its great losses, he could return vitually alone to France and make himself master. Even after the disastrous Moscow campaign and the loss of the flower of his Grande Armée and his banishment to Elba, he could make a bold return to France and reinstate himself as the Emperor, only to lose all at Waterloo. Thereafter he became a prisoner banished to a desolate island, thousands of miles from Europe, cut off from France and the world and without news of his wife and of his innocent son, the tragic King of Rome.

'What was left to him? No future, only ultimate death on the island. How could this extraordinary man adapt himself to this position? After activity and glory on such a heroic scale how could he be content to do nothing but wait patiently for death? How impotent, frustrated, and hopeless he must have felt. A magnificent past, an impotent present, a hopeless future. How could he pass the time? He made a definite effort and buried himself in his memoirs, but how futile these reminiscences of past greatness and glory as contrasted with his present circumstances. An ordinary man may have submitted and adapted himself to the situation, but not an extraordinary man such as the Emperor. How could he, with his past, find any satisfaction confined in a disused stable, dealing with the petty quarrels of his staff, futilely being involved in the most minor of intrigues and trying to carry on a vendetta with an impossible governor, whom he could merely irritate and over whom he could score no victory? How pathetic it was that this great man should be reduced to getting a thrill out of a pot-shot at Madame Bertrand's pet goat or a straying cow belonging to the Company. Under such circumstances only corrosion of the soul, asphyxiation of the spirit and consequent degeneration of the body could occur.

'The peculiar psychological situation leading to physical deterioration is thus, in my opinion, the main factor which contributed to his final end.

'The English may not have killed the Emperor of the French, as the French allege, by exposing him to tropical diseases, or even by poisoning him with arsenic, but they slowly killed him by imprisoning him on the island, with no hope, and so strangled his spirit. It is of course possible that a general metabolic disturbance also contributed to the Emperor's end. Perhaps the obesity and indolence depended also on a hypothalamic lesion. His brain was not examined at the post mortem and it is also stated that he had no pubic hair. Such a diagnosis is, however, based on pure speculation and has no firm basis. Perhaps the kindest thing would have been, after his surrender, to have stood him against a wall and shot him, as he unhesitatingly did to the Duke of Enghien, and as he would possibly have done to the fat Louis XVIII if he had managed to capture him.'

BIBLIOGRAPHY

Abell, L. E., *Recollections of the Emperor Napoleon*. John Murray, London, 1848.

Abrantès, Duchesse d', *Mémoires*. Mame, Paris, 1835.

Ali, *Souvenirs*. Payot, Paris, 1926.

Antommarchi, Dr. F., *Les derniers moments de Napoléon*. Paris, 1825.

Arthur-Lévy, *Les dissentiments de la famille impériale*. Calmann-Lévy, Paris, 1932.

Aubry, Octave, *Sainte-Hélène*. Flammarion, Paris, 1935.

Augustin-Thierry, A., *Madame Mère*. Albin Michel, Paris, 1939.

Bertrand, Général, *Cahiers de Sainte-Hélène*. Flammarion, Albin Michel et Sulliver, Paris, 1959.

Bonaparte, Joseph, *Lettres d'exil*. Charpentier, Paris, 1912.

Bourrienne, *Bonaparte intime*. Hachette, Paris.

Brice, R., *Le secret de Napoléon*. Payot, Paris, 1936.

Brooke, T. H., *A History of the Island of St. Helena*. London, 1808.

Brookes, Dame Mabel, *St. Helena Story*. Heinemann, London, 1960.

Broughton, Lord, *Recollections of a Long Life*. John Murray, London.

Cabanès, Dr., *Au chevet de l'Empereur*. Albin Michel, Paris, 1943.

Cahuet, A., *Après la mort de l'Empereur*. Emile-Paul, Paris, 1913.

Caulincourt, Général de, *Mémoires*. Plon, Paris, 1933.

Chaplin, Dr. A., *A St. Helena Who's Who*. A. Humphreys, London, 1919.

Chateaubriand, A. de, *Mémoires d'outre-tombe*.

Couchoud, P. L., *Voix de Napoléon*. Milieu du Monde, Geneva, 1949.

Fabre, M. A., *Jérôme Bonaparte*. Hachette, Paris, 1952.

Fain, Baron, *Manuscrit de 1814*. Bossange, Paris, 1825.

Firmin-Didot, G., *La captivité de Sainte-Hélène, rapports du marquis de Montchenu*. Firmin-Didot, Paris, 1894.

Fleury de Chaboulon, *Mémoires*. Rouveyre, Paris, 1901.

Forshufvud, Sten, *Napoléon a-t-il été empoisonné?* Plon, Paris, 1961.

Forshufvud, Sten, Dr. Hamilton Smith, Dr. Anders Wassen, 'Arsenic content of Napoleon's Hair Probably Taken Immediately After His Death, *Nature*, October 1961.

Forsyth, William, *History of the Captivity of Napoleon at St. Helena*. John Murray, London, 1853.

Ganière, Dr. P., *Napoléon à Sainte-Hélène*. Paris, 1961.

Génies et Réalistes (collection), *Napoléon*. Hachette, Paris, 1962.

Goldsmith, Lewis, *Procès de Buonaparte*. J. Moronval, Paris, 1815.

Gourgaud, Général, *Journal de Sainte-Hélène*, 1815-1818. Flammarion, Paris, 1947.

Hauterive, E. d', *Sainte-Hélène au temps de Napoléon et aujourd'hui*. Calmann-Lévy, Paris, 1903.

Hegemann, W., *Napoleon, or Prostration Before the Hero*. Constable & Co., London, 1931.

Heine, Heinrich, *Poésies*. Mercure de France, Paris, 1924.

Hortense, Queen, *Mémoires*. Plon. Paris, 1927.

Itinéraire de Buonaparte de l'île d'Elbe à Sainte-Hélène. Paris, 1817.

Jackson, E. L., *St. Helena*. Ward, Lock & Co., London, 1903.

Kemble, James, *Napoleon Immortal*. John Murray, London, 1959.

Korngold, R., *The Last Years of Napoleon*. Gollancz, London, 1960.

Las Cases, Comte de, *Le Mémorial de Sainte-Hélène*. Flammarion, Paris, 1951.

Las Cases, Emmanuel de, *Notice*. Remquet, Paris, 1854.

Lutyens, Captain G., *Letters*. J. Lane, London, 1915.

Madelin, Louis, *Histoire du Consulat et de l'Empire*. Hachette, Paris.

Malcolm, Lady, *A Diary of St. Helena*. Allen & Unwin, London, 1899.

Manceron, C., *Le dernier choix de Napoléon*. Robert Laffont, Paris, 1960.

Marchand, Louis, *Mémoires*. Plon, Paris, 1955.

Martineau, G., *Bulletin de Sainte-Hélène*, No. 7, 'De quoi est mort Napoléon?'

Masson, F., *Une journée de Napoléon*. Flammarion, Paris, 1934.

Melchior-Bonnet, C., *Dictionnaire de la Révolution et de l'Empire*. Larousse, Paris, 1965.

Mellis, J. C., *St. Helena*. London, 1872.

Misciatelli, P., *Lettere di Letizia Buonaparte*. U. Hoepli, Milan, 1936.

Montholon, Général de, *Récits de la captivité de l'Empereur Napoléon*. Paulin, Paris, 1847.

Nabonne, B., *Joseph Bonaparte*. Hachette, Paris, 1949.

Napoléon I, *Dictionnaire des opinions et jugements*. Club de l'Honnête Homme, Paris, 1964.

Correspondance, Librairie Impériale, Paris, 1869.

Napoléon, Prince, and J. Hanoteau, *Lettres personnelles des souverains à l'Empereur Napoléon*. Plon, Paris, 1939.

O'Meara, Dr. B., *Napoleon in Exile, or A Voice from St. Helena*. London, 1827.

Pardee, M. A., *Sainte-Hélène*. 1933.

Rémusat, Madame de, *Mémoires*. Calmann-Lévy, Paris, 1881.

Rosebery, Lord, *Napoleon, The Last Phase*. A. Humphreys, London, 1900.

Scott, Sir Walter, *Life of Napoleon*.

Seaton, R. C., *Napoleon's Captivity in Relation to Sir Hudson Lowe*, London, 1903.

Shorter, C., *Napoleon and His Fellow Travellers*. Cassell & Co., London, 1908.

Sieburg, F., *Napoléon*. Robert Laffont, Paris, 1957.

Stendhal, *Napoléon*.

Stokoe, Dr. J., *With Napoleon at St. Helena*. London, 1902.

Talleyrand, Prince de, *Mémoires*. Plon, Paris, 1957.

Thomson, J. M., *Napoleon Bonaparte, His Rise and Fall*. Blackwell, Oxford, 1958.

Tschudi, C. de, *La mère de Napoléon*. Fontemoing, Paris, 1910.

Vaulabelle, A. de, *Histoire des deux restaurations*. Perrotin, Paris, 1855.

Wolseley, Vicomte, *Le déclin et la chute de Napoléon*. Ollendorff, Paris, 1894.

MANUSCRIPTS

Paris   Bibliothèque Nationale
            Archives du Ministère des Affaires Etrangères
London British Museum
            Public Record Office
Moscow Diplomatic Archives

INDEX

Aboukir, 71
Aix, Ile d', 27, 29, 204
Ajaccio, 71, 86
Alabama, 203
Alarm House, 10, 41, 46, 70, 82, 122, 128, 150
Alexander I, Tsar of Russia, 74, 100–101, 106, 112–18, 140, 148
Alexandria, battle of, 71
Ali (*see* Saint-Denis, Louis Etienne)
Alison, Sir Archibald, 76
Amiens, Peace of, 71
Angola, 63
Angoulême, Louis, Duc d', 29
Angoulême, Marie-Thérèse, Duchesse d', 93
Anti-Gallican, The, 193–5
Antommarchi, Dr., xi, 7, 23, 60, 142, 208, 211–21, 223, 225
Archambault brothers, 13, 33, 35, 46, 60, 149, 200–2, 204
Arnott, Dr., 208, 213–17, 220
Austerlitz, battle of, 1, 17, 27, 43

Bacchiocchi, Marie Anne Elisa, 190
Bagly, John, 164
Balcombe, Betsy, xiii, 6, 10, 12–14, 17, 23, 104, 128, 133, 147, 152, 176–7, 180
Balcombe, Mrs., 12, 14, 23, 127–8, 189
Balcombe, William, 10, 12, 14–15, 23, 36, 56, 59–60, 127, 133, 136–7, 165, 176, 188–9, 198
Balcombe family, the, xii, 12–15, 17, 45, 151, 158, 176–7, 180, 189
Balmain, Alexander Ramsay, Count de, relations with Hudson Lowe, 68, 73, 76, 117–19; his dispatches quoted, 72, 84, 86, 94, 108, 113–20, 123–4; marriage, 80, 118–119; relations with the Longwood

party, 87, 106–7, 115–16, 132; character and career, 111–13, 118–119; ill health, 117–18, 140–1
Barn, the, 41
Bassano, Hugues Maret, Duke of, 50
Bathurst, Henry, 3rd Earl, issues security regulations for St. Helena, 3, 17–19, 79, 90; and Napoleon's finances, 51, 60, 198–9; and Sir Hudson Lowe, 57, 75, 84, 96, 98, 111, 119, 205; and Metternich, 147
Bautzen, 72
Baxter, Dr., 70, 85–6, 140, 147, 161, 174
Beale, Onesiphorus, 160
Beauharnais, Eugène de, 25, 51, 53, 60–2
Beauharnais, Hortense de, Queen of Holland, 194
Beauharnais, Josephine de (*see* Josephine, the Empress)
Bellerophon, the, 6, 31, 39, 130, 203
Bennet, Captain, 161
Beresina, river, 27
Bernard (valet to the Bertrands), 48
Bernardin de Saint-Pierre, J. H., 15, 49, 157
Bernadotte, Marshal, 112
Berthier, Marshal, 25
Bertrand, Arthur, 145
Bertrand, Fanny, Countess, Napoleon's companion in exile, 2, 21, 46–7, 54, 56–7, 162–3, 206, 226; character and career, 22, 25; at Hutt's Gate, 26, 34, 36, 46; sleeps while Napoleon reads aloud, 49; liked by Lady Lowe, 80; friendly with the British Navy, 133; illness 141; miscarriages, 145; credited with love affair with Napoleon, 147; and plans for Napoleon's escape, 199